WARM
WELCOMES
IN
BRITAIN

WARM WELCOMES IN BRITAIN

'More than 500
Great Little Places to Stay'

FROM GUESTACCOM COUNTRY HOMES
AND EXECHOTEL LISTINGS

MIKE STONE & ROGER RUSSELL

David & Charles
Newton Abbot   London

British Library Cataloguing in Publication Data

Stone, Mike
  Warm welcomes in Britain.
  1. Great Britain. Hotels
  I. Title II. Russell, Roger
  647'.944101

  ISBN 0–7153-9784–2

Printed in Great Britain
by Billings and Sons Ltd Worcester
for David & Charles Publishers plc
Brunel House Newton Abbot Devon

Contents

Foreword

It is my pleasure to introduce you to some of the lovely homes, guesthouses and small hotels that I have visited and enjoyed over the last ten years. In making my selection, I have always considered the general 'all-round' ambience of a particular place of prime importance. This is created, I believe, by the character and attitude of the host which can make or break one's visit – (after all, Fawlty Towers would not have been so awful without Basil!). The places featured in this book deliver outstanding service; for example, have you ever stayed in a guesthouse where breakfast continues indefinitely throughout the morning, so that guests can get to know one another (Exmouth)? It is this kind of atmosphere – homely, friendly and relaxing – that makes this selection so special.

Historically, some of the estates have been mentioned in the Domesday Book, and some of the houses are very old, dating as far back as the 13th century – one, for instance, has heavy shutters which originally doubled as combat shields, and on the site of another a major battle of the War of the Roses was fought.

I hope you enjoy each location as much as I have, but please feel free to write to inform me of your impressions, whether it be a compliment or a complaint. I am well aware that you cannot always please all of the folks all of the time!

Happy travelling!

MIKE STONE
(Claremont House, Second Avenue, Hove, E. Sussex BN3 2LL)

Acknowledgements

Thanks to:
Our Hosts
for providing so much useful local information.

Susie Behar
for her invaluable help in collating this material, the enormous amount of additional research which was necessary and for providing her journalistic expertise in bringing it all together.

Introduction

In 1976 I decided to leave the manufacturing industry, and become a freelance hotel inspector. After three years I formed 'Guestaccom', a consortium of quality guest houses, small hotels with an average size of six bedrooms – its advisory booklet was called *The Good Room Guide*, and it proved to be an immediate success. I travelled Britain whilst my brother supplied office facilities and my sister supported the operation at home. In 1981 we formed 'ExecHotels': a group of smaller than usual, independent, proprietor-operated, hotels in the 2/3 star range; I found all these were of exceptionally high standard and good value in comparison with some 'group' hotels. In 1987 we formed 'Country Homes', aimed at the more discerning traveller: this is a guide to country houses, old rectories and the occasional castle, each with just two or three letting bedrooms, but all of an exceptionally high standard. For instance, dinner may be served at a refectory table, resplendent with the family's finest tableware, with your hosts joining you *en famille*.

All properties featured in this book have been selected and inspected, and are continually vetted with the help of the travelling public. Such a massive undertaking required additional help, however, and Roger Russell, whom I have known for several years, joined me in 1988; since then we have collaborated in selecting and inspecting new places, and he has made many contributions to this book.

How to Use This Book

Our selections are divided into areas: the West Country, London and the South East, Central England, the North, Scotland and Wales. In each section you will find an introduction to the area with a map and a list of Regional Tourist Board offices, followed by a complete listing of all our selected places, arranged alphabetically by town or village (as shown on the map). The listings include basic details and approximate room rates, and will indicate those prepared to accept the voucher system (for details see page 9). To whet your appetite further, each listing is followed by detailed descriptions of some of our favourite places.

Room Rates
We have included an indicator as to the cost for bed and cooked breakfast, service (which is rarely levied) and VAT (Value Added Tax) per person per night sharing a double/twin bedroom.

(A) under £15
(B) £15– £20   *This is an indication of room rates for 1990*
(C) £20 – £25   *Bed and Breakfast per person per night*
(D) over £25

Where you see A/B or maybe A/C it means there is a variety of rooms available, possibly some rooms with bathroom and some without. It could also indicate where a hotel is seasonal: some reduce rates in winter, and many offer winter or weekend breaks.

Please check costs and ascertain the types of room you are booking when making your reservation.

Pets
Dogs and other pets are allowed at some places, but only by arrangement with your host; we have specified when a place featured states clearly 'Sorry, No Pets'. Guide dogs, however, should be announced when booking and will normally be accepted.

Children
Are normally welcome, but sometimes hosts express a wish not to take young children. Please enquire.

Licensed Premises
Most that offer dinner are licensed. If they are not, hosts will normally allow you to bring your own bottle and may often not charge corkage. Please enquire.

Dinner
This is not always offered; however, your hosts will usually direct you to, or often give you a local map of recommended eating places. When offered, it is usually by arrangement. Please enquire at time of booking. It could be a set meal at a set time. Please enquire. Special diets can normally be catered for with advance warning.

Packed Lunches
Can be arranged with your host. It is advisable to request this the evening before.

Payment Cards
Credit or charge cards are often accepted. Please enquire how payment can be made.

Book Early
Many of our places have fewer than five bedrooms and you should

book early, especially in the months of June, July and August.

Tea and Coffee
These facilities are normally provided in the bedroom but if not early morning beverages and afternoon tea should be requested from your hosts.

En Suite – Private Bathroom
The term 'en suite' used in this book means bathroom adjoining bedroom; 'bathroom' could also include shower and WC (also known as toilet, loo, the privvy and the 'John', for our American visitors!). 'Private bathroom' could mean across a corridor or down the hallway.

Activities
We have mentioned some of the most popular things to do when staying in the area, but this list is by no means comprehensive. Your hosts will supply you with detailed information on request.

Award Winners
You will see this mentioned occasionally throughout the book. They are always unsolicited awards, and could have been given in any of the last few previous years by motoring authorities, tourist authorities, or by leading guide books. It is by no means comprehensive.

Transport
It is nearly always advisable to travel by car, but many hosts will pick you up from the nearest railway station, airport, or seaport, and some offer a chauffeuring service for special occasions.

Voucher System
Vouchers are accepted by 321 places listed, as indicated in the area indexes, and are valid until 30 June 1991. Each voucher is for £5 and is to be used against 'Bed and Breakfast' for a stay of at least three days for two people. Please note that only one voucher can be used at any single establishment, and that they are not valid on Bank Holidays, and can only be allowed against full rack rates. See back page of this book.

In English law a booking is a contract. You may be charged for cancellation.

To the best of our knowledge all details are correct at the time of going to press.

THE WEST COUNTRY

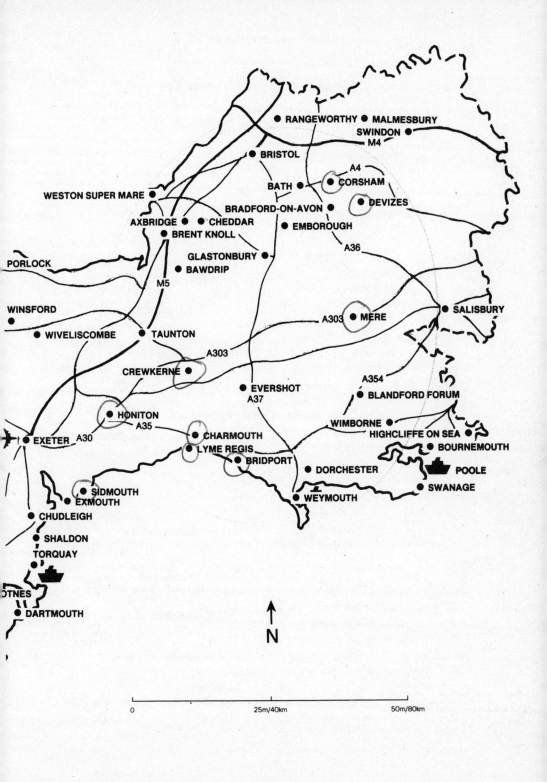

The West Country

*Covering the counties of: Avon, Cornwall, Devon, Dorset (part),
Somerset and Wiltshire*

People flock to the West Country every summer. They seek its famously warm climate – the South Hams district of Devon enjoys the mildest climate in Great Britain, and on the south coast of Cornwall sub-tropical plants and palm trees flourish; its long sandy beaches like those in the National Trust's Golden Cap estate in Dorset; and its excellent sea-side resorts such as Torquay in Devon, and Weston-super-Mare in Avon. In addition to the coastal pleasures, there are many popular beauty spots: the awe-inspiring Cheddar Gorge in Somerset; the great untrammelled moors of Exmoor in Somerset, Bodmin Moor in Cornwall, and the bleakest, most windswept of them all, Dartmoor in Devon. And in total contrast to the latter, the gentle rolling Quantock hills in Somerset, beloved by the poets Wordsworth and Coleridge.

Picturesque villages, harbours, and small towns dot the countryside and coast. Some – like Clovelly in Devon, with its boat-lined harbour, and steep main street (no cars either!) – are almost too pretty to be true; others – like Lacock in Wiltshire, once a centre of the wool trade and today one of the best preserved medieval towns in the country – are notable for their historical and architectural heritage.

The great towns and cities of the West Country are no less interesting or attractive. Bath, in Avon, is one of the most complete Georgian cities in the country; Salisbury, a wonderful hotch-potch of architectural styles and periods ranging from the 14th century onwards, is home to a pure Gothic cathedral with a magnificent 14th-century spire – the tallest in the country; Exeter, the West Country's premier city, was severely damaged in the war, but despite the despoliation, it remains a city of great charm and character, and its cathedral is renowned, not least for its two sturdy and imposing Norman towers.

Ancient history is abundant in the West Country. The stone circles of Avebury and Stonehenge in Wiltshire are the most important in Europe; the moors are littered with fascinating archaeological sites; and in Cadbury, in Somerset, a massive earthwork (once a Celtic fortification) is believed to be the true Camelot of the real King Arthur.

If all of this is not enough to keep the tourist busy, the wealth and grandeur of the West Country's stately homes is quite staggering. They range from the elegant Kingston Lacy in Dorset, a 17th-century house with a very fine art collection, to the Elizabethan mansion, Longleat House, in Wiltshire, with its modern safari park stretching across its once peaceful grounds.

A review of the West Country would not be complete without mention of the most westerly point on the British mainland – Land's End. Here the sea hurls itself tirelessly against jagged rocks, whilst in the distance the lonely Longships lighthouse stands sentinel in the cold Atlantic – it takes one's breath away.

Regional Tourist Board:
Trinity Court, Southernhay East, Exeter, Devon EX1 1QS
Tel: (0392) 76351

ASHBURTON   THE DARTMOOR MOTEL
Peartree Cross, Ashburton, Devon TQ13 7JW. *Tel*: Ashburton (0364) 52232.
Hosts: The Stepney Family.
Rates: C/D   Vouchers accepted.
   Conveniently situated well back from A38, this attractive motel is ideal for touring Dartmoor and beautiful Holne Valley. Near ancient stannary town nestling in foothills of moor, Exeter and Plymouth 30 minutes. Easy reach coast. Two 4-posters, one with jacuzzi bath. Syndicate rooms available.

AXBRIDGE   COMPTON HOUSE
Townend, Axbridge, Somerset BS26 2AJ. *Tel*: Axbridge (0934) 732928. *Hosts*:
Dr Piers & Polly Blakeney-Edwards.
Rates: C   Vouchers accepted.
   Elegant, spacious Georgian/medieval house overlooking unspoilt country-side. Charming en suite bedrooms, colour televisions. Secluded gardens, panelled dining room. Licensed. Hostess qualified in cuisine. Winter breaks. A38/M5 nearby, Cheddar, Wells, Bath. Older children welcome. Sorry, no pets.

BARNSTAPLE   ROBOROUGH HOUSE HOTEL AND
RESTAURANT
Barnstaple, North Devon EX31 4JG. *Tel*: Barnstaple (0271) 72354. *Hosts*:
Roger Porter and Robert Dolman
Rates: D   Vouchers accepted.
   Country house hotel in 14 acres gardens and woodlands. Breathtaking views over lovely countryside and estuary to Dartmoor. Off A39 Lynton road. Two 4-posters available. Proprietors are proud of their reputation for good food and wine.

BATH   EAGLE HOUSE
Church Street, Bathford, Avon BA1 7RS. *Tel*: Bath (0225) 859946. *Hosts*:
John & Rosamund Napier.

Rates: B/C   Vouchers accepted.
(See page 30 for description)

BATH   PARADISE HOUSE
Holloway, Bath, Avon BA2 4PX. *Tel*: Bath (0225) 317723. *Hosts*: David &
Janet Cutting.
Rates: B/D   Vouchers accepted.
(See page 30 for description)

BATH   THE ORCHARD
80 High Street, Bathford, Bath BA1 7TG. *Tel*: Bath (0225) 858765. *Hosts*:
Olga & John London.
Rates: B/C
(See page 31 for description)

BAWDRIP (Nr. Bridgwater)   TUDOR COURT FARM
East Side Lane, Bawdrip, Bridgwater, Somerset TA7 8QB. *Tel*: Puriton (0278)
683361. *Hosts*: The Foletti Family.
Rates: B
> Very comfortable and attractive 16th-century Tudor farmhouse. Original
> wall murals. Riding and stabling. Nr Quantock Hills and Exmoor. M5. Exit
> 23. Glastonbury 10 m, Wells 15 m. No smoking in bedrooms. Reduced rates
> 3 nights or more. Phone for directions.

BIDEFORD   MOUNT HOTEL
Northdown Road, Bideford, Devon EX39 3LP. *Tel*: Bideford (0237) 473748.
Hosts: Mike & Janet Taylor.
Rates: B   Vouchers accepted.
(See page 32 for description)

BIDEFORD (Parkham)   THE OLD RECTORY
Parkham, Nr Bideford, North Devon EX39 5PL. *Tel*: Horns Cross (0237)
451443. *Hosts*: Jean & Jack Langton.
Rates: C/D   Vouchers accepted.
> Charming, peaceful small country house decorated in English country
> cottage style. Home cooking using local and garden produce. Most rooms
> en suite. Children over 12 welcome. Sorry, no pets. Many beaches within
> 5 miles. Walking and fishing nearby.

BLANDFORD FORUM   THE CROWN HOTEL
West St, Blandford Forum, Dorset DT11 7AJ. *Tel*: Blandford (0258) 56626.
Telex: 418292 BADGER G. *Host*: James Mayo.
Rates: D
> Comfortable, warmly attractive hotel, overlooking river and Crown Mead-
> ows in elegant country town, in heart of historic Dorset. Kingston Lacy,

Badbury Ring, Bryanston School nearby. Central for Salisbury, Shaftesbury, Dorchester and Poole. 4-poster available.

BOSCASTLE   ST. CHRISTOPHER'S COUNTRY HOUSE
Boscastle, Cornwall PL35 0BD. *Tel*: Boscastle (08405) 412. *Hosts*: Brian & Brenda Thompson.
Rates: A/B   Vouchers accepted.
(See page 33 for description)

BOURNEMOUTH   HINTON FIRS HOTEL
Manor Road, East Cliff, Bournemouth, Dorset BH1 3HB. *Tel*: Bournemouth (0202) 25409. *Fax*: 0202 299607. *Host*: Graham Robinson.
Rates: C
Friendly, family-run hotel set in almost rural surroundings in the heart of the East Cliff. Four south-facing lounges overlook outdoor pool, sheltered gardens and sun terrace. Newly opened indoor pool with swimjet, spa pool and sauna. Solarium. Lift. Annexe. Conference facilities available.

BOURNEMOUTH   PARKLANDS HOTEL
4 Rushton Crescent, Bournemouth, Dorset BH3 7AF. *Tel*: Bournemouth (0202) 22529. *Hosts*: Sylvia and Alan Clark
Rates: B
Elegant hotel with charm and character. Central quiet residential area, easy reach of beach, shops, entertainment, most sports incl golf. Good access for touring New Forest, Purbecks and 'Hardy' country. Sorry, no pets.

BOVEY TRACEY   THE BLENHEIM HOTEL
Brimley Road, Bovey Tracey, South Devon TQ13 9DH. *Tel*: Bovey Tracey (0626) 832422. *Hosts*: John & Dea Turpin.
Rates: B/C   Vouchers accepted.
Traditionally furnished country house, attractive lawns and gardens. Views Dartmoor National Park. Stately homes and Stover golf nearby. Nature Reserve. Salmon and trout fishing. Wonderful walks. Home cooking, own and local produce. Also vegetarian menu. Pets welcome.

BRADFORD-ON-AVON   WIDBROOK GRANGE
Trowbridge Road, Bradford-on-Avon, Wiltshire BA15 1UH. *Tel*: Bradford-on-Avon (02216) 3173/4750. *Hosts*: John & Pauline Price.
Rates: B/C   Vouchers accepted.
200-year-old country house, elegantly restored, very secluded. Antique furniture throughout. Fine examples of bee-bowls in grounds. Most rooms en suite, all have colour TV. Access, Amex and Visa. Half tester. Bath 9 miles.

BRENT KNOLL   BATTLEBOROUGH GRANGE HOTEL
   AND RESTAURANT
Brent Knoll, Nr. Burnham-on-Sea, Somerset TA9 4DS. *Tel*: Brent Knoll

78) 760208. *Fax*: 0278 760208 *Hosts*: Tony & Carol Wilkins.
tes: D   Vouchers accepted.
Very comfortable country house hotel, with private drive, off A38, 3
miles from coast and Burnham-on-Sea. Easy access M5, exit 22, turn right
then ½ mile. Area of ancient and historic interest. Golf. 4-poster and spa
baths available.

BRIDPORT   BRITMEAD HOUSE LICENSED GUEST HOUSE

154 West Bay Road, Bridport, Dorset DT6 4EG. *Tel*: Bridport (0308) 22941.
Hosts: Dan & Ann Walker.
Rates: A/B   Vouchers accepted.
Detached house with scenic views in residential area of market town. Har-
bour and beach nearby. Ground floor room available. Golf, fishing, riding,
tennis, bowling. Nature reserve. Wildlife Park. Cliff walks. Home-cooking.
Reduced rates 3 nights or more. All rooms colour TV.

BRIDPORT   ROUNDHAM HOUSE HOTEL

Roundham Gardens, West Bay Road, Bridport, Dorset DT6 4BD. *Tel*:
Bridport (0308) 22753/25779. *Telex*: 817182 enel G ROUNDHAM. *Fax*:
0308 421145 *Hosts*: David & Pat Moody.
Rates: C/D   Vouchers accepted.
(See page 34 for description)

BRISTOL   PARK HOUSE

19 Richmond Hill, Clifton, Bristol BS8 1BA. *Tel*: Bristol (0272) 736331. *Host*:
Delia Macdonald.
Rates: B/C
Large, elegant and comfortable Georgian house in this quiet and attrac-
tive residential area of Clifton, near suspension bridge. Wide variety of
restaurants and wine bars within walking distance. Colour TV all rooms.
Sorry, no pets.

BUDE   HARTLAND HOTEL

Bude, Cornwall EX23 8JY. *Tel*: Bude (0288) 55661. *Hosts*: The Barker Family.
Rates: D
South-facing comfortable hotel in superb position overlooking summer-
lease beach on north Cornish coast; only short walk to town. Heated
freshwater swimming pool. Surfing, sailing, riding, fishing, golf. Closed
November to Easter. 4-poster bed.

BURNHAM-ON-SEA   PINE GRANGE HOTEL

Berrow Road, Burnham-on-Sea, Somerset TA8 2EY. *Tel*: Burnham-on-Sea
(0278) 784214. *Hosts*: Bob & Lynda Walker.
Rates: C
Small and comfortable family-run hotel with warm, friendly atmosphere.
Large well-stocked bar. Close to beach, town centre, Berrow golf course

and tennis courts. Cheddar, Wells and Glastonbury all within easy reach. 2 miles from M5 (junc.22).

CHAGFORD   TORR HOUSE
Thorn Cross, Chagford, Newton Abbot, Devon TQ13 8DX. *Tel*: Chagford (0647) 432228 and 433343. *Hosts*: John & Hazel Cork.
Rates: B   Vouchers accepted.
(See page 35 for description)

CHARMOUTH   HENSLEIGH
Lower Sea Lane, Charmouth, Dorset DT6 6LW. *Tel*: Charmouth (0297) 60830. *Hosts*: Malcolm & Mary Macnair.
Rates: B   Vouchers accepted.
Friendly family atmosphere in Georgian-style house, residential area 300 yards from lovely beach. Spectacular cliff walks. Fossil hunting. Near the Golden Cap (NT), highest point on south coast. Home-cooking, local produce.

CHEDDAR (Axbridge)   THE PARSONAGE
Parsonage Lane, Cheddar Road, Axbridge, Somerset BS26 2DN. *Tel*: Axbridge (0934) 733078. *Hosts*: Pat and Peter Filer.
Rates: B   Vouchers accepted.
Charming and friendly home with superb views. Quiet location near medieval Axbridge on the edge of the Mendip Hills. No evening meals but several pubs and restaurants within ½ mile. Wells 10 miles, Bath 27 miles. All rooms with hospitality trays and colour TV. Children over 14 welcome. Sorry, no pets.

CHUDLEIGH   (A 'no smoking' house) WADDON HOUSE
Chudleigh, Nr Exeter, Devon TQ13 ODJ. *Tel*: Chudleigh (0626) 853216.
Host: Sylvia Frowd.
Rates: B   Vouchers accepted.
(See page 36 for description)

CLAWTON (Holsworthy)   COURT BARN COUNTRY HOUSE
Clawton, Holsworthy, Devon EX22 6PS. *Tel*: North Tamerton (040927) 219.
Hosts: Robert & Susan Wood.
Rates: C/D
Beautiful country house hotel set in 5 acres park-like grounds with putting green and championship croquet lawn. Lovely panoramic views. Recommended by leading guides for food and wine. Combined with peace and tranquillity, a perfect place for touring Devon/Cornwall and the moors. Two merit awards. 4-posters and half-testers available.

CORSHAM (Nr Bath)   THE METHUEN ARMS HOTEL
Corsham, Nr Bath, Wiltshire SN13 0HB. *Tel*: Corsham (0249) 714867. *Fax*: 0249 712004. *Hosts*: Mike, Wren & Mark Long.
Rates: C/D

nunnery, to medieval country home, to inn in 1608, with surviving stone walls and mullioned windows. 500-year-old Long Bar has genuine old 100-foot skittle alley. Half-tester. M4 exit 17 to Chippenham, then A4. 8 miles Bath. Cottage Annexe.

CRACKINGTON HAVEN   (A 'no smoking' house) MANOR FARM

Crackington Haven, North Cornwall EX23 0JW. *Tel*: St Gennys (084 03) 304. *Hosts*: Paul & Muriel Knight.
Rates: B

Warm and welcoming Domesday listed manor house surrounded by gardens and 40 acre farm. Peace and tranquillity. Beach 1 mile, Boscastle harbour 4 miles, Bude 12 miles. All rooms en suite or with private facilities. Log fires. Snooker room. Phone for directions. Sorry, no children or pets.

CREDITON (Barnstaple Cross)   THE THATCHED COTTAGE

Barnstaple Cross, Nr Crediton, Devon EX17 2EW. *Tel*: Crediton (03632) 3115. *Hosts*: Daphne & Michael Nightingale.
Rates: B

Delightful historic 16th-century cottage in lovely gardens, with panoramic views over rolling farmland and hills to Dartmoor. Off A377. Touring, golf, fishing. Dinner by arrangement only. Colour TV all rooms.

CREWKERNE   BROADVIEW

43 East Street, Crewkerne, Somerset TA18 7AG. *Tel*: Crewkerne (0460) 73424. *Hosts*: Gillian & Robert Swann.
Rates: A
(See page 37 for description)

DARTMOUTH   FORD HOUSE

44 Victoria Road, Dartmouth, Devon TQ6 9DX. *Tel*: Dartmouth (08043) 4047 (from March 1990 (0803) 834047). *Hosts*: Henrietta and Richard Turner.
Rates: B   Vouchers accepted.
(See page 38 for description)

DEVIZES (Westbrook)   THE COTTAGE

Westbrook, Bromham, Nr Chippenham, Wiltshire SN15 2EE. *Tel*: Devizes (0380) 850255. *Host*: Gloria Steed.
Rates: B   Vouchers accepted.
(See page 39 for description)

DORCHESTER   KING'S ARMS HOTEL

30 High East Street, Dorchester, Dorset DT1 1HF. *Tel*: Dorchester (0305) 65353. *Fax*: 0305 60269. *Host*: Anthony D Roach.
Rates: D

Comfortable and busy traditional coaching inn in the heart of historic

Dorchester. On important West Country approach cross-roads. Walking on Dorset hills, fishing, riding, golfing. Free entry arranged to all National Trust properties in area. Two rooms with 4-poster beds. Family rooms: children under 10 free, 10 and over reduced rates.

DORCHESTER (Affpuddle)   THE OLD VICARAGE
Affpuddle, Nr Dorchester, Dorset DT2 7HH. *Tel*: Puddletown (0305) 848315. *Hosts*: Michael & Anthea Hipwell.
Rates: A/B
Lovely spacious Georgian country house in an acre of mature gardens. Historic area, NT. Walking coastline and riding. Fishing arranged. Off A35 to B3390, 8 miles east of Dorchester, 4 miles Puddletown. Colour TV all rooms. No lounge. Sorry, no pets.

EMBOROUGH (Nr Bath)   THE COURT HOTEL
Chilcompton, Emborough, Nr Bath, Somerset BA3 4SA. *Tel*: Stratton-on-the-Fosse (0761) 232237/233237. *Hosts*: Lynda & Stephen Hayes.
Rates: D
Early 18th-century country manor house in 3 acres of lawns and gardens, tennis court, croquet, lovely tranquil countryside, three golf courses, fishing and hot air ballooning arranged. Off A37 and A367. Bath 11 miles. Free parking for Bristol Airport.

EVERSHOT   THE ACORN INN
Evershot, Nr Dorchester, Dorset DT2 0JW. *Tel*: Evershot (093583) 228. *Hosts*: Denise & Keith Morley.
Rates: B/D   Vouchers accepted.
16th-century licensed inn, in quaint village. All rooms en suite. 4-poster with jacuzzi. Ideal location for picturesque walks in Hardy countryside, surrounded by places of interest. Proprietors proud of their popularity locally for excellent selection and quality food and drink.

EXETER   ST ANDREWS HOTEL
28 Alphington Road, Exeter, Devon EX2 8HN. *Tel*: Exeter (0392) 76784. *Hosts*: Wally & Marie Nobbs and Sally & David Bailey.
Rates: D   Vouchers accepted.
Comfortable detached Victorian house, ½ mile city centre, near sports centre in historic city. Follow signs off M5 to Marsh Barton, then to Alphington Road. Maritime Museum nearby, shopping centre and cathedral easy walk.

EXMOUTH   KERANS HOTEL
Esplanade, Exmouth, Devon EX8 1DS. *Tel*: Exmouth (0395) 275275. *Hosts*: Pat & Alfred Woods.
Rates: B/C   Vouchers accepted.
Small, intimate, friendly hotel overlooking Lyme Bay. 2 miles sandy beach. Direct dial phones. Excellent for touring, watersports. Guided nature walks

and winter bird-watching cruises available. Many NT properties nearby. M5 (exit 30) 8 miles.

FALMOUTH (Penryn)   PROSPECT HOUSE
1 Church Road, Penryn, Cornwall TR10 8DA. *Tel*: Falmouth (0326) 73198. *Hosts*: Cliff Paul & Barry Sheppard.
Rates: B/C   Vouchers accepted.
(See page 40 for description)

GLASTONBURY (West Pennard)   LAVERLEY HOUSE
West Pennard, Glastonbury, Somerset BA6 8NE. *Tel*: Pilton (074 989) 696. *Hosts*: Stephen & Cheryl Staines.
Rates: A/B   Vouchers accepted.
(See page 41 for description)

HAYTOR   BEL ALP HOUSE
Haytor, Dartmoor, South Devon TQ13 9XX. *Tel*: Haytor (03646) 217. *Hosts*: Roger & Sarah Curnock.
Rates: D
A small elegant country house hotel in a most spectacular setting on the edge of Dartmoor. Resident owners are proud of their country house atmosphere, comfort, good food and personal service. Between Bovey Tracey and Haytor. BTA commended, three merit awards.

HIGHCLIFFE ON SEA (Nr Christchurch)   BEVERLY GLEN
1 Stuart Road, Highcliffe-on-Sea, Christchurch, Dorset BH23 5JS. *Tel*: Highcliffe (0425) 273811. *Hosts*: Mary & Peter Bourn.
Rates: A   Vouchers accepted.
Detached corner house in residential area, close to cliff walks, sandy beaches and shops. Golf. Sea and coarse fishing on Stour and Avon. 10 mins drive New Forest. Bournemouth 9 miles. Colour TV all rooms. Home-cooking, fresh produce. Dinner not available during August. Restaurants close by.

HONITON (Colestocks)   COLESTOCKS HOUSE
Colestocks, Honiton, Devon EX14 0JR. *Tel*: Honiton (0404) 850633. *Hosts*: Henri & Jacqueline Yot.
Rates: B
Lovely thatched country house with mature gardens in peaceful hamlet. Feature beds and 4-poster. All rooms en suite, colour TV. English and French home- cooking. Bargain breaks all year. Ground-floor rooms. Children over 10 welcome. Sorry, no pets.

HORRABRIDGE   OVERCOMBE HOTEL
Horrabridge, Nr Yelverton, Devon PL20 7RN. *Tel*: Yelverton (0822) 853501. *Hosts*: Maurice & Brenda Durnell.
Rates: B
Country house with panoramic views of Dartmoor National Park. Off A386, 1 mile north of Yelverton. Proprietors take pride in their

home-cooked meals. Children and dogs welcome. Disabled persons welcome.

IVYBRIDGE (Ermington)   ERMEWOOD HOUSE HOTEL
Totnes Road, Ermington, Ivybridge, South Devon PL21 9NS. *Tel*: Modbury (0548) 830741. *Hosts*: Jack & Jennifer Mellor.
Rates: C/D
   South-facing country house hotel overlooking beautiful River Erme valley, close to South Hams, sandy beaches and Dartmoor. 4-poster available. Off A38 at Ivybridge, through Ermington to B3210, turn right 200 yards. Easy access Plymouth 10 miles.

KINGSBRIDGE   KINGS ARMS HOTEL
Fore Street, Kingsbridge, South Devon TQ7 1AB. *Tel*: Kingsbridge (0548) 2071. *Fax*: 0548 2977. *Hosts*: Derek & Paula Budge.
Rates: D
   Attractive, warm 16th-century coaching inn, in interesting old country town. Plymouth 15 miles. Nice beaches nearby. Eight 4-posters & one half-tester available. Indoor heated swimming pool. Ballroom. Two golf courses, walking, touring, watersports.

KINGSTON   TREBLES COTTAGE HOTEL
Kingston, Nr Kingsbridge, South Devon TQ7 4PT. *Tel*: Bigbury-on-Sea (0548) 810268. *Hosts*: David & Georgiana Kinder.
Rates: B   Vouchers accepted.
(See page 42 for description)

LADOCK (Nr Truro)   BISSICK OLD MILL
Ladock, Nr Truro, Cornwall TR2 4PG. *Tel*: St Austell (0726) 882557. *Hosts*: Ray and Jean Giles.
Rates: C
(See page 43 for description)

LAND'S END   BOSCEAN COUNTRY HOTEL
St Just-in-Penwith, Penzance, Cornwall TR19 7QP. *Tel*: Penzance (0736) 788748. *Hosts*: Roy & Joyce Lee.
Rates: A/B
(See page 44 for description)

LISKEARD   THE OLD RECTORY HOTEL
Duloe Road, St Keyne, Liskeard, Cornwall PL14 4RL. *Tel*: Liskeard (0579) 42617. *Hosts*: Kate & Ron Wolfe.
Rates: C
(See page 45 for description)

LIZARD   PENMENNER HOUSE
Penmenner Road, The Lizard, Cornwall TR12 7NR. *Tel*: The Lizard (0326) 290370. *Hosts*: Peter & Liza Gembarski.

: B   Vouchers accepted.

Comfortable house in own secluded grounds, close to famous Lizard Head and lighthouse. Magnificent coastal scenery on Britain's most southerly point. Sandy coves. Cliff walks, fishing. Local produce, home-cooking.

LOOE   THE SNOOTY FOX
Morval, Looe, Cornwall PL13 1PR. *Tel*: Widegates (05034) 233. *Hosts*: Richard & Jacqui Rix, Anne & Peter Faulkner.
Rates: C   Vouchers accepted.

Lovely views of Cornish countryside from this comfortable modern inn. Sailing, fishing, riding and golf with special terms. Proprietors are proud of their reputation for their food and hospitality. Off A38 on A387 Liskeard/Looe (3 miles) road.

LYDFORD   LYDFORD HOUSE HOTEL
Lydford, Okehampton, Devon EX20 4AU. *Tel*: Lydford (082282) 347: *Hosts*: Ron & Ann Boulter.
Rates: C   Vouchers accepted.

Country house peacefully set on the edge of Dartmoor. All rooms with bathroom en suite. Just off A386, halfway between Okehampton and Tavistock. Ideal touring centre for Devon and Cornwall. Own fishing on River Lyd. Own riding stables in grounds, hourly or for full holidays. Children over 5 welcome. 4-poster bed.

LYME REGIS (Uplyme)   AMHERST LODGE FARM
Uplyme, Lyme Regis, Dorset DT7 3XH. *Tel*: Lyme Regis (02974) 2773. *Hosts*: Ian & Betty Collier.
Rates: C   Vouchers accepted.

Lovely 16th-century, comfortable house with attractive garden in 160 acres of woodland, lakes and pasture. Working sheep/cattle farm. All rooms en suite and colour TV. Licensed. Phone for directions. Supper every night, dinner Tues and Thurs. Children over 10 welcome. Reduced rates 2 nights or more. Sorry, no pets. Clay pigeon shooting. 5 acres of own trout lakes.

LYNMOUTH   HEATHERVILLE
Tors Park, Lynmouth, Devon EX35 6NB. *Tel*: Lynton (0598) 52327. *Hosts*: Sylvia & Frank Bilney.
Rates: B   Vouchers accepted.

Impressive location in south-facing Tors Park, with lovely views of Lynmouth village on the Lyn estuary. Short walk to harbour, beach and cliff railway to Lynton. Traditional English home-cooking. Reduced rates 2 nights or more. Lovely honeymoon suite. Sorry, no pets.

LYNMOUTH   THE BATH HOTEL
Lynmouth Street, Lynmouth, North Devon EX35 6EL. *Tel*: Lynton (0598) 52238. *Hosts*: The Braunton & Dalgarno Families.
Rates: C/D   Vouchers accepted.

In prominent position overlooking Lynmouth quayside and river estuary.

Friendly family-run hotel in very attractive North Devon coastal resort. Use of Tors Hotel facilities, including swimming pool. Swimming, fishing. Restaurant serves salmon from hotel's own trap.

LYNTON NEUBIA HOUSE HOTEL
Lydiate Lane, Lynton, North Devon EX35 6RH. *Tel*: Lynton (0598) 52309. *Hosts*: Brian & Dorothy Murphy.
Rates: B/C Vouchers accepted.
Centrally situated in picturesque old hill-top village. Quiet cul-de-sac, ample parking. Spectacular cliff walks and cliff railway to harbour and beach. Cordon bleu cooking. Vegetarian/wholefoods available. Reduced rates 2 nights or more.

MALMESBURY MARSH FARMHOUSE
Crudwell Road, Malmesbury, Wilts SN16 9JL. *Tel*: Malmesbury (0666) 822208. *Hosts*: David & Sarah Clarke.
Rates: B
Cotswold stone farm buildings converted to comfortable accommodation. All rooms en suite and colour TV. No smoking in bedrooms. Good food at pub ½ m away. A mile from the centre of historic Malmesbury. Cirencester, Chippenham 10 miles. On A429, 5 miles from M4 (junc 17).

MARAZION (A 'no smoking' house) CASTLE GAYER
Marazion, Cornwall TR17 0AQ. *Tel*: Penzance (0736) 711548. *Hosts*: John Trewhella & Brian Ivory.
Rates: C Vouchers accepted.
Victorian sea captain's house in superb position on peninsula in Mount Bay. All rooms en suite with colour TV and tea/coffee facilities. Log fires. No evening meals but many restaurants near. Safe sandy beach. Coastal path. Sailing, windsurfing, golf and walking area. Penzance 3m, St Ives 7m, Land's End 10m. Sorry, no children or pets.

MERE CHETCOMBE HOUSE HOTEL
Chetcombe Road, Mere, Wiltshire BA12 6AZ. *Tel*: Mere (0747) 860219. *Hosts*: Colin & Sue Ross.
Rates: C Vouchers accepted.
(See page 46 for description)

MORCHARD BISHOP (A 'no smoking' house) WIGHAM
Morchard Bishop, Nr Crediton, Devon EX17 6RJ. *Tel*: Morchard Bishop (036 37) 350. *Hosts*: Lesley & Stephen Chilcott.
Rates: D (incl dinner) Vouchers accepted.
(See page 47 for description)

MORTEHOE SUNNYCLIFFE HOTEL
Mortehoe, Devon EX34 7EB. *Tel*: Woolacombe (0271) 870597. *Hosts*: Victor & Betty Bassett.
Rates: B/C Vouchers accepted.
(See page 48 for description)

NEWQUAY (Pentire)   CORISANDE MANOR HOTEL

Riverside Avenue, Pentire, Newquay, Cornwall TR7 1PL. *Tel*: Newquay (0637) 872042. *Hosts*: David & Anne Painter.

Rates: C   Vouchers accepted.

On quiet Pentire, lovely location, all rooms overlooking Gannel estuary with private foreshore. 3 acres secluded landscaped gardens. Peace, tranquillity. Putting, croquet, rowing boats, outdoor giant chess and draughts. Children over 3 welcome. Closed mid Oct–early May. Chef-proprietor. Linked annexe.

NEWTON FERRERS   COURT HOUSE HOTEL

Newton Ferrers, South Devon PL8 1AQ. *Tel*: Plymouth (0752) 872324. *Hosts*: Alan & Mary Gilchrist.

Rates: C/D   Vouchers accepted.

Quiet, comfortable country house hotel in 3 acres of wooded grounds in middle of village by church. Heated swimming pool. 4–poster available. Log fires. Sailing, walking, golf and many National Trust houses nearby. Plymouth 10 miles, Dartmoor 10 miles. Children over 8 welcome.

PENZANCE   MOUNT PROSPECT HOTEL

Britons Hill, Penzance, Cornwall TR18 3AE. *Tel*: Penzance (0736) 63117. *Fax*: 0736 50970. *Hosts*: The Blakeley Family.

Rates: D   Vouchers accepted.

(See page 48 for description)

PLYMOUTH   TRILLIUM GUEST HOUSE

4 Alfred Street, The Hoe, Plymouth, Devon PL1 2RP. *Tel*: Plymouth (0752) 670452. *Hosts*: The Cross Family.

Rates: B

Comfortable guest house with a homely and friendly atmosphere close to city centre, the Hoe and the Barbican. Imaginative home-cooked food. French, Italian, German and Spanish spoken. Children welcome. Reservation for car park necessary. Sorry, no pets.

POLPERRO   NATAL HOUSE

The Coombes, Polperro, Cornwall PL13 2RH. *Tel*: Polperro (0503) 72532. *Hosts*: Archie & Mavis Lund.

Rates: B

Comfortable house situated in quaint and historic fishing village, flanked by NT land, affording picturesque cliff walks and nature rambles. All rooms with colour TV and bathrooms en suite. Sorry, no pets.

PORLOCK (A 'no smoking' house) TERRELLS COTTAGE HOTEL

By Old Lane, Minehead Road, Porlock, Somerset TA24 8EY. *Tel*: Porlock (0643) 862638. *Hosts*: Marjorie & Graham Plumb.

Rates: B

Attractive, Georgian-style house, large peaceful garden, edge of village, in Exmoor National Park. Close Selworthy, Dunster and Dunkery Beacon. Colour TV all rooms. Good value 4-day breaks. Sorry, no pets. Children over 12 are welcome. Closed Oct–May.

POUNDSGATE   LEUSDON LODGE

Poundsgate, South Dartmoor, Devon TQ13 7PE. *Tel*: Poundsgate (03643) 304. *Hosts*: Don, Betty & Lynne Moses.
Rates: B   Vouchers accepted.
   A 150-year-old granite house set in its own hillside grounds with panoramic views. Off A38 towards Princetown, after Poundsgate turn right to Leusdon and Lower Town. Home-cooking, local produce. British Tourist Authority commended. Pets welcome.

RANGEWORTHY   RANGEWORTHY COURT HOTEL

Church Lane, Wotton Road, Rangeworthy, Bristol, Avon BS17 5ND. *Tel*: Rangeworthy (0454 22) 347 & 473. *Fax*: 045422 8945. *Hosts*: Mervyn & Lucia Gillett.
Rates: D   Vouchers accepted.
   Comfortable, elegant 17th-century, manor house built for Lord Chief Justice. 2½ acres well tended gardens. Oak beams. Log fires. 4-poster room and half-tester. Antiques throughout. 10 mins M5 (junc 14), 15 mins M4. Bristol 20 mins, Bath 30 mins.

SALISBURY   STRATFORD LODGE

4 Park Lane, Castle Road, Salisbury, Wiltshire SP1 3NP. *Tel*: Salisbury (0722) 25177 (from summer 1990 (0722) 325177). *Host*: Jill Bayly.
Rates: B   Vouchers accepted.
   Elegant Victorian home furnished with antiques, opposite Victoria Park. Dinner by prior arrangement, NOT Sunday. Imaginative breakfasts and dinners using own and local produce. Non-smokers preferred. Children over 8 welcome. All rooms colour TV and en suite. Castle Road is A345 to Amesbury, turn at post office/store. Sorry, no pets.

ST AGNES   ROSEVEAN HOTEL

Rosemundy, St. Agnes, Cornwall TR5 0UD. *Tel*: St. Agnes (087 255) 2277. *Hosts*: Derek & Edna Brierley.
Rates: C/D   Vouchers accepted.
   Imposing early Victorian building with secluded gardens, near pretty village square. Close to three attractive bays with beautiful coastal walks. All rooms with colour TV. Ample parking. Golf, riding, fishing nearby.

ST AUSTELL (St Blazey)   (A 'no smoking' house) NANSCAWEN HOUSE

Prideaux Road, St Blazey, Par, Cornwall PL24 2SR. *Tel*: Par (0726 81) 4488. *Hosts*: Janet & Keith Martin.
Rates: B/C   Vouchers accepted.
   Quiet, comfortable and elegant Georgian home in 2 acres of gardens. Du

aurier country. Saints Way, Luxulyan Valley, Lanhydrock House, many aches and coves nearby. All rooms en suite. Children over 12 welcome. rry, no pets. Closed Jan. Log fires. Heated outdoor pool. St Austell 4 miles, Fowey 5 miles.

ST IVES   THE GARRACK HOTEL
Burthallan Lane, St Ives, Cornwall TR26 3AA. *Tel*: Penzance (0736) 796199. *Fax*: 0736 798955. *Hosts*: The Kilby Family.
Rates: D   Vouchers accepted.

Country house atmosphere in creeper-covered granite hotel in 2 acres of gardens overlooking Porthmeor beach and St Ives. Ideal centre for exploring Cornish peninsula. 4-posters available, indoor pool, sauna, solarium, whirl-pool spa. Land's End side of St Ives – well signposted.

ST IVES   THE OLD VICARAGE HOTEL
Parc-an-Creet, St Ives, Cornwall TR26 2ET. *Tel*: Penzance (0736) 796124. *Hosts*: Jack & Irene Sykes.
Rates: A/B   Vouchers accepted.

Exceptionally well converted Victorian rectory with great character and charm. In wooded grounds, just over ½ mile from town centre off St Ives/Lands End Road B3306. Moorland and beaches within easy reach.

SHALDON   GLENSIDE HOTEL
Ringmore Road, Shaldon, South Devon TQ14 0EP. *Tel*: Shaldon (0626) 872448 *Hosts*: Derek & Ann Newbold.
Rates: B   Vouchers accepted.
(See page 49 for description)

SIDMOUTH   GREENWAY HOUSE
Greenway Lane, Sidmouth, Devon EX10 0LZ. *Tel*: Sidmouth (0395) 514487. *Hosts*: Barbara & Peter Chittenden.
Rates: A   Vouchers accepted.

Comfortable Edwardian house in 'area of outstanding natural beauty'. Ideal centre for touring Devon. Good local pubs and restaurants. Children over 10 welcome. 2 miles from Sidmouth town and beach on B3176. Sorry, no pets.

SOUTH BRENT   COOMBE HOUSE
North Huish, South Brent, South Devon TQ10 9NJ. *Tel*: Gara Bridge (054882) 277. *Hosts*: Alan & Bunny Jaques.
Rates: C   Vouchers accepted.
Sorry, no pets.
(See page 50 for description)

SOUTH BRENT   (A 'no smoking' house) THE ROCK
South Brent, South Devon TQ10 9JL. *Tel*: South Brent (0364) 72185. *Hosts*: George & Avril Chapman.
Rates: B   Vouchers accepted.

Early Victorian listed building set in lovely garden with mill stream beside

River Avon, Lydia Falls and Lydia Bridge. One bedroom with lounge and bathroom en suite. One with private bathroom and WC. Outdoor swimming pool. Closed Dec and Jan. Dinner by arrangement only. Good local pub. Children over 8 welcome. Phone for directions.

SPREYTON (Nr Crediton) DOWNHAYES
Spreyton, Crediton, Devon EX17 5AR. *Tel*: Bow (0363) 82378. *Hosts*: Mr & Mrs Hines.
Rates: B/C Vouchers accepted.
(See page 51 for description)

SWANAGE CROWTHORNE HOTEL
24 Cluny Crescent, Swanage, Dorset BH19 2BT. *Tel*: Swanage (0929) 422108.
Hosts: Clive Doran & Cathy Bridge
Rates: A/B Vouchers accepted.
Discover the natural beauty of the Dorset coast whilst staying in an attractive Victorian property overlooking Swanage Bay. Close to beach and town centre. Watersports, fishing and golf available. Home-cooking. Special weekly rates, half board and children sharing. Sorry, no pets.

SWINDON (Cricklade) CRICKLADE HOTEL AND COUNTRY CLUB
Common Hill, Cricklade, Nr Swindon, Wiltshire SN6 6HA. *Tel*: Swindon (0793) 750751. *Fax*: 0793 751767. *Host*: Else-Marie Kearney.
Rates: D
Very attractive, comfortable hotel in 25 acres secluded grounds. Off A419, Swindon 7 miles, Cirencester 8 miles. Golf course, tennis court, indoor swimming pool, spa bath, steam room, gym, solarium and snooker available. Children over 14 welcome and accommodated free when sharing parents' room. Honeymoon suites. Sorry, no pets. Annexe.

TAUNTON THE FALCON HOTEL
Henlade, Taunton, Somerset TA3 5DH. *Tel*: Taunton (0823) 442502. *Hosts*: Tony & Glen Rutland.
Rates: D Vouchers accepted.
Country house style hotel in an acre of gardens 1 mile east of M5 at junct 25, on A358 to Yeovil. 4-poster available. Some no-smoking rooms. Children welcome. Merit award. Sorry, no pets except guide dogs.

TAUNTON (Beercrocombe) WHITTLES FARM
Beercrocombe, Taunton, Somerset TA3 6AH. *Tel*: Hatch Beauchamp (0823) 480301. *Hosts*: Clare & John Mitchem.
Rates: B
(See page 52 for description)

TAUNTON (Norton Fitzwarren) OLD MANOR FARMHOUSE
Norton Fitzwarren, Taunton, Somerset TA2 6RZ. *Tel*: Taunton (0823) 289801.
Hosts: Eric & Vera Foley.

Rates: B   Vouchers accepted.
Pleasant Edwardian property in village on A361, 3 miles west of Taunton. Verdant cider country. Easy access M5 exit 25. Proprietors proud of high-class regional cooking using own produce. Varied menu. Selection vegetarian dishes. All rooms with bathroom en suite, colour TV and direct dial 'phone.

TORQUAY FAIRMOUNT HOUSE HOTEL
Herbert Road, Chelston, Torquay, Devon TQ2 6RW. *Tel*: Torquay (0803) 605446. *Hosts*: Noel & Maggie Tolkien.
Rates: B   Vouchers accepted.
(See page 53 for description)

TOTNES (Harberton) FORD FARM HOUSE
Harberton, Nr Totnes, South Devon TQ9 7JS. *Tel*: Totnes (0803) 863539.
Hosts: Mike & Sheila Edwards.
Rates: B   Vouchers accepted.
(See page 54 for description)

WESTON SUPER MARE THE COMMODORE HOTEL
Beach Road, Sand Bay, Kewstoke, Weston-super-Mare, Avon BS22 9UZ. *Tel*: Weston-super-Mare (0934) 415778. *Fax*: 0934 636483. *Host*: Mr J Stoakes.
Rates: D
Bright and cheerful hotel on bay outside town. Wide range of walks through woods and by the sea. NT headland and riding facilities nearby. Restaurant and bars. Golf arranged with local courses. Conference facilities available.

WESTON-SUPER-MARE (Hutton) MOORLANDS
Hutton, Weston-super-Mare, Avon BS24 9QH. *Tel*: Bleadon (0934) 812283.
Hosts: Margaret & David Holt.
Rates: A/B   Vouchers accepted.
(See page 55 for description)

WEYMOUTH BAY LODGE
27 Greenhill, Weymouth, Dorset DT4 7SW. *Tel*: Weymouth (0305) 782419.
Hosts: Barbara & Graham Dubben.
Rates: A/B   Vouchers accepted.
Imposing house in own grounds overlooking Weymouth Bay and next to Lodmoor Country Park. All rooms colour TV. Log fires. Oak panelled dining room. Ferry crossing Cherbourg. Hydrofoil Channel Islands. Breaks available November to March.

WEYMOUTH MOONFLEET MANOR HOTEL
Moonfleet, Nr Weymouth, Dorset DT3 4ED. *Tel*: Weymouth (0305) 786948.
Hosts: Bruce & Jan Hemingway.
Rates: D   Vouchers accepted.
Georgian manor house in the country, by the sea. Indoor heated swimming pool open all year, sauna, solarium, 3 squash courts, full snooker table. 2

hard tennis courts. Cellar Club. Off B3157 Bridport/Weymouth (5 miles) road. Two miles down private drive. Indoor 4-rink bowls hall. 4-poster. Superior ground floor rooms. Sorry, no pets.

WIMBORNE (A 'no smoking' house) KENILWORTH COTTAGE
Colehill Lane, Wimborne, Dorset BH21 7AW. *Tel*: Wimborne (0202) 883159. *Hosts*: Pattie and Ray Dutton.
Rates: B Vouchers accepted.
Pretty thatched cottage in an acre of garden. Beautiful touring area. NT Kingston Lacy House 2 miles. Thomas Hardy country. Badbury Rings, Wimborne Minster 2 miles. Bournemouth 9 miles. Phone for directions. Sorry, no pets.

WINSFORD KARSLAKE HOUSE HOTEL
Winsford, Somerset TA24 7JG. *Tel*: Winsford (064 385) 242. *Hosts*: Jane Young & Fred Alderton.
Rates: C
Small friendly 15th-century country hotel in centre of Exmoor National Park. Enthusiastic chefs. Reduced rates for 2-day breaks. Hunting, shooting, fishing, riding and walking area. Tarr Steps and Dunkery Beacon nearby.

WIVELISCOMBE WATERCOMBE HOUSE
Huish Champflower, Nr Wiveliscombe, Taunton, Somerset TA4 2EE. *Tel*: Wiveliscombe (0984) 23725. *Host*: Moira Garner-Richards.
Rates: A Vouchers accepted.
Charming country home with river frontage and pool, Exmoor close. 3½ acres copse and paddock. Fly fishing, sailing, riding, lovely walks. Log fires and home-cooking. 20 mins coast. No smoking in bedrooms. Phone for directions. Children over 10 welcome. Sorry, no pets.

Eagle House   Bed and Breakfast only
Church Street
Bathford
Avon
BA1 7RS

☎ Bath (0225) 859946

John and Rosamund Napier

Off A4, 3 miles from Bath

This is a small, listed, Georgian mansion built round an Elizabethan malt-house, which is still intact within the newer, larger building. It is an elegant, comfortable house, with a most attractive landscaped garden which descends the hillside in steps, with very fine views over the Avon valley. There are six bedrooms, all with their own private facilities and colour TV, furnished in period and antique furniture. The public rooms are all very pleasant with open fires, antiques and the family's 17th- and 18th-century portrait collection. The drawing room is a quite spectacular octagonal room, with a 17-foot ceiling.

  John has a wealth of experience in the hotel business, having worked for some of the largest chains in the country including a stint at the Savoy in London. He and his journalist wife, Rosamund, are very welcoming and helpful hosts; they take great trouble to ensure their guests enjoy their stay at Eagle House to the full, booking sports activities (including hot air ballooning), theatre seats, and dinner reservations. As there is no dinner served at Eagle House, it is quite usual for John and Rosamund to find their guests dinner bookings, and they consider it their responsibility to find an eating establishment to suit the purse and palate of each guest.

Easily Accessible: Please see entry on The Orchard, Bathford, p.32.

Paradise House   Bed and Breakfast only
Holloway   Sorry, no pets
Bath
BA2 4PX

☎ Bath (0225) 317723

David and Janet Cutting

The views of Bath and the surrounding hills from the rear of this beautiful Georgian house are quite wonderful. Situated in a quiet residential cul-de-sac, it is only a seven-minute walk from the town centre.

David was a squadron leader in the Royal Air Force, and Janet was a fashion designer, so running a guest house was a radical change for them both – but as it turned out, a happy and successful one. They have worked very hard over the last nine years to create a warm, comfortable and gracious environment from a building which was, on their arrival, fairly dilapidated. Today there is a fresh, light breakfast room, a pretty sitting room, and nine bedrooms, each equipped with a colour TV.

The spacious walled garden is quite lovely, with neat lawns and rose-covered pergolas – and of course, those splendid views of the elegant Georgian town of Bath.

There is no evening meal, but Bath has restaurants to suit all tastes.

Easily Accessible: Please see entry on The Orchard, Bath, p.32.

The Orchard
80 High Street
Bathford
Bath

BA1 7TG

☎ Bath(0225) 858765

Olga and John London

Three miles from Bath

Closed Nov–Feb
Children over 11 welcome
Sorry, no pets
No smoking in bedrooms
Bed and Breakfast only

This beautiful listed Georgian country house lies in the conservation village of Bathford, just 3 miles from Bath. Guests have a wing with a lounge and dining room to themselves; the rooms are spacious and elegant, furnished with antiques, and have marvellous views of the grounds and surrounding hills. Each bedroom has a private bathroom and colour television, and one has an orthopaedic queen-size bed which has proved very popular with guests. The walled garden is quite lovely, with sloping lawns and a wide variety of mature trees.

A healthy breakfast is served, consisting of home-made muesli, live yogurt, wholemeal bread and free-range eggs. Dinner is not offered, but the local pub is recommended by the Londons and there are many pubs and restaurants in Bath.

Easily Accessible: Bathford is an attractive stone-built village dating mainly from the 1700s. There is a very pretty walk around Bathford, another to Bath along the canal towpath, and yet another in the nearby Limpley Stoke valley, recently designated an area of outstanding natural beauty. Bath is a beautiful city well known for its spa, its Roman baths and the excellence of its Georgian architecture, an example of which is the supremely elegant Crescent. The Huntingdon Centre in the Paragon has a fascinating display on Bath's history. There is a wealth of interesting shops, and a wide variety of museums – for example, the museum of costumes in the Assembly Rooms. In May and June the prestigious Music and Arts Festival is held. There is a regular bus service from Bathford to Bath, with a stop conveniently situated just a minute's walk from The Orchard. Corsham Court (5 miles) has some fine Georgian state rooms, and grounds with a 15th-century gazebo. There are many beauty spots in the surrounding countryside, including the quite spectacular Cheddar Gorge (28 miles) with its signposted walks and underground caves to explore.

Local Activities: Walks, golf, tennis, horse-riding, hot-air ballooning, cycling.

Mount Hotel
Northdown Road
Bideford
Devon
EX39 3LP

No smoking in bedrooms
Sorry, no pets

☎ Bideford (0231) 473748

Mike and Janet Taylor

Close to town centre, phone for directions.

This small, attractive Georgian house is situated near to the centre of the riverside town of Bideford; it has a delightful secluded garden dominated by a beautiful 100-year old copper beech, and also a protected patio. Inside, the décor is elegant and traditional, the gentle colour scheme creating a relaxing ambience. Guests tend to congregate in the lounge for a chat over a drink from the 'snug' bar, or to watch TV. There are seven bedrooms, three of which are en suite. The Taylors' main aim is to make their guests feel very welcome and as committed Christians they are happy to see the Mount Hotel used as a retreat.

The restaurant is open to residents and guests of residents. The diet is a wholesome one; healthy foods such as salads, wholemeal bread and semi-skimmed milk are used. To counteract all this healthy eating, real Devonshire clotted cream is often available and there is a small bar serving a variety of drinks - draught beer is not available due to lack of space! Vegetarian meals can be provided, and packed lunches are available on request.

Easily Accessible: Bideford itself is a charming place to amble through, with its narrow streets, picturesque quay and famous medieval bridge. A two-hour boat trip will take you to Lundy Island, once famous for its pirates and now for its puffins. There are numerous footpaths in the area, the most notable being the long-distance South West Coastal Path. There are also some interesting local walks, including nature trails around the Tamar lakes. Of the many pretty villages to see, Clovelly, ten miles away, with its narrow winding cobbled streets and its ban on cars, is a delight. Barnstaple, the principal town of North Devon, is only a mile away. There are several excellent beaches; the most famous must be that at Westward Ho!, just two miles away. Incidentally, Westward Ho! was named after Charles Kingsley's book and not, as one would expect, the other way around.

Local Activities: Walks, fishing, golf, horse-riding, bowls, tennis, swimming.

St Christopher's Country House Closed Nov-Feb
Boscastle
Cornwall
PL35 OBD
Boscastle (08405) 412

Brian and Brenda Thompson

In Boscastle village

This cosy hotel is situated in the unspoilt harbour village of Boscastle on the North Cornwall coast. Boscastle is a truly delightful place, which looks very much the same as it must have done 600 years ago with its narrow winding streets and pretty 14th-century cottages.

The house is full of character and Cornish charm, with a slate floor in the reception area and a large comfortable sitting room with an open fire. Eight of the nine bedrooms have en suite facilities, and two have excellent views over the village towards the coast. The décor throughout the house is simple but tasteful.

The food is fresh and home-cooked. Specialities of the house are the crab soup, made from locally caught crabs, and homemade sweets. Brian

renda Thompson, who previously ran a restaurant, are cheery and
y and will help you make the most of your stay.

Easily Accessible: There are 300 miles of unspoilt coastline and moors to
explore. The walk from Boscastle to Tintagel(3 miles away) takes you
through spectacular coastal scenery. Another, from the harbour to St
Juliot's Church through the delightful Valency Valley (where Thomas
Hardy courted his Emma), is particularly lovely in spring, when you
tread upon a carpet of bluebells and primroses. The whole area is
steeped in legend and history. Boscastle itself has long been associated
with smuggling and witchcraft, and today has a witchcraft museum.
At Camelford (Tennyson's Camelot) you can visit the North Cornwall
Museum and the ancient stone circles. Tintagel with its ruined castle is
closely associated with the legend of King Arthur.

Local Activities: Walks, surfing, golf, diving, fishing, bird-watching,
pleasure boat trips, sandy beaches.

Roundham House Hotel
Roundham Gardens, West Bay Rd
Bridport
Dorset
DT6 4BD

☎ Bridport (0308) 22753

David and Pat Moody

Closed Nov–Jan, please check
Chauffeuring service to and
  from station

1 mile south of Bridport past Crown Inn, left of West Bay Rd

This Victorian stone house standing in an elevated position on the edge
of Bridport has very fine views of both the sea and country. There is a
pretty secluded garden and a sunny terrace. The decor is full of period
charm and colour. The spacious porch leads into an elegant hall, from
which access is made to the lounge, bar and dining room. The bedrooms
are comfortable with co-ordinated furniture and fittings and all have
private facilities and a colour TV.
    David and Pat Moody are very professional hosts – it was Pat's
grandmother who started the business in 1911 and Pat was born in
the hotel.
    Dinner is offered: a table d'hôte menu of six inventive courses.
This is served from the end of May to the end of October; otherwise a
'meagre' four courses are available! The proprieters describe the food as
a mixture of traditional British (such as 'Rabbit with juniper berries') and
French. Produce is, when possible, taken from the kitchen garden and

fruit trees and good use is made of local game, freshly caught shellfish and local cheeses – Dorset Blue Vinney is a favourite. Lunch and packed lunches are available.

Easily Accessible: Bridport is an interesting Saxon town, historically famous for its rope-making – a hangman's noose used to be known as a Bridport dagger. To the south is West Bay, a small port with a shingle beach. The coastal road to Weymouth from Bridport has spectacular scenery and half way along it, you pass through the unspoilt village of Abbotsbury, lined with thatched cottages. Fifteen miles away is Forde Abbey , a 900-year old Cistercian monastery with gardens. Parnham House 6 miles away is the home of Viscount Linley's furniture business. Dorchester, the 'Casterbridge' of Hardy's novels, is 15 miles away. Take a day trip to Wells and Glastonbury, both within a 30-mile radius.

Local Activities: walks, golf, fishing, horse-riding, bowling.

Torr House
Thorn Cross
Chagford
Newton Abbot
Devon
TQ13 8DX

☎ Chagford(06473)2228

John and Hazel Cork

Follow sign through Chagford to Fernworthy/Kestor Rock.

Torr House is an attractive granite building, dating from the early 18th century, and was home, originally, to a woollen merchant. It is situated in the Dartmoor National Park, amidst gentle rolling hills and woods where buzzards nest. Herons can be seen fishing in the tumbling stream. Today it is the home of John and Hazel Cork who renovated it after years of neglect and a serious fire. As they put it, they feel that they have 'put back the life into a very contented house'. They have managed to do this without losing the original character of the building; marble fireplaces, Victorian and Georgian chests, a collection of clocks and a grand piano which has been in the house since the turn of the century, all seem to be very much at home here. The house faces south and has a delightful sheltered terrace and two acres of garden which is host to a splendid bank of rhododendrons and a copse of red cedar, beech, willow and prunus. There are four bedrooms, all with en suite or private facilities and fine views.

Breakfast is plentiful and Hazel's home-baked bread is delicious. The four-course evening meal is served by candlelight and afterwards coffee is served in the drawing room by a log fire. The cheeseboard offers a good selection of locally produced cheeses such as applewood smoked cheese and the wonderfully named Cornish Yarg.

Easily Accessible: The whole of Dartmoor spreads before you. In addition to their wild natural beauty, the moors contain interesting ancient relics and sites that are well worth investigating. Four miles away you can visit Castle Drogo, a splendid private house, designed by Sir Edwin Lutyens, now owned by the National Trust. At Okehampton, you can visit the Dartmoor Centre with its museum of Dartmoor life, working craft studios and Victorian tea rooms.

Nearby, in the small village of Sticklepath, the Museum of Rural Industry gives one a clear understanding of the skills and hard work involved in living in such a remote area.

Local Activities: walks, golf, horse-riding, fishing, bird-watching.

Waddon House

Chudleigh
Nr Exeter
Devon
TQ13 ODJ

Children over 10 welcome
A 'no smoking' house

☎ Chudleigh (0626) 853216

Sylvia Frowd

Just outside village of Chudleigh

After a long drive this charming house with its friendly and welcoming hostess is most refreshing. It stands in gardens landscaped over a period of two years (which were designed to ensure an array of colours and scents throughout the year), and woodlands resplendent with over one hundred species of trees and shrubs, the home of owls, badgers, green woodpeckers, pheasants and foxes. The house was built in the 1930s and faces south with glorious views of Dartmoor, shared by all the principal bedrooms. The interior is airy, elegant and newly furnished in an Edwardian style. There are six bedrooms, all en suite or with adjoining bathrooms, and provided with colour TV. One has a four-poster bed and another, a half-tester, which reputedly once belonged to Lily Langtry.

Guests are invited to join Sylvia Frowd in the elegant drawing room for cocktails before the four-course evening meal. Local and home produce is used.

Easily Accessible: Of course, the best walks are on Dartmoor, fifteen minutes away by car. Just 2 miles away, you can visit Ugbrooke stately home and park, a Robert Adam mansion built circa 1778 with a fine collection of furniture and paintings. Killerton House and gardens, 10 miles away, has fifteen acres of beautiful hillside gardens, and some splendid views. The house, rebuilt in 1778, houses a splendid collection of costumes. At Rockbeare, the English Lace School (the only one in the country) invites you to watch and even participate in the lacemaking. Plymouth and Exeter and the coast at Torquay are easily reached for day trips.

Local Activities: sauna and tennis at Waddon House, walks, trout-fishing, horse-riding, golf.

Broadview   Unlicensed
43 East Street
Crewkerne
Somerset
TA18 7AG

☎ Crewkerne (0460) 73424

Gillian and Robert Swann

On the Yeovil road, on edge of town

This colonial-style bungalow stands in an elevated position, set back from the main road, with fine views of the small Somerset town of Crewkerne and the surrounding hills. It faces south, in over an acre of landscaped gardens with a feature water-garden. Inside, the décor is inventive with an imaginative mix of old-fashioned elegance and a co-ordinated mish-mash of plants, caged finches and colourful rugs. The sun lounge with its comfortable settees is ideal to relax in. All the bedrooms have views over the garden and Crewkerne. Each has been individually decorated and is equipped with a colour TV and en suite facilities.
    Dinner is a home-cooked, traditionally English meal – for example, home-made chicken soup; roast beef and Yorkshire pudding; and fresh fruit flan. Gillian relies on fresh produce and quality food.

Easily Accessible: Broadview is well situated for visits to Somerset, Devon and Dorset. Crewkerne itself has many interesting historical buildings and antique shops, and many local walks start here. The Cricket St Thomas Wildlife Park, consisting of 1000 acres of land given over to (amongst other things) a working dairy farm, wildlife, a pets' corner and an aviary for tropical birds, is only ten minutes' drive away. The coast which offers some splendid walks, can be reached in thirty-five minutes. There is a multitude of stately homes and historic sites to visit, including Glastonbury Abbey and Tor, where Joseph of Arimathea is said to have buried the chalice used at the Last Supper; and Montacute House, a very fine Elizabethan mansion with formal gardens. Compton House, another stately home, houses a fine collection of butterflies from all over the world. In the ancient village of Mulchelney you will find the second oldest monastery in the county, with buildings surviving from the 16th century. Just south of Mulchelney you can visit the John Leach pottery.

Local Activities: Walks, fishing (sea and river), golf, bird-watching, horse-riding.

Ford House   Unlicensed
44 Victoria Road   Will collect guests from
Dartmouth   station
Devon
TQ6 9DX

☎ Dartmouth (08043) 4047
(From March 1990 (0803) 834047)

Henrietta and Richard Turner

This is an attractive listed building within easy reach of the centre of Dartmouth. It is elegantly furnished, light and spacious, and the atmosphere is very relaxed – breakfast, for instance, is served until midday, so there is never any pressure to hurry. There is a small walled garden at the front. The character of the original house is very much intact, with open fireplaces, shutters and servants' bells echoing a previous age.

Richard and Henrietta set up the business in 1987. Richard, who hails from Australia, and his wife Henrietta have travelled extensively through Europe, China and India. Meeting people from all over the world became a hobby for them and they were both very happy to turn it into a way of life.

Henrietta is a trained cook with a varied repertoire including French, Italian and Oriental food, and is happy to cater for special diets. Evening meals include such delights as 'fresh sea bass, wrapped in lettuce leaves and filled with sorrel and tarragon', and desserts such as 'lime mousse with passionfruit sauce'. Vegetables are fresh from their allotment breakfast jams and marmalade are home-made. If guests feel like a out, there are numerous pubs and restuarants in Dartmouth.

Easily Accessible: Ford House is situated in an area of Devon known as the South Hams – 'Hamme' is old English for a 'sheltered place' – and the climate here is particularly kind as the coasts are washed by the Gulf Stream. Walks abound, along the coastal and cliff paths and the river, and through local woods. Dartmouth itself is a very pretty town, with wealth of historic buildings (including a 15th-century castle) and considerable 'olde worlde' charm. On Tuesdays and Fridays, Dartmouth market, which has existed since 1828, still bustles. Totnes, 8 miles away, can be reached by boat; amongst other attractions, it has a motor museum, Elizabethan museum and the country's only horse-drawn double-decker bus service. All around there are numerous pretty villages and many miles of gentle rolling countryside to explore.

Local Activities: Walks, golf, sailing, fishing, river cruises, sandy beaches, open-air swimming pool, tennnis, bird-watching.

The Cottage
Westbrook
Bromham
Nr Chippenham
Wiltshire
SN15 2EE

☎ Devizes (0380) 850255

Gloria Steed

On the A3102 Calne-Melksham road

Bed and Breakfast only
Sorry, no pets

This delightful 15th-century cottage (grade II listed) shelters in the tiny hamlet of Westbrook. It was once the home of the Irish poet Thomas Moore. Surrounded by beautiful countryside, it is an ideal rural retreat. Its large landscaped garden (which includes an orchard with a nine-hole putting course) is lovingly tended by your hosts, gardening enthusiasts Gloria and Richard, who will gladly give cuttings.

The guest accommodation is an attractive converted barn attached to the main house. The three double rooms, all with en suite shower, are 'attic'-style with fresh flowers and wonderful views of the garden, surrounding fields and woodland, which is home to rabbits, pheasants and deer.

Breakfast (strawberries and raspberries in season) is served in a

pretty room with white stone walls and beams made of ships' timber.
No dinner is provided but Gloria and Richard will recommend local
restaurants and make reservations.

Easily Accessible: Walkers will be delighted to know that Wiltshire has
over 4,000 miles of footpath. Nearby is a Roman road and a little further afield is the Ridgeway, the Wansdyke Path and the Tan Hill Way.
Within a 15-mile radius you can visit: the National Trust village of
Lacock with 13th-century abbey; the Fox Talbot Museum of Photogra-
phy; Bowood House with gardens and adventure playground; Sheldon
Manor, Wiltshire's oldest inhabited manor house; Castle Combe, a very
pretty village; Devizes with a market on Thursdays; Bradford-on-Avon
with a Saxon church; Avebury Stone Circle, the largest in Europe and
owned by the National Trust.

Local Activities: walks, golf, horse-riding.

Prospect House

1 Church Road
Penryn
Cornwall
TR10 8DA

Children over 12 welcome
Chauffeuring service (Rolls
   or Landrover)

☎ Falmouth (0326) 73918

Cliff Paul and Barry Sheppard

Prospect House is an attractive town house, with a pretty, secluded
garden. Situated close to the harbour its nautical connections (it was
once owned by a local shipowner) are very evident – all the bedrooms
are named after local sailing ships. Built in 1830, it retains many of its
original features: the elaborately painted plaster cornices, stained-glass
'Cornish' porch and panelled mahogany doors. It has been very styl-
ishly furnished by Cliff and Barry with great attention to detail. The
dining room, for instance, has William IV dining chairs in walnut, and
a specially commissioned refectory table, a small Cornish stove and the
original (restored) window shutters. All four bedrooms have en suite
facilities and are furnished individually with great care; the prettiest
is perhaps the Waterwitch room, with its low bay window looking
over the garden.
    Cliff Paul and Barry Sheppard began taking in paying guests as an
extension of their enthusiasm for entertaining friends. They deliberately
limit the number of guests to six at any one time as they aim to preserve

the home-from-home atmosphere. Cliff is the cook, and loves the job, especially as he can use produce from the greenhouse and herb garden. A long-established vine provides grapes in season. Cliff is only too pleased to prepare a celebratory meal for any special occasion.

Easily Accessible: Within an hour's drive from Prospect House, there are many of Cornwall's favourite beauty spots: beaches, gardens, and National Trust and English Heritage properties. Pendennis Castle, which withstood a Roundhead siege during the Civil War for five months, is only 3 miles away. Penryn itself is unspoilt, and its old and narrow streets are under a preservation order. As for walks – well, Barry and Clive will help you find your feet (so to speak): there are twelve which begin locally and are recommended by the Ramblers Association.

Local Activities: Walks, sailing, wind-surfing, deep-sea fishing, golf, sandy beaches.

Laverley House   Unlicensed
West Pennard   Children welcome
Glastonbury
Somerset
BA6 8NE
Pilton (074989) 696

Stephen and Cheryl Staines

On the A361 4 miles east of Glastonbury.

Laverley House is a listed Georgian farmhouse built in 1820 with five acres of land with spectacular views towards the Mendip hills, and an attractive garden in which highly scented roses blossom in the summer. On your arrival you may be greeted by the pretty Welsh Palamino pony nodding to you from the field beside the car park, or by the friendly Great Dane, known as 'Puppy'.

The house is spacious and homely. There are three bedrooms, each with a private bathroom, a comfortable guest lounge, and a dining room. The full English or Continental breakfast offered is freshly prepared using local produce. Dinner can be provided at twenty-four hours' notice, and in addition, your hosts will recommend local pubs and restaurants. English, Italian, Chinese and Indian food can be enjoyed in Glastonbury, four miles away.

Easily Accessible: This is an unique area of the West Country, where history and legend blend. The origins of English Christianity can be found in Glastonbury Abbey, where the first Christian sanctuary in the British Isles was established and where, according to legend, King Arthur was buried. Glastonbury Tor, with the ruined tower of St Michael's church, can be seen for miles around. At the foot of the Tor lies the Chalice Well, where, it is said, the Holy Grail was hidden by Joseph of Arimathea. The surrounding countryside is very beautiful, with limestone hills, caves, moors and a rich diversity of wildlife. The climate is particularly favourable and the area is known for its cider-making and vineyards. There are numerous walks around the house, to the top of Pennard Hill, through local woods, and across the moor.

Local Activities: walks, bird-watching, fishing, clay-pigeon shooting, horse-riding. Special arrangements for guests at Wells golf club.

Trebles Cottage Hotel
Kingston
Nr Kingsbridge
South Devon
TQ7 4PT

☎ Bigbury-On-Sea (0548) 810268

David and Georgiana Kinder

Easily accessible off the A379

Trebles Cottage can be found in the picturesque village of Kingston in the South Hams, an area of fertile farming land in South Devon designated as being 'of outstanding natural beauty' and notable for its mild climate. Trebles Cottage, built in 1801, lies in an acre of secluded grounds. At its front is a walled garden with camellias and fuschias, and a palm tree. At the back David and Georgiana have planted flower beds, a small orchard, a heather garden and a vegetable patch. The latter is already yielding fresh produce and fresh fruit is expected from the orchard in the not too distant future.

Inside, the cottage is comfortable and tastefully furnished. Each of the five pretty bedrooms is individually furnished with a particular theme in mind, such as the 'apple room', 'rose room' and 'almond room'. All are en suite and are equipped with colour TV; one with a double king-size bed is particularly luxurious and is often used as a bridal suite.

The food, cooked in Georgiana's beloved Aga, is excellent. There is plenty of choice and whenever possible locally produced foods are used, such as Devon crabs and, of course, Devon clotted cream. The wine list is comprehensive and if you feel like a pre-prandial treat, there is a small, well-stocked cocktail bar.

Easily Accessible: Kingston is a very pretty village with thatched cottages, just one mile from a sandy beach and some stunning coastal walks, and yet Dartmoor with its rugged tors and crags is only 10 miles away. Five miles away you can visit the National Shire Horse Centre. Plymouth is 12 miles away, and the sailing centres of Kingsbridge and Salcombe are 10 and 13 miles respectively. Dartmouth, 25 miles away, has a famous naval college and a very attractive waterfront. Here you can take a boat on the estuary or a river trip to Totnes, or take a steam train on the Dart Valley Railway.

Local Activities: walks, golf.

Bissick Old Mill
Ladock
Nr Truro
Cornwall
TR2 4PG

☎ St Austell (0726) 882557

Ray and Jean Giles

On A39 5 miles north of Truro

This 17th-century house was once a working mill, powered by two enormous water-wheels – one wheel alone was twenty-four feet high. Today, after a careful conversion it is a very comfortable and elegant country home. It has three pretty bedrooms, decorated in well-chosen fabrics, and furnished with antiques and pine. Each room has a colour TV, mini-fridge with fresh fruit, soft and alcoholic drinks. There are always fresh flowers on show. The beamed sitting room has an open fire and the appropriately named 'honesty bar' where guests are invited to help themselves to drinks, and then record their indulgences on a slate – charges are then made at the end of the visit. It may seem a little naive but Ray and Jean believe it works and it really helps to preserve the 'home-from-home' atmosphere. A fresh, wholesome meal is served every evening in the attractive dining room.

Easily Accessible: Bissick is centrally situated and so most of Cornwall with its glorious countryside, picturesque villages, lush gardens and ancient sites, is accessible. The north and south coasts are 14 miles equidistant. The village of Ladock itself is surrounded by woods through which a nature trail runs and there are many local foopaths and, of course, the long coastal walks to enjoy. Nearby Truro has a modern cathedral, river trips down the River Fal with its many creeks to Falmouth, a country museum and country park. Four miles south of Truro are the National Trust's Trelissick Gardens with their abundant magnolias, camellias and rhododendrons. There is also a very pleasant woodland walk here. In Falmouth, you can visit St Mawes Castle, and the Maritime Museum, and enjoy the sandy beaches and safe bathing.

Local Activities: walks, golf, fishing.

Boscean Country Hotel
St Just-in-Penwith
Penzance
Cornwall
TR19 7QP

Closed Dec–Jan
Award winner

☎ Penzance (0736) 788748

Roy and Joyce Lee

The walled gardens surrounding Boscean Country Hotel are a shelter for wildlife – badgers, foxes and a wide variety of birds make their home here in the shadow of two ancient Celtic crosses. The house was built by an Edwardian doctor using only the best materials – oak cured for eight years for the lower rooms' panelling, fine teak for the window frames and mahogany for the fireplace. The furniture is very much in keeping with the original character of the house. All the bedrooms are en suite and have superb views of the sea or across the wild moorland.

The food is home-cooked. Produce is fresh: soft fruits, salads and vegetables come from the garden. The sweet trolley in particular is very tempting, with a choice of five or six home-made sweets. Vegetarians and special diets are catered for on request.

Roy and Joyce Lee will arrange activities for you, including trips to the local theatre, and horse-riding. They very much enjoy having guests to stay on a house-party basis and they will arrange daily activities and entertainments for most evenings.

Easily Accessible: St Just-in-Penwith, an old mining town, is 7 miles away from Penzance, one of the first Cornish resorts and the county's third largest town. Penzance has fine views of St Michael's Mount, a fairytale castle built on an island reached at high tide by boat and at low tide by a causeway, which is owned by the National Trust. The moorland and seemingly endless miles of coastal path (accessible only a few yards from the hotel) beckon many walkers. Wherever you are on it, the cliff scenery is always spectacular. Within a 10-mile radius there are several archaeological sights, stone circles and museums to visit.

Local Activities: Walks, fishing, golf, swimming, horse-riding, pleasure flights (airfield at St Just).

The Old Rectory Hotel
Duloe Road
St Keyne
Liskeard
Cornwall
PL14 4RL

Disabled guests welcome
Pets welcome by arrangement

☎ Liskeard (0579) 42617

Ron and Kate Wolfe

On B3254 St Keyne/Duloe road.

This gracious and well-proportioned early 19th-century building has a varied past: it started out life as a rectory, became a farmhouse, and is now a comfortable country hotel. It stands in three acres of garden, and overlooks the picturesque valley of Looe. To say that it is peaceful is an understatement; it is so quiet as to be almost unsettling for anyone used to the never-ending noise of the city.

The rooms are spacious and furnished to suit the Victorian features of the house, such as the marble fireplaces in the lounge and drawing room and heavy panelled doors. The lounge (with adjacent bar) is a particularly warm and welcoming room, with Persian rugs, comfortable sofas, and in winter a blazing log fire. Two of the bedrooms have four-poster beds, and there are also facilities for the disabled. A five-course dinner of traditional English cooking is offered.

Easily Accessible: The Old Rectory is ideally place for touring the area, and offers access to many splendid walks, including those encompassing the coastal path and Bodmin Moor. The latter is smaller and less well-known than Exmoor or Dartmoor but is still very beautiful in a bleak windswept way, and, like the others, has its fair share of ancient sites and wildlife. There are several historic houses nearby, including Cotehele House, a Tudor manor house with spectacular grounds; and Buckland Abbey, with its beautiful gardens and medieval tithe barn.

:actions are the slate caverns, Cheesewring stone circles and ellham tin mine.

....*ities*: Walks, golf, boating, sailing, fishing, beaches.

Chetcombe House Hotel

No smoking in bedrooms

Chetcombe Road
Mere
Wiltshire
BA12 6AZ

☎ Mere (0747) 860219

Colin and Sue Ross

Off A303 on slip road into Mere from the East

The guest sitting room opens onto a terrace which in turn leads out into the garden and a romantic avenue of apple trees. It is quite lovely; the views which are enjoyed by most of the main south-facing rooms take one's eyes across the beautiful countryside way out into the distance to Blackmore Vale.

One of the first things Colin and Sue Ross did when taking over Chetcombe was to refurbish the bedrooms in pretty Laura Ashley papers and fabrics, and to put them en suite. The guests' lounge is comfortable, with a wood-burning stove used for cooking chestnuts in the winter.

There is a small à la carte menu, and a table d'hôte menu, which changes daily. The cuisine is traditional English fare. Lunch is available on request. The food is freshly cooked using produce from the kitchen garden and local produce as much as possible.

Easily Accessible: Mere is an attractive town dating back to Saxon times with pretty stone cottages and fine views of Blackmore Vale from Castle Hill, where once stood a medieval fortification. There are many unrestricted walks around Mere, onto White Sheet Hill, with its nature reserve, over the chalk downlands, and along the Roman road. There are several pretty villages nearby including Maiden Bradley, with its 14th-century church and Bradley House and Park, the ancestral house of the Dukes of Somerset. Three miles away, the National Trust's Stourhead House and Gardens have delightful landscaped gardens which are quite beautiful with follies and grottos and Greek temples creating an unusual atmosphere. The house, a fine Georgian mansion, has a magnificent collection of paintings and Chippendale furniture. Longleat House and safari park is only 9 miles away.

Local Activities: walks, horse-riding, tennis, golf, cycling.

Wigham

Morchard Bishop
Nr Crediton
Devon
EX17 6RJ

A 'no smoking' house
Sorry, no pets or small
   children
Must book in advance

☎ Morchard Bishop (03637) 350

Lesley and Stephen Chilcott

1½ miles outside Morchard Bishop

This is the house to a thirty-acre farm, with three-quarters of an acre of fruit, vegetable and herb garden and a pretty cottage garden. The house is very picturesque, with honeysuckle, jasmine, clematis, passionflower and virginia creeper growing up its walls, a thatched roof, oak panelled walls, beams, original ovens, and inglenook fireplaces. The interior is pretty with 'cottagey' wallpapers, interesting black and white prints, locally made furniture including a unique solid yew four-poster bed in the honeymoon suite. All five bedrooms have colour TV, video, and full private bathrooms. There are two cosy sitting rooms, a dining room and bar, and a fourth public room, given over to a snooker table.

The four-course evening meal is taken around a magnificent yew table, and offers a set starter with garlic bread or home-baked wholemeal, with the farm's own butter. The main course is set, with dishes such as coq au vin or boeuf en croute and vegetables fresh from the garden. There is choice of desserts which may include home-made ice-cream, strudel or cheesecake. Vegetarian diets are catered for.

Easily Accessible: Here, you are right in the depths of the Devon countryside, surrounded by woods, farmland and gentle hills. The parish of Morchard Bishop, just 1½ miles away, has forty footpaths. Dartmoor and Exmoor are easily reached for day trips. Crediton, 8 miles away, is an ancient town, once known for its wool industry, now for its cider making. Thirteen miles away at Tiverton, there are several historically and architecturally interesting buildings including a medieval castle, now incorporated into a private house. Exeter, 16 miles away, has a fine 13th-century cathedral, a modern university, and an attractive waterfront.

Local Activities: heated swimming pool and stabling at Wigham.

Sunnycliffe Hotel

Mortehoe
Devon
EX34 7EB

☎ Woolacombe (0271) 870597

Victor and Betty Bassett

Phone for directions

Closed Dec and Jan
Sorry, no pets
Children over 12 welcome
Award winner

Sunnycliffe is indeed an appropriate name for this small hotel perched on a cliff overlooking the pretty bay of Woolacombe. To its rear are miles and miles of open moorland and on a clear day the views from all aspects are quite spectacular. All eight bedrooms have sea views, colour TV, and en suite facilities. There is a comfortable lounge bar, a reading lounge, and a spacious dining room.

The Bassetts have developed Sunnycliffe for over twenty years. Betty is the front-of-house person with all the gregariousness needed to put her guests at ease and in the holiday spirit, whilst Victor is the (trained) chef. He prepares the delicious four-course evening meal with home-made soups and traditional English dishes as his speciality.

Easily Accessible: Directly from Sunnycliffe you can explore sandy beaches, rocky coves, moors and the coastal path with spectacular cliff scenery. Many of the small, pretty inland and coastal villages can be incorporated into walks. A little further away you can enjoy the natural beauty of Exmoor National Park. Barnstaple, the premier market town for most of North Devon, has a 14th-century bridge across the River Taw, and among the modern high street shops, several small traders with a craft market during the summer months. Six miles north of Barnstaple the Braunton Burrows is thought to be the largest area (2000 acres) of sand dunes in the country. Within this vast area is a National Nature Reserve with a wide variety (some rare) of wildlife. Braunton itself has a 13th-century church and a medieval church house, now a museum. You can take a boat trip along the coast to Lundy Island, the famous bird sanctuary.

Local Activities: walks, swimming, sandy beaches, fishing, horse-riding, donkey rides, surfing.

Mount Prospect Hotel

Britons Hill
Penzance
Cornwall
TR18 3AE

No-smoking rooms available

☎ Penzance (0736) 63117

The Blakeley Family

Just minutes from Heliport, station and shops

This is a very comfortable, warm and sunny place to stay with
a prize-winning garden laden with tropical and sub-tropical plants
and an outdoor heated swimming pool bordered by palm trees. Its
outlook is spectacular, with panoramic views across Mount's bay to St
Michael's Mount. The decor is simple but tasteful. There are twenty-six
individually decorated bedrooms, each with its own colour TV, video
link-up, and daily supply of fresh fruit.

The atmosphere is relaxed and convivial and friendships are often
forged after dinner in the lounge. Alexander Blakeley (a keen yachts-
man) has a wealth of experience, and he runs Mount Prospect Hotel
very professionally with his wife and daughter. They are particularly
proud of the food; the breakfast is enormous and includes foods such
as local smoked haddock and lamb's kidneys. Bar lunches, full lunches
and a four-course evening meal are available. Fish features strongly as
nearby Newlyn has the third highest fish landings in England.

Easily Accessible: the south coast of Cornwall is most spectacular, with
its cliffs and coves, magnificent gardens and sandy beaches. Penzance,
once a centre of smuggling, is now very much a holiday resort. St
Michael's Mount, 2 miles away, can be reached by foot when the tide
is out or by motor launch at high tide. Six miles away, at the open-air
Minack Theatre, plays are performed with the sea as a backdrop. To
the North there are great expanses of beaches. St Ives, 7 miles away,
is an old fishing port, with an artists community, and good surfing. A
very popular day excursion is to the Isles of Scilly, either by helicopter
or ferry. These islands have a history of shipwrecks and smuggling; St
Mary's has a busy harbour, and Tresco has a beautiful tropical garden.

Local Activities: free golf, squash, and offshore sailing at local venues,
swimming pool at Mount Prospect, fishing, wind-surfing, water-skiing.

Glenside Hotel   Dogs welcome (small charge)
Ringmore Road
Shaldon
South Devon
TQ14 0EP

☎ Shaldon (0626) 872448 or 873722

Derek and Ann Newbold

Glenside Hotel is beautifully situated on the southern bank of the River Teign, ½ mile from the unspoilt village of Shaldon. It is a white cottage-style residence, built as a private home in 1820. There are well-kept gardens to the front and rear, and in the latter there grows a very fine example of a Judas tree. Inside, Glenside is comfortable and attractive, and the homely lounge with separate bar provides a welcoming atmosphere for a relaxing evening drink. Each bedroom has a colour TV; most have en suite facilities; some have lovely views of the river.

Dinner is home-cooked, and soups and sauces are home-made at Glenside. Special diets are catered for, but please let the proprietors know in advance.

Easily Accessible: Shaldon is a pretty village well-known for its narrow streets of Regency and Georgian cottages. There is plenty to do and see in the area and if you like long walks, Britain's longest footpath, the South West Way, is on your doorstep – in total it is 560 miles long. The old town of Widecombe-in-the-Moor (famous for its fair) has several historic buildings, while Becky Falls, also on Dartmoor, are quite spectacular. Buckfast Abbey, built at the beginning of this century, is famous for its wine and honey. Along the coast there are several interesting old mining, and fishing villages to visit. Children will enjoy Paignton Zoo. Plymouth, Exeter and Torquay are all easily reached for day trips.

Local Activities: Deep-sea and river fishing, sailing, bird-watching, wind-surfing, golf, bowling, tennis.

Coombe House   Closed mid Dec-Feb
North Huish   Sorry, no pets
South Brent
South Devon
TQ10 9NJ

☎ Gara Bridge (054882) 277

Alan and Bunny Jacques

Phone for directions

In the grounds of Coombe House, at the top of a valley, in an area designated of outstanding natural beauty, wildlife flourishes: buzzards, herons, sparrow hawks and tawny owls, wild flowers and the occasional stoat playing with its young can all be seen. The origins of Coombe House lie in the 14th century (the surrounding farms date back to the 10th and 11th); today it is a Georgian building with an attractive garden, the perimeter of which has been left to flourish without the interfering hand of man. Two streams run through the four-acre grounds and a pond has been built which attracts local birdlife.

Bunny and Alan Jacques set up Coombe House as a semi-retirement project after a business career in Africa. The house is spacious and comfortable, with four bedrooms all en suite, a lounge, dining room, and sun lounge/bar.

Bunny loves cooking (she is trained to cordon bleu standard) and after a lifetime's experience of entertaining, cooking for her guests presents no problem. The cuisine is English and Continental and the four-course evening meal uses fresh local ingredients.

Easily Accessible: Dartmoor, with its woods, tors and ancient sites, and the long coastal path provide numerous walks. Totnes, 7 miles away, is a pretty, busy town with an Elizabethan market and Norman castle. The Dartmoor Wildlife Park and Falconry Centre, near Plymouth, 16 miles away, is set in thirty acres of beautiful countryside and has a good collection of big cats. There are numerous picturesque villages to visit including Berry Pomeroy, a small village which forms part of the Duke of Somerset's estates, and which has a haunted castle. Exeter, 30 miles away, is an attractive city with a splendid Gothic cathedral.

Local Activities: walks, horse-riding, pony trekking, golf, beaches, swimming, wind-surfing, sailing.

Downhayes

Spreyton
Crediton
Devon
EX17 5AR

☎ Bow (0363) 82378

Mr and Mrs Hines

Phone for directions

Children over 12 welcome
Sorry, no pets
Unlicensed, guests welcome to
 bring own wine

This fine example of a 16th-century longhouse, with thick cob walls and open fireplaces, is set in fifteen acres of rolling countryside and commands magnificent panoramic views. Inside, the rooms are light and spacious; some are beamed ; all have character. Guests have use of a dining room, a comfortable lounge with a colour television and open fire, a long clematis-clad verandah, a colourful garden, a barn converted into a games room and artist's studio. Two of the three guest bedrooms are en suite.

Mr and Mrs Hines are welcoming and helpful. They describe themselves as 'emigrés from the South East' and truly delight in sharing their lovely home with visitors from all over the world. Prue Hines is the cook, offering a four-course meal in the evening accompanied by fine china and candlelight. Fresh vegetables and local produce such as quail and fish feature. Vegetarian meals are provided by prior arrangement.

In summer and autumn embroidery courses under the tutelage of Jocelyn James are held. Organised on house party lines, they have proved most popular.

Easily Accessible: Downhayes is set in an area of small working farms with few public footpaths in the immediate area. However Dartmoor National Park with its wild rocky scenery and prehistoric remains is a short drive away. Exeter with its 13th-century cathedral, maritime museum is only twenty miles away. Within a 22-mile radius there are several National Trust properties including: Castle Drogo, a splendid private house; Knightshayes Court, a fine Victorian mansion; the old mining village of Lydford with its spectacular gorge; and Killerton House, an 18th-century residence with an outstanding garden. Both the north and south coasts can be reached for day trips.

Local Amenities: golf, fishing, walking.

Whittles Farm
Beercrocombe
Taunton
Somerset
TA3 6AH

No dinner Nov–Dec but
    arrangements made
Sorry, no pets
Children over 12 welcome
Award winner

☎ Hatch Beauchamp (0823) 480301

Claire and John Mitchem

M5 exit 25

Whittles Farm is a 200-acre dairy and beef farm, situated in the rich vale of Taunton Deane, between the Quantock and Blackdown Hills, one mile from the pretty village of Beercrocombe. The house is built of locally hewn blue lyas stone, and originated in 1580, with a new front added in 1850. This is now almost completely covered by stunning 150 year old virginia creeper which sets the wall alight in autumn with its fiery russet colours. Inside, the pretty cushions and curtains, exposed beams, inglenook fireplace, log burners and freshly cut flowers (beautifully arranged by a friend) contribute to Whittles' delightful 'cottagey' atmosphere. The rooms are spacious and light with large windows. All the bedrooms are en suite with colour TV. There are two lounges, one with a TV. Dinner is served in the attractive dining room at one shared table.

John and Claire are charming and welcoming hosts (although John is really too busy on the farm to help with the day-to-day running of the house). Claire greatly enjoys the business, after a career as the Assistant Head of a laboratory. She enjoys the cooking and it shows in her wholesome and hearty meals. A four-course evening meal offers local and home-produced foods including beef, lamb, turkey, vegetables, milk and home-baked bread, and local cheddar cheese.

Easily Accessible: There are plenty of splendid walks in the area in the Quantocks and Blackdown Hills, but if you feel like a gentle stroll, you are welcome to explore the farm. Taunton is an interesting place with a castle reputedly haunted. Just outside the town you can visit the Sheppey Cider Works. Two miles away, at Hatch Court, a fine Bath stone mansion built in the Palladian style with a fine collection of paintings and furniture. Ten miles away you can visit Poundisford Park, a beautiful tudor house with a charming garden. Brympton d'Evercy, 16 miles away, is a magnificent country home, vineyard, and distillery. At the Wookey Hole caves and mill, 2 miles outside Wells, you can visit the spectacular caves and Victorian working paper mill. Dartmoor and Exmoor are within easy driving distance.

Local Activities: walks, golf.

Fairmount House Hotel
Herbert Road
Chelston
Torquay
Devon
TQ2 6RW

☎ Torquay(0803) 605446

Noel and Maggie Tolkien

Closed Nov–Feb
Award winner

The pretty south-facing conservatory-type bar (overlooking a terraced garden), the sunny patio and the wire-haired Daschunds all contribute towards the homely holiday atmosphere that Maggie and Noel Tolkien have created in this small Victorian hotel. The terraced garden is dominated by an absolutely magnificent magnolia tree that blossoms every April – it is not surprising that people tend to return year after year. The lounge is cosy, with an open fire, and all eight bedrooms are en suite.

Food is fresh, and everything from soups to sweets is home-made. Herbs, vegetables and soft fruits come from the garden. Maggie describes the cuisine as basically British, with occasional pasta dishes and some French and Eastern favourites. Noel keeps a small but interesting wine cellar.

Easily Accessible: Fairmount House is situated away from the hustle and bustle of the centre of the popular resort of Torquay and closer to the peace of the old and pretty village of Paignton. Torquay itself is all that a seaside resort should be, with discos, restaurants, cabaret and museum. It is part of the 'English Riviera'– so called because of the mild climate and sandy beaches. The surrounding countryside offers a bewildering number of activities. There are numerous historical sights, museums, parks, gardens and picturesque villages. There is an excellent zoo, some spectacular caves, a steam railway, and much more. For walkers there is the excitement of exploring Dartmoor National Park and the miles of scenic coastal path. Your hosts, incidentally are able to recommend over one hundred walks!

Local Activities: Walks, horse-riding, golf courses, river and sea fishing, water-skiing, boating, swimming.

Ford Farm House
Harberton
Totnes
Devon
TQ9 7SJ

Unlicensed
Children over 12 welcome
Small dogs welcome

☎ Totnes (0803) 863539

Mike and Sheila Edwards

Phone for directions

Ford Farm House is a picturesque 17th-century farmhouse with cob and stone walls painted white with black shutters, situated in a small village, close to Dartmoor. It has a secluded garden bordered by a stream. Nearby is a lovely 14th-century church with the equally old Church House Inn next door. Inside, it is small but comfortable and furnished with antiques. The dining room has a beamed ceiling and a wood-burning stove within a stone fireplace. The bedrooms are pretty; one, the Patchwork Room, has a king-sized bed with a colourful patchwork quilt and an en suite shower.

Sheila and Mike Edwards are charming and helpful hosts who enjoy looking after their guests. They will, for instance, bring an early morning cup of tea to your bedroom. Sheila is an excellent cook, cordon bleu trained. She and her husband ran a restaurant for eleven years before opening up Ford Farm in 1978. Dinner is offered most nights (twenty-four hours notice required). Fresh local produce is used whenever possible, and herbs come from the garden, but weight-watchers beware, real Devon ice-cream is conspicuously present at meals. If you prefer to eat out, there are several places locally including the Church House Inn which serves good fresh local produce, and a little further away, two riverside pubs, the Waterman's Arms and Maltster's Arms.

Easily Accessible: There are several local walks from the farm, on Dartmoor, 10 miles away, and the South Devon Coastal Path, 7 miles away. There are some good beaches at Torbay and Start Bay, including Slapton Sands, where there is a nature reserve. Nearby are several National Trust properties including Compton Castle, a medieval fortified manor house. Three miles away, you can visit Dartington Hall, a medieval estate with gardens and theatre.

Local Activities: walks, golf, swimming pool.

Moorlands
Hutton
Weston-super-Mare
Avon
BS24 9QH

☎ Bleadon (0934) 812283

Margaret and David Holt

From M5 (junc 21) 5 miles (off A 370)

Moorlands gives one the impression of a house that is well lived in – that is, in the best possible sense. It is a large, friendly and comfortable Georgian building with a delightful landscaped garden which looks out to a paddock, and some thick wooded hills beyond. The rooms are simply but prettily furnished. Four out of a total of nine are en suite and two are attic rooms with marvellous views over the village and hills. The spacious lounge has a TV and in suitable weather, an open fire.

David and Margaret Holt run Moorlands with both professionalism and warmth. They are even willing to give parents a much needed rest in the evenings by listening out for the children (once settled), thereby allowing the parents time off. When guests arrive they are welcomed with a cup of tea, and every evening a hot or cold drink is offered.

The food is freshly cooked and wholesome. Margaret's daughter Anita is a trained patisserie chef, who comes in for three days a week to delight people with her delicious home-baked brown bread and scrumptious desserts. Special diets are catered for on request.

Easily Accessible: The village of Hutton is over a thousand years old, and has many buildings of historic interest, in particular Hutton Court, dating from the late 15th or early 16th century. Only ten minutes away from the peace of Hutton, is the hustle and bustle of the resort of Weston-super-Mare with its beaches, donkey rides and piers. Cider making (from early September) and cheddar cheese making are open to the public and well worth seeing. Bath, Glastonbury, Bristol and Berkeley Castle (home of the Berkeley family for eight hundred years) all make excellent day trips. There are numerous walks around Hutton, on the Somerset moors, the Mendips and, thirty miles away, the Quantocks and Exmoor.

Local Amenities: Pony rides for children (in the Holts' paddock), golf, angling (fly, course, sea), horse-riding. Moorlands has a special arrangement for guests with a local Country Club.

LONDON & SOUTH EAST

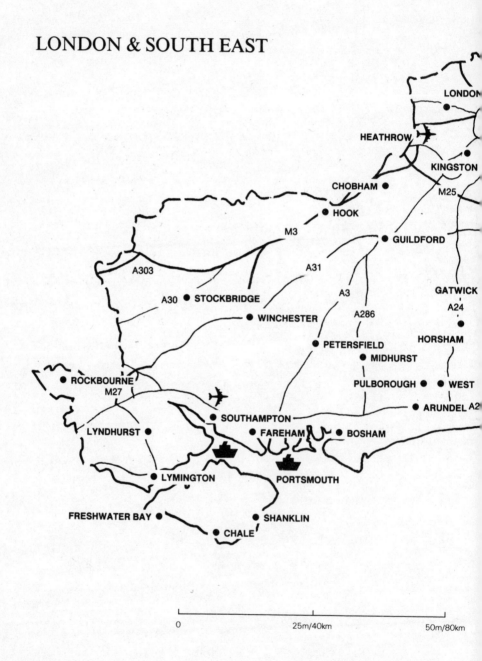

LONDON

HEATHROW

KINGSTON

M25

CHOBHAM

HOOK

M3

GUILDFORD

A303

A31

A30 STOCKBRIDGE

A3

GATWICK

A24

WINCHESTER

A286

HORSHAM

PETERSFIELD

MIDHURST

ROCKBOURNE

PULBOROUGH WEST

M27

SOUTHAMPTON

ARUNDEL A2

LYNDHURST

FAREHAM BOSHAM

LYMINGTON

PORTSMOUTH

FRESHWATER BAY

SHANKLIN

CHALE

0   25m/40km   50m/80km

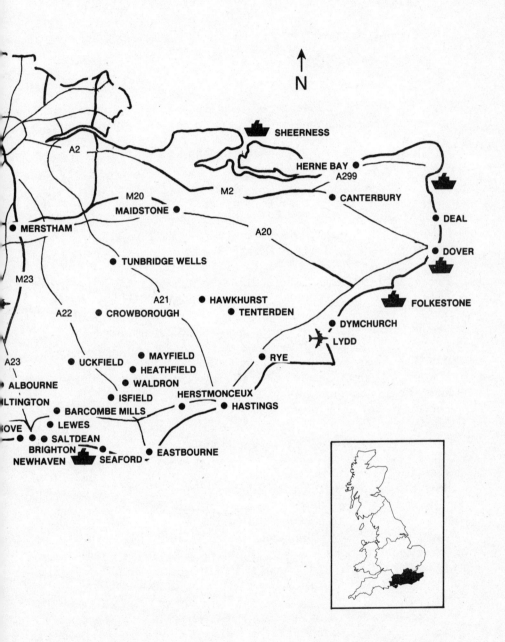

N

SHEERNESS

HERNE BAY
A299

M20   M2
MAIDSTONE   CANTERBURY

A2

MERSTHAM   A20   DEAL

                                                         DOVER

M23   TUNBRIDGE WELLS
                                                         FOLKESTONE

        A21   HAWKHURST
A22   CROWBOROUGH   TENTERDEN
                                        DYMCHURCH
A23   LYDD
        MAYFIELD
UCKFIELD   HEATHFIELD   RYE
ALBOURNE   WALDRON
LTINGTON   ISFIELD   HERSTMONCEUX
        BARCOMBE MILLS   HASTINGS
OVE   LEWES
        SALTDEAN
BRIGHTON
NEWHAVEN   SEAFORD   EASTBOURNE

London and the South East

*Covering the counties of: London, Dorset (part), Hampshire,
Isle of Wight, Kent, Surrey and Sussex*

This is a prosperous, densely populated area, dominated authoritatively by London whose financial, cultural, and commercial institutions act as a magnet for tourists, immigrants, high flyers, and culture-vultures. Suburbia stretches far and wide, yet within an hour's train ride the tranquillity and beauty of the countryside await the traveller: the New Forest in Hampshire, covering 145 square miles and one of the largest open spaces in the South, is one of the oldest forests in England; the North and South Downs of Surrey and Sussex provide numerous footpaths (many of them ancient) for energetic walkers; and sandwiched between the Downs, the lush, fertile Weald with its orchards, hop fields and woods.

Throughout the South and South East, historic buildings attract multitudes of visitors. Some – like Petworth House in West Sussex – are notable for their great art collections, others – like Hampton Court Palace in Surrey – for their history and the sheer magnificence of their state rooms. There are also the houses of the great and famous, many of which are open to the public – Charleston Farmhouse in East Sussex, for example, a famous haunt of the Bloomsbury Group, and Chawton in Hampshire, home of Jane Austen.

The many attractive towns of the region exhibit a wealth of fine architecture, ranging from Tudor through to Queen Anne, Georgian and Victorian. Towns like Winchester in Hampshire and Canterbury in Kent are dominated by their splendid cathedrals. Others like Brighton in East Sussex are dominated by the sea, and the dictates of the tourist industry; Brighton, the uncrowned 'queen' of the southern resorts, is the proud owner of some very fine Regency crescents, as well as the marvellous and eccentric oriental palace of the Prince Regent, the Pavilion. In towns like Chichester in West Sussex, the legacy of the Roman conquerors can still be seen in the original Roman street pattern, and just outside the town, Fishbourne Roman Palace, the largest Roman villa in Britain, boasts some magnificent mosaics.

The area is also rich in gardens: the Leonardslee Gardens in West Sussex, the Wisley Gardens in Surrey, and probably most famous of all, Kew Gardens in London. Amongst the many other delights awaiting you, here are grand hothouses, a lovely rose garden, and a large variety

60

of quite magnificent trees, some of which were unfortunately damaged in the gales of 1987.

Off the coast of Hampshire lies the Isle of Wight. Small and picturesque, it can be reached by ferry or hovercraft from Southampton and Portsmouth. Famous for its sandy beaches, sunny climate, miles and miles of National Trust footpath, and multi-coloured sandstone cliffs, it is a very popular holiday destination.

Regional Tourist Boards:
London – 26 Grosvenor Gardens, London SW1W 0DU
Tel: (01) 730 3450
Southern – 40 Chamberlayne Road, Eastleigh, Hampshire SO5 5JH
Tel: (0703) 616027
South East – The Old Brew House, Warwick Park, Tunbridge Wells, Kent TN2 5TU
Tel: (0892) 540766
West Country Tourist Board for part of Dorset – Trinity Court, Southernhay East, Exeter, Devon EX1 1QS
Tel: (0392) 76351

ALBOURNE GREAT WAPSES FARM
Wineham, Nr Henfield, West Sussex BN5 9BJ. *Tel*: Henfield (0273) 492544.
Hosts: Michael & Eleanor Wilkin.
Rates: A/B   Vouchers accepted.
 Lovely Tudor/Georgian house, attractive gardens, peaceful setting, lovely views. Mixed farm. Free use of tennis court. Gatwick 12 miles.. Off A23 and B2116. 1 mile up farm road. 4–poster available. Dinner by arrangement winter months. No lounge.

ARUNDEL PORTREEVES ACRE
The Causeway, Arundel, West Sussex BN18 9JJ. *Tel*: Arundel (0903) 883277.
Hosts: Pat & Charles Rogers.
Rates: A/B   Vouchers accepted.
(See page 73 for description)

BARCOMBE MILLS (Lewes) (A 'no smoking' house)   CRINK
  HOUSE
Barcombe Mills, Lewes, East Sussex BN8 5BJ. *Tel*: Brighton (0273) 400625.
Hosts: Ray & Hazel Gaydon.
Rates: B   Vouchers accepted.
 Comfortable Victorian family house, rural setting, beautiful views. Walking, touring, easy reach Glyndebourne, Gatwick, Newhaven and Brighton.

4-poster. All rooms with private facilities. Pubs, restaurants nearby. Sorry, no pets.

BOSHAM (Nr Chichester)   WHITE BARN
Crede Lane, Bosham, West Sussex PO18 8NX. *Tel*: Bosham (0243) 573113. *Hosts*: Susan & Antony Trotman.
Rates: C   Vouchers accepted.
(See page 73 for description)

BRIGHTON   THE TWENTY ONE HOTEL
21 Charlotte Street, Marine Parade, Brighton, East Sussex BN2 1AG. *Tel*: Brighton (0273) 686450. *Host*: Janet Power.
Rates: B/D   Vouchers accepted.
Small elegant hotel just off seafront, specialising in high standard French country cooking. Charming rooms. 4-poster available. Colour TV all rooms. Executive singles available weekdays only. Restaurant closed Sun and Wed.

BRIGHTON   TOPP'S HOTEL
17 Regency Square, Brighton, East Sussex BN1 2FG. *Tel*: Brighton (0273) 729334. *Telex*: 877159 BHV Ref TOPPS. *Fax*: 0273 779192. *Hosts*: Paul & Pauline Collins.
Rates: D
(See page 75 for description)

CANTERBURY (Bridge)   WYCH ELM
13, High Street, Bridge, Canterbury, Kent CT4 5JY. *Tel*: Canterbury (0227) 830242. *Hosts*: Barry & Pleasance Kirk.
Rates: B
Regency house with pretty walled garden. Small village 2 m Canterbury. Dover and Folkestone 15 miles (day trips to France). Howletts Zoo. Historic area. Lounge/dining room. No smoking in bedrooms. Early breakfast arranged. Sorry, no pets.

CHALE (Isle of Wight)   CLARENDON HOTEL AND WIGHT MOUSE INN
Chale, Isle of Wight PO38 2HA. *Tel*: Niton (0983) 730431. *Hosts*: John & Jean Bradshaw.
Rates: C   Vouchers accepted.
Charming 17th-century coaching hotel in extensive grounds with own country pub attached (150 malt whiskys, many real ales). Two mins from Blackgang Chine, overlooking the sea and Needles. Book car ferry. Colour TV all rooms.

CHOBHAM (Knaphill)   KNAPHILL MANOR
Carthouse Lane, Woking, Surrey GU21 4XT. *Tel*: Chobham (0276) 857962. *Hosts*: Kevin & Teresa Leeper.
Rates: C   Vouchers accepted.

Comfortable and secluded manor house (1780) with very relaxing family atmosphere. Beautiful and extensive gardens. All rooms en suite or with private bathroom. Sorry, no pets. Children over 8 welcome. Sun terrace. Tennis court. Ascot 20 mins, Windsor 25 mins. Heathrow ½hr. Gatwick less than 1 hr, London ½hr by rail.

CROWBOROUGH ROCKS HOUSE
Alice Bright Lane, Stone Cross, Nr Crowborough, East Sussex TN6 3SJ. *Tel*: Crowborough (0892) 655612. *Hosts*: Carol & Gore Johnston.
Rates: A/B
Quiet Victorian country house with large garden, south of Crowborough off A26. Beautiful views over South Downs. Large outdoor swimming pool, heated in summer. Lounge/dining room. Sorry, no pets.

DEAL SUTHERLAND HOUSE
186 London Road, Deal, Kent CT14 9PT. *Tel*: Dover (0304) 362853. *Hosts*: The Pitman Family.
Rates: B
(See page 75 for description)

DOVER LODDINGTON HOUSE
14 East Cliff, Dover, Kent CT16 1LX. *Tel*: Dover (0304) 201947. *Hosts*: The Cupper Family.
Rates: A/B
Superbly positioned small hotel in Georgian terrace. Comfortable and welcoming. Yards from Dover East ferry terminal. Children welcome. Private parking available. Sorry, no pets.

DYMCHURCH THE CHANTRY HOTEL
Sycamore Gardens, Dymchurch, Romney Marsh, Kent TN29 0LA. Dymchurch (0303) 873137. *Host*: Paul Airey.
Rates: B/C Vouchers accepted.
On quiet green and private road south of A259 near town centre with own direct access to the sandy beach. Near famous Romney Hythe and Dymchurch Steam Railway. Pets by arrangement. Home-cooking, good choice of wines.

EASTBOURNE FLAMINGO HOTEL
20 Enys Road, Eastbourne, East Sussex BN21 2DN. *Tel*: Eastbourne (0323) 21654. *Hosts*: Ron & Margaret Smith.
Rates: B
Comfortable detached house and garden in quiet residential area, easy reach town centre. All rooms with colour TV and bathrooms en suite. Enys Road is opposite junction A259 (the Goffs) and A22 (Upperton Road). Dinner only by prior arrangement. Sorry, no pets.

FAREHAM AVENUE HOUSE HOTEL
22 The Avenue, Fareham, Hants PO14 1NS. *Tel*: Fareham (0329) 232175. *Hosts*: Hilary & Stewart Mitchell.

Rates: B/C Vouchers accepted.
  Comfortable small hotel with charm and character in mature gardens close to central Fareham. All rooms have colour TV, radio and telephone. Many pubs and restaurants within 5 mins walk. Standing back from A27 on west of town, short drive from M27 (juncs 9/10/11).

FRESHWATER BAY, ISLE OF WIGHT   SAUNDERS HOTEL
Coastguard Lane, Freshwater Bay, Isle of Wight PO40 9QX. *Tel*: Freshwater (0983) 752322. *Hosts*: Keith & Marion Brettell.
Rates: B
  Comfortable Victorian house with large garden. Quiet situation, 50 yards from Bay beach. Beautiful West Wight NT countryside with many walks. Golf ¼ mile. Home-cooking. Children and pets welcome. Book car ferry during high season.

GUILDFORD   QUINNS HOTEL
Epsom Road, Guildford, Surrey GU1 2BX. *Tel*: Guildford (0483) 60422. *Hosts*: Mr & Mrs A. M. Mhani.
Rates: B/C
  Large comfortable Victorian house, popular touring area. Only 35 mins by train London. Convenient for both Gatwick and Heathrow airports, each 40 mins by car. Ample parking, easy walking distance town centre and many good restaurants.

HASTINGS (St Leonards-on-Sea)   THE CHIMES HOTEL
1 St Matthew's Gardens, Silverhill, St Leonards-on-Sea, East Sussex TN38 0TS. *Tel*: Hastings (0424) 434041. *Hosts*: John & Elsie McConnell.
Rates: A/B
  In a quiet residential area, overlooking private park. Good home-cooking. Close Battle Abbey and other interesting visits. One mile seafront. Weekend breaks available. All rooms colour TV. Sorry, no pets.

HAWKHURST   WOODHAM HALL HOTEL
Rye Road, Hawkhurst, Kent TN18 5DA. *Tel*: Hawkhurst (0580) 753428. *Hosts*: John & Jean Bennett.
Rates: A/B   Vouchers accepted.
  Part 16th-century estate house in 2½ acres of attractive gardens on A268 at edge of village. Full snooker table, donkey paddock, hard tennis court. Golf and squash very close. Riding and fishing arranged. Bodiam, Hever, Scotney and Leeds castles and Sissinghurst gardens within 10 m. Coast (Rye) 13 miles, Dover 30 miles.

HEATHFIELD (A 'no smoking' house)   RISINGHOLME
High Street, Heathfield, East Sussex TN21 8LS. *Tel*: Heathfield (04352) 4645. *Hosts*: June & Bryan Farmer.
Rates: B   Vouchers accepted.
  Comfortable spacious Victorian house set in 3 acres of mature terraced

garden. Off A265 opposite GPO up private drive. Colour TV all rooms. Whirlpool, sauna available. Dinner by arrangement. Children over 12 welcome. Sorry, no pets.

HERNE BAY   NORTHDOWN HOTEL
Cecil Park, Herne Bay, Kent CT6 6DL. *Tel*: Herne Bay (0227) 372051. *Hosts*: Norman & Julia Sands.
Rates: A/B   Vouchers accepted.
   Comfortable small hotel in quiet residential area, few mins walk from sea and downs, town centre and cliff walks. Historic Canterbury 8 miles. Water sports, walking, angling, riding, historic houses and gardens. Sorry, no pets.

HERSTMONCEUX   CLEAVERS LYNG
Church Road, Herstmonceux, Nr Hailsham, East Sussex BN27 1QJ. *Tel*: Herstmonceux (0323) 833131. *Hosts*: Marylin, Neil & Gavin Holden.
Rates: A   Vouchers accepted.
   Picturesque oak-beamed, 16th-century country house in lovely grounds near South Downs; about 5 miles from Hailsham. Adjacent to unusual, brick-built Herstmonceux Castle (Royal Greenwich Observatory). Traditional home-cooking.

HOOK   OAKLEA
London Road, Hook, Nr Basingstoke, Hampshire RG27 9LA. *Tel*: Hook (0256) 762673. *Hosts*: Mr & Mrs T. R. Swinhoe.
Rates: A/C   Vouchers accepted.
   Large detached Victorian house, nicely modernised with very attractive walled gardens and large lawns. 1 mile from Exit 5 on M3. Heathrow 35 mins drive. Basingstoke 5 miles. Easy access to London and West Country.

HORSHAM (Slinfold)   (A 'no smoking' house) PARK HOUSE
Stane Street, Slinfold, Horsham, West Sussex RH13 7QX. *Tel*: Slinfold (0403) 790723. *Hosts*: Paul & Barbara Sparrow.
Rates: C   Vouchers accepted.
   Once a coaching inn (date 1670) on A29 Bognor road. Horsham 4 miles. Gatwick airport 12 miles (20 mins), Heathrow 1 hr. Collection and delivery available. Dining room/lounge. Local pubs and restaurant. Sorry, no pets.

HOVE   CLAREMONT HOUSE
Second Avenue, Hove, East Sussex BN3 2LL. *Tel*: Brighton (0273) 735161/2.
Fax: 0273 24764. *Hosts*: Colin & Sue Humber.
Rates: D
(See page 76 for description)

ISFIELD (Nr Uckfield)   BIRCHES FARM
Isfield, Nr Uckfield, East Sussex TN22 5TY. *Tel*: Isfield (082 575) 304. *Host*: Lesley Robertshaw.
Rates: B
   Lovely 16th-century oak-beamed farmhouse in 26 acres of paddocks,

woods and garden. Swimming pool. En suite room available. No smoking in bedrooms. Glyndebourne, Bentley Wildfowl Trust and Bluebell Railway near. No dinner but good pubs near, good restaurants in nearby Lewes.

KINGSTON (Hampton Wick) CHASE LODGE
10 Park Road, Hampton Wick, Kingston-upon-Thames KT1 4AS. *Tel*: London (01) 943-1862. *Hosts*: Denise & Nigel Dove.
Rates: B/C   Vouchers accepted.
(See page 78 for description)

LEWES (A 'no smoking' home)   MILLERS
134 High Street, Lewes, East Sussex BN7 1XS. *Tel*: Lewes (0273) 475631. *Hosts*: Tére & Tony Tammar.
Rates: B
(See page 79 for description)

LEWES (Rodmell) BARN HOUSE
Rodmell, Lewes, East Sussex BN7 3HF. *Tel*: Brighton (0273) 477865. *Hosts*: Ian & Bernadette Fraser.
Rates: B/C   Vouchers accepted.
(See page 80 for description)

LONDON (Maida Vale) COLONNADE HOTEL AND NEW CASCADES RESTAURANT
2 Warrington Crescent, London W9 1ER. *Tel*: London (01) 289 2167. *Telex*: 298930. *Fax*: 01 286 1057. *Host*: Robin Richards.
Rates: D   Vouchers accepted.
   In quiet residential district off Edgware Road, 1½ miles from Marble Arch, ten mins by bus or Underground to the West End. Ten rooms with 4-posters. Some rooms air-conditioned. Limited off-street parking. Spa baths.

LONDON (Ealing) KENTON HOUSE HOTEL AND RESTAURANT
Hillcrest Road, Ealing, London W5 2JL. *Tel*: London (01) 997 8436. *Telex*: 8812544. *Fax*: 01 998 0037. *Hosts*: The Knowles Family.
Rates: D
   Quiet residential location opposite park with par-3 nine-hole golf course. Mid-way between central London and Heathrow airport, both within easy reach by car, taxi or underground. Ample free parking. Ealing's Broadway & Waterglade shopping centre 10 mins walk.

LONDON (Knightsbridge) THE KNIGHTSBRIDGE
10 Beaufort Gardens, London SW3 1PT. *Tel*: London (01) 589 9271. *Fax*: 01 823 9692. *Host*: Mohmed Jetha.
Rates: D
   In elegant Victorian terrace cul-de-sac, off Brompton Road, two blocks west of Harrods, 3 mins walk Underground station. Reduced rates for

Continental breakfast. No restaurant, but bar snacks available, and many local restaurants. Sorry, no pets.

LONDON (Harrow)   VINTAGE HOUSE
134 Hindes Road, Harrow, Middlesex HA1 1RR. *Tel*: London (01) 427-7637. *Hosts*: Gerald & June Firkins & Eve Eckstein.
Rates: B   Vouchers accepted.
Attractive, Victorian family home in quiet cul-de-sac, adjoining parkland. Easy reach Heathrow and can arrange to meet. Very convenient Underground central London. Antiques advice and sales. Over 20 restaurants nearby. Sorry, no pets.

LONDON (Shepperton)   WARREN LODGE HOTEL
Church Square, Shepperton-on-Thames, Middlesex TW17 9JX. *Tel*: Walton-on-Thames (0932) 242972. *Telex*: 923981 Warren. G. *Fax*: 0932 253883. *Host*: Douglas Gordon.
Rates: D   Vouchers accepted.
Very comfortable and attractive old lodge, part 1752 with historic links. Lovely garden and terrace overlooking river. Easy access M3 exit 2, M25 exit 11, to B375 to Chertsey. M4 15 mins, Heathrow 20 mins. Annexe. BTA commended. Sorry, no pets.

LYMINGTON (Sway)   WHITE ROSE HOTEL
Village Centre, Sway, Lymington, Hampshire SO4 OBA. *Tel*: Lymington (0590) 682754. *Hosts*: The Winchcombe Family.
Rates: D
Family-run country house hotel in New Forest village, halfway between Southampton and Bournemouth. Beaulieu 7 miles, Lymington and Isle of Wight ferries 4 miles. 6 acres lawns and gardens with pool.

LYNDHURST   KNIGHTWOOD LODGE
Southampton Road, Lyndhurst, Hampshire SO43 7BU. *Tel*: Lyndhurst (042128) 2502. *Hosts*: Paul & Jackie Sanderson.
Rates: B   Vouchers accepted.
Comfortable and friendly small hotel in 'the capital of the New Forest'. Overlooking open forest where deer and ponies roam free. All rooms en suite, colour TV, mini-bars and radio alarm. Indoor Health Club – sauna, steamroom etc. Ample car parking. Southampton 10 miles, Lymington 8 miles.

MAIDSTONE   THE BOXLEY HOUSE HOTEL
Boxley, Maidstone, Kent ME14 3DZ. *Tel*: Maidstone (0622) 692269.*Fax*: 0622 683536. *Hosts*: Malcolm & Elizabeth Fox.
Rates: D
Attractive Georgian-style country house, built in 1600 and set in 20 acres picturesque mature parkland. Outdoor heated swimming pool and 4-poster available. Maidstone 2 miles. M20 exit 6, 1 mile. Proprietors are proud of their excellent cuisine. Annexe.

MAIDSTONE (East Malling) BLACKLANDS HOUSE
Blacklands, East Malling, Kent ME19 6DS. *Tel*: West Malling (0732) 844274.
Hosts: Ann & Vernon Leonard.
Rates: A Vouchers accepted.
(See page 80 for description)

MAYFIELD HUGGETTS FURNACE FARM
Stonehurst Lane, Five Ashes, Nr Mayfield, East Sussex TN20 6LL. *Tel*:
Hadlow Down (082 585) 220/722. *Hosts*: Gillian & John Mulcare.
Rates: B/C Vouchers accepted.
(See page 81 for description)

MERSTHAM (near Gatwick) WEAVERS
Warwick Wold, Merstham, Surrey RH1 3DG. *Tel*: Merstham (07374) 5491
(from mid 1990 (0737) 645491). *Hosts*: The Rayner Family.
Rates: B/C
(See page 82 for description)

MIDHURST (A 'no smoking' house) MIZZARDS FARM
Rogate, Petersfield, Hampshire GU31 5HS. *Tel*: Rogate (073080) 656 (from
end May 1990: (0730) 821656). *Hosts*: Mr & Mrs J. C. Francis.
Rates: B Vouchers accepted.
(See page 83 for description)

PETERSFIELD (Trotton) SOUTH DOWNS COUNTRY HOUSE
  HOTEL
Trotton, Rogate, Petersfield, Hampshire GU31 5JN. *Tel*: Rogate (073 080)
521 & 763. *Telex*: 86658 SHR PLC G. *Fax*: 073 080 790. *Hosts*: Nic Vedovato,
Richard Lion.
Rates: D
  Large traditional English country house, in lovely peaceful South Downs
  area. 4 miles from historic Midhurst, 7 miles east of Petersfield off A272.
  Goodwood and Fontwell Park race-courses, polo in Cowdray Park, golf.
  4-poster available. Indoor heated pool, sauna and solarium. Conference fa-
  cilities available.

PULBOROUGH CHEQUERS HOTEL AND RESTAURANT
Church Place, Pulborough, West Sussex RH20 1AD. *Tel*: Pulborough (07982)
2486. *Fax*: 07982 2715. *Hosts*: The Searancke Family.
Rates: D Vouchers accepted.
(See page 84 for description)

PULBOROUGH (Coldwaltham) BARN OWLS GUESTEL AND
  RESTAURANT
London Road, Coldwaltham, Nr Pulborough, West Sussex RH20 1LR. *Tel*:
Pulborough (07982) 2498. *Hosts*: Pat & Marion Hellenberg.
Rates: B/C Vouchers accepted.
  Cosy Victorian farmhouse with open fires in South Downs countryside. 2

miles south Pulborough on A29. Petworth 5 miles. Arundel 6 miles. Rates include en suite facilities. Proprietors take pride in their gourmet menus. Gourmet breaks available. Sorry, no children. Dogs welcome.

ROCKBOURNE   SHEARINGS
Rockbourne, Fordingbridge, Hampshire SP6 3NA. *Tel*: Rockbourne (07253) 256. *Hosts*: Colin & Rosemary Watts.
Rates: B   Vouchers accepted.
(See page 85 for description)

RYE (Northiam)   THE HAYES ARMS HOTEL
Northiam, Nr Rye, East Sussex TN31 6NN. *Tel*: Northiam (07974) 3142. *Hosts*: Michael & Barbara Pithie.
Rates: D
   Tudor/Georgian country house hotel in 1½ acres, on A28 between Hastings and Tenterden. Log fires, beams. Proprietors proud of their fine food and friendly welcome. 4-poster available. Ideal for Rye, Hastings, Bodiam and much more.

RYE   THE OLD VICARAGE GUEST HOUSE
66 Church Square, Rye, East Sussex TN31 7HF. *Tel*: Rye (0797) 222119. *Hosts*: Julia Lampon & Paul Masters.
Rates: B/C   Vouchers accepted.
(See page 86 for description)

RYE   LITTLE ORCHARD HOUSE
West Street, Rye, East Sussex TN31 7ES. *Tel*: (0797) 223831. *Hosts*: Robert & Geraldine Bromley.
Rates: D   Vouchers accepted.
   Elegant Georgian home with panelled rooms, period furnishings, old English walled garden, at the heart of an ancient town. Generous country breakfasts. All rooms en suite and colour TV. 4-poster bed, antiques, log fires. No dinner – reservations and guidance gladly given. 3-day winter breaks available. Sorry, no children or pets.

SALTDEAN (East Brighton)   LINBROOK LODGE HOTEL
74, Lenham Avenue, Saltdean, Brighton BN2 8AG. *Tel*: Brighton (0273) 303775. *Hosts*: David & Josie Doyle.
Rates: B/C
   Large family house in residential area off Cranleigh Avenue with wide views over Saltdean Vale. Rottingdean ½ mile, Newhaven 5 miles. Lovely cliff and undercliff walks. All rooms with private facilities and colour TV. Home-cooking. Winter breaks available.

SEAFORD (West Dean)   THE OLD PARSONAGE
West Dean, Seaford, E Sussex BN25 4AL. *Tel*: Alfriston (0323) 870432. *Hosts*: Raymond & Angela Woodhams.
Rates: C/D   Vouchers accepted.
(See page 87 for description)

SHANKLIN, Isle of Wight   LUCCOMBE HALL HOTEL
Luccombe Road, Shanklin, Isle of Wight P037 6RL. *Tel*: Shanklin (0983 86)
2719. *Telex*. 869441 UT IVKG Ref LH1. *Fax*: 0983 867482. *Hosts*: John &
Michael Drewery.
Rates: C   Vouchers accepted.
   Overlooking Shanklin/Sandown Bay with beautiful views. Extensive
   grounds with heated indoor and outdoor pools and grass tennis court.
   Squash court. Sauna, solarium. 4-poster available. Ferry can be booked.

SHANKLIN   CULVER LODGE HOTEL
Culver Road, Shanklin, Isle of Wight PO37 6ER. *Tel*: Isle of Wight (0983)
863515. *Hosts*: Bob & June Ward.
Rates: A/B   Vouchers accepted.
(See page 88 for description)

SOUTHAMPTON (Cadnam)   BARTLEY LODGE AND CRYSTAL
   RESTAURANT
Cadnam, New Forest, Hampshire SO4 2NR. *Tel* Southampton (0703) 812248.
Fax: 042 128 3719 *Host*: Mr Parry.
Rates: D
   Gracious Georgian (1759) country mansion, lovely views New Forest.
   Attractive bedrooms in 'Country Style' prints. Country house hospitality,
   crystal chandeliers, oak panelling. Children over 6 welcome. 4-poster &
   half-tester available. M27 exit 1, south to Cadnam. At roundabout take
   A337 towards Lyndhurst.

SOUTHAMPTON   NIRVANA
384–386 Winchester Road, Bassett, Southampton, Hampshire SO1 7DH. *Tel*:
Southampton (0703) 790087. *Hosts*: Douglas & Eileen Dawson.
Rates: B/C   Vouchers accepted.
   Conveniently situated town house. Cosy Tudor bar. Near university and
   general hospital. Golf, tennis nearby. 2 miles city centre. Colour TV, private
   telephone, radio alarm and intercom all rooms. Home-cooking. Annexe.

STOCKBRIDGE (Nether Wallop)   BROADGATE FARM
Stockbridge, Hampshire SO20 8HA. *Tel*: Andover (0264) 781439. *Hosts*: Susan
& Richard Osmond.
Rates: A
   Comfortable 18th-century farmhouse in 300 acres with walled garden in
   picturesque village. Test valley fishing, lovely walks. Salisbury 11 miles,
   Stonehenge 11 miles. New Forest near. Off M3, A303 and A30 to The
   Wallops. Restaurants and pubs in village. Sorry, no pets.

TENTERDEN   WEST CROSS HOUSE HOTEL
2 West Cross, Tenterden, Kent TN30 6JL. *Tel*: Tenterden (05806) 2224. *Hosts*:
Mr G. & Mrs M. L. May.

Rates: A

Comfortable elegant Georgian house in attractive town on A28 near edge of Weald and Romney Marshes. Touring, historic area. NT gardens and properties. 25–30 miles Channel ports. Dinner by arrangement. Own parking.

TENTERDEN   (A 'no smoking' house) BRATTLE HOUSE
Cranbrook Road, Tenterden, Kent TN30 6UL. *Tel*: Tenterden (05806) 3565. *Host*: Maureen Rawlinson.
Rates: C   Vouchers accepted.

Elegant Georgian farmhouse in one acre of garden amidst rolling countryside. Rooms en suite or with private bathroom. Two-day winter and spring breaks. Reduced terms 3 days or more, summer to autumn. Children over 12 welcome. Home-cooking, fresh produce, vegetarians catered for. Sorry, no pets. Steam trains. Antiques. 10–15 mins drive to Sissinghurst and Great Dixter.

TUNBRIDGE WELLS   WELLINGTON HOTEL
Mount Ephraim, Tunbridge Wells, Kent TN4 8BU. *Tel*: Tunbridge Wells (0892) 542911. *Telex*: 23152 Ref: 8211. *Hosts*: John Hogg with Jim & Andrée Porter.
Rates: D

A building of Regency beauty with its own secluded lawns, overlooking the Common in this elegant Royal Spa town. Famous Pantiles shopping area within easy reach. Solarium, sauna, gymnasium facilities available. Lift. Video show. Eight 4-posters available.

UCKFIELD (Halland)   HALLAND FORGE HOTEL AND RESTAURANT
Halland, Nr. Lewes, East Sussex BN8 6PW. *Tel*: Halland (082584) 456. *Fax*: 0825 84773. *Host*: Jean Howell.
Rates: D   Vouchers accepted.

Near South Downs and Ashdown Forest, charming family-run hotel in 40 acres gardens and lawns. Touring. 4 miles from Uckfield on A22 Eastbourne road, at junction of B2192. 7 miles Lewes, 6 miles Glyndebourne, 14 miles Newhaven, 28 miles Gatwick.

WALDRON (Nr Heathfield)   (A 'no smoking' house) HARLYN HOUSE
Back Lane, Waldron, Nr Heathfield, Sussex TN21 0NL. *Tel*: Horam Road (04353) 2775. *Hosts*: John & Diana Allies.
Rates: D   Vouchers accepted.

Superb Edwardian country residence in one acre of gardens. Beautiful, superbly furnished rooms both en suite. Separate child's bedroom available. All-weather tennis court. Loose boxes available. Bodiam Castle, Mickleham Priory, Battle and Seven Sisters Nature Reserve nearby.

WEST CHILTINGTON   NEW HOUSE FARM
Broadford Bridge Road, West Chiltington, Nr Pulborough, West Sussex RH20 2LA. *Tel*: West Chiltington (07983) 2215. *Hosts*: Alma & Mac Steele.

Rates: B   Vouchers accepted.

Charming old farmhouse, 1450 with Jacobean addition. Near South Downs Way. Fishing, golf and riding. Gatwick 40 mins drive. Most rooms en suite. Closed December. Reduced rates weekly. Pubs within walking distance. Dairy annexe. Children over 12 welcome. Sorry, no pets.

WINCHESTER   EAST VIEW
16 Clifton Hill, Winchester, Hants SO22 5BN. *Tel*: Winchester (0962) 62986.
Hosts: The Parker Family.
Rates: B

Warm and welcoming Victorian house with pleasant garden on hill with views over city. 10 min walk from historic cathedral. Many restaurants in city centre. No smoking in bedrooms. Southampton 12 miles, Portsmouth 23 miles, Salisbury 25 miles. On A3090 (towards Romsey) ¼m from city centre.

Portreeves Acre   Bed and Breakfast only
The Causeway
Arundel
West Sussex
BN18 9JJ

☎ Arundel (0903) 883277

Pat and Charles Rogers

Pat and Charles came to Arundel in 1974 as the tenants of the Red
Lion public house, and took over this distinctive modern house in
1985 from some very good friends. By now they are well acquainted
with the area and its people and have nothing but good to say about
both. The house itself was built by a local architect in 1974, and is set
in an acre of garden, bordered on one side by the gently flowing River
Arun, and on the other by green fields. The background is dominated
by the castle. Guest accommodation (which does not include a lounge)
is in a linked annexe. All five bedrooms are on ground-floor level with
private bathrooms and colour TV and they all overlook the garden. No
dinner is served but there is a substantial choice of restaurants within
five minutes walking distance.

Easily Accessible: Arundel itself is an interesting historical town with
many attractions, including the Wildfowl Trust nature reserve, a Sat-
urday antiques market, and a picturesque park. The pride and joy of
the town is the splendid castle, which originated in the 11th century
and has been restored through the ages. There are also enjoyable cruises
along the River Arun and in August a lively arts festival takes place.
The surrounding countryside is quite lovely and you can take a pleasant amble along the river or a more challenging hike along the South
Downs Way, which passes nearby. Just outside Arundel you can visit the
archaeological remains at Fishbourne Roman Palace and Bignor Roman
Villa, the latter being the remains of the largest villa in the country.
Goodwood House and race course are only 10 miles away, and within
a 15-mile radius there are numerous historic houses to see. If you feel
like taking a day trip to the coast, Portsmouth with its naval heritage
is only 25 miles away and the pleasant seaside resort of Brighton only
20 miles away.

Local Activities: walks, boat cruises, swimming pool, golf, horse-riding.

White Barn

Crede Lane
Bosham
West Sussex
PO18 8NX

Closed Christmas
No dinners August
Sorry, no pets
Unlicensed, guests welcome
    to bring own wine

☎ Bosham (0243) 573113

Susan and Antony Trotman

Off A27 from Chichester to Portsmouth

This is a modern, single-storied, open-plan house of considerable character. It is situated in a private road in the pretty, ancient harbour village of Bosham. Exposed rafters, wall-to-wall pine panelling and the extensive use of beech and oak endow it with a warmth that is too often absent from modern architecture. The dining room has a thirty foot wall of glass which enables guests to view the attractive landscaped garden and which looks out to a small patio for guests to enjoy in the summer. There are three bedrooms; the two doubles are en suite, and the single has an adjacent bathroom.

Breakfast and dinner are sociable affairs – both are served at one large table (although guests may use separate tables). The food is original, tasty and well presented. Susan particularly enjoys mixing luxury items with traditional English ingredients. Special diets can be prepared. No dinner is served in August but there are several good restaurants nearby including a well-recommended Indian restaurant.

Easily Accessible: Bosham is where, according to legend, King Cnut tried and failed to turn back the sea and the village is depicted on the Bayeux Tapestry. Today one can enjoy a relaxing boat tour around the harbour. The surrounding countryside is delightful and the South Downs are a very popular walking area. Chichester, a charming town with a notable festival theatre and Norman cathedral, is 3 miles east. The Weald and Downland open air museum, 6 miles north of Chichester, has a fascinating collection of houses of historical interest including a 15th-century farmhouse and working smithy which have been saved from dereliction, brought here and restored. Historic Arundel with its medieval castle (much altered and restored) is 12 miles to the east. Portsmouth is 15 miles to the west and here one can visit the *Mary Rose*, *HMS Warrior* and *HMS Victory*. There are numerous stately homes nearby including Petworth House with its excellent fine-art collection.

Local Activities: walks, golf, tennis, sailing, swimming, horse-riding.

Topp's Hotel

17 Regency Square
Brighton
East Sussex
BN1 2FG

☎ Brighton (0273) 729334

Paul and Pauline Collins

10 minute drive Brighton station, near sea-front

No dinner Wed or Sunday
Sorry, no pets
Large car park opp. hotel

Topp's Hotel is an engaging blend of the old and the new. A beautiful grade II listed Regency building, it is furnished in both an antique and modern style. It is superbly situated in Regency Square in the heart of Brighton, only one hundred yards from the sea-front.

The rooms are spacious and light with refreshing colour schemes. Nothing is heavy or ponderous. All the bedrooms have en suite bathrooms and come complete with writing desk, mini-bar and colour TV. Two rooms have four-poster beds and sun-catching balconies.

The Bottoms restaurant, in the hotel basement, is run by Topps' proprietors, Paul (who has been in the business for twenty-three years) and his wife, Pauline. It is open to guests and non-guests. The food is fresh, simple French and British cuisine accompanied by tasty home-baked rolls. Pauline does all the cooking using only top quality produce.(She also does all the lovely flower arrangements for which she has won an award.)

Easily Accessible: Brighton has much to offer the visitor. Apart from the sea and its attendant attractions, there is a wealth of elegant Georgian and Victorian architecture, the Pavilion, the Dome, an Aquarium and Dolphinarium, the Theatre Royal, nine cinema screens, interesting shops and for the 'foody' – over three hundred restaurants. In spring there is a fascinating arts festival and in November the famous London to Brighton Car Run. Just outside Brighton there are the lovely South Downs to walk on and numerous pretty village to visit. The quaint village of Rottingdean is just 4 miles along the sea-front.

Local Activities: As above plus golf, swimming, horse-racing, sea-fishing.

Sutherland House

186 London Road
Deal
Kent
CT14 9PT

Sorry, no pets
Children over 5 welcome
Private dinner parties
    catered for

☎ Dover (0304) 362853

The Pitman Family

This attractive Victorian house, situated near the centre of Deal, is run by the Pitman family. Both Mr Pitman Senior and Junior were reps who grew progressively despondent over the standard of rooms and services they encountered on their travels. Their intention when they opened Sutherland House was to create a homely, clean and warm environment. This is very evident here, and in addition the period furniture, pot plants, unusual porcelain animals, and delicately patterned and coloured fabrics give Sutherland House a very distinctive look and atmosphere. All the bedrooms have en suite facilities and the pleasant lounge has a colour TV.

The food (up to cordon bleu standard) is home-cooked by Janet Pitman using fresh ingredients. Dinner is open to non-residents.

Easily Accessible: Deal is an attractive resort, with an unspoilt promenade, a pier – ever popular with fishermen – and two outstanding Tudor castles. Deal Castle was constructed by order of Henry VIII and is the largest in the network of Tudor coastal defences; Walmer Castle, shaped like a Tudor rose, is the official residence of the Lord Warden of the Cinque Ports, who, at the present time, is Her Majesty the Queen Mother. The port of Dover, twenty minutes away, has a splendid castle, and a Roman painted house with well-preserved wall paintings and heating system. There are numerous picturesque villages (inland and coastal) to visit. There are stunning walks along the coast and inland over the North Downs Way. The Pitmans are agents for P & O Ferries and can arrange bookings for day trips to France.

Local Activities: walks, golf, beaches.

Claremont House
Second Avenue
Hove
East Sussex
BN3 2LL

☎ Brighton (0273) 735161

Colin and Sue Humber

Facilities for reception/cocktail
  party etc of up to 80 people

Bed, breakfast and
  bar snacks

This sunny Victorian house is situated in a wide tree-lined avenue just off the sedate Hove sea-front. The rooms are high-ceilinged, with large windows and marble fireplaces (some with 'coal effect' fires), and are very prettily decorated in light, flowery wallpapers and fabrics. All twelve bedrooms have en suite facilities, and are equipped with remote control colour TV; the larger suites have mini bars, large bathrooms (one with a corner bath, another with a jacuzzi), and one has a very pretty four-poster bed with lace trimmings. The spacious lounge with its well-stocked bar is furnished in soft peachy colours and attractive cane-backed chairs.

Colin and Sue Humber took over Claremont House in early 1989, from myself and my partner Mary Behar. It had been my first venture into the hotel business and probably my last – I take my hat off to anyone who makes it work. It is hard work. Mary and I upgraded the hotel considerably, but the strain of running two businesses at once proved too much. Colin and Sue took it off our hands and have made further excellent improvements. I may be a little biased about this one, but I now consider it to be of a very high standard. Amongst the many things Sue and Colin have worked on, the walled garden is much improved with very pretty herbaceous borders and a lawn laid out with parasoled tables and chairs, where guests can relax with a drink on a warm summer's evening.

Bar snacks are served at lunchtime and in the evening, either in the bar or, weather permitting, in the garden. The menu is varied and if you choose to do so, you could make a full meal of it – for instance you could choose calamari, followed by Scottish salmon, followed by delicious fudge brownies.

Easily Accessible: Hove is considered a rather more genteel town than Brighton. As the centre of the latter is only a half hour's walk away, many of its attractions are the same (and for these please see entry for Topp's Hotel). In Hove, the beaches are a little less crowded, the streets less bustling. Hove has its own museum and art gallery, which holds some fascinating 'off beat' exhibitions (such as 'The Pioneer Movie-Makers of Hove'); the King Alfred Sports Centre, with a leisure pool and water slide; and for steam enthusiasts, the Hove Engineerium.

Chase Lodge   Unlicensed
10 Park Road
Hampton Wick
Kingston-upon-Thames
KT1 4AS

☎ London (01) 943 1862

Denise and Nigel Dove

20 mins train central London

Chase Lodge is well-placed, lying near the banks of the Thames in a conservation area, bordered by the Royal Bushy Park. It is very well served for public transport and is one of the few places in this book where a private car is not essential. The Lodge has an interesting history; built in 1870, it was once owned by a wealthy coal merchant who provided Hampton Court Palace (just down the road) with fuel. Later as the home of the local prison warder it became known as 'the cage'. Today, it is a comfortable period-style house – something achieved after much restoration work. To its rear is a gate leading directly to the Palace through the Royal Park with its free-roaming wild deer. There are three bedrooms, all with colour TV, and en suite facilities and a fridge. One has a four-poster bed. There is a small patio garden full of colour and pot plants.

There is a three-course dinner, home-cooked with fresh vegetables. The menu is simple, with a choice for all courses – Carrott soup, followed by beef in beer, and for dessert a rich chocolate mousse would be typical. Wine can be purchased at a local store. There are many restaurants in the area – your hosts will advise.

Easily Accessible: The centre of London with myriad attractions is only twenty minutes away. Hampton Court, Cardinal Wolsey's splendid palace, can be reached in fiteen minutes by foot. Boats will take you up and down the river, stopping off at Kew Gardens, Richmond and its beautiful park and Greenwich Observatory and park, and the National Maritime Museum. Kingston iself is a historic town; prosperous since Anglo-Saxon days, it has a famous coronation stone where reputedly seven Anglo-Saxon kings were crowned. During the summer months, the Wimbledon Tennis Tournament, the Oxford and Cambridge Boat Race and the Twickenham, Kingston and Richmond boat regattas are all to hand. Richmond Theatre, a popular touring theatre, frequently shows West End productions.

Millers
134 High Street
Lewes
East Sussex
BN7 1XS

Bed and breakfast only
A 'no smoking' house
Sorry, no pets

☎ Lewes (0273) 475631

Tére and Tony Tammar

Short drive from railway station

Situated in a conservation area in the historical town of Lewes, Millers derives its name from the millers who in the 19th century sold their produce from the front parlour (now the dining room). In 1939 it was bought by two genteel but eccentric sisters, Caroline Lucas and Frances Byng-Stamper, who were closely associated with the Bloomsbury group. They converted the stables into a gallery and here staged art exhibitions, concerts and lectures, and later set up a printing press.

The small timber-framed house dates from the 16th century. There are three bedrooms for visitors all with private bathrooms and individual character – one has an iron-framed antique rose-painted four-poster bed with lace hangings and a Victorian screen, another has oak beams and a closet (now a shower) where priests are reputed to have hidden during times of persecution.

A good English breakfast or a vegetarian equivalent including home-made preserves and bread rolls made from locally ground flour is served in the beamed dining room. There is no dinner but Lewes has a good range of restaurants. The proprietors recommend the Sussex Kitchen at the Pelham Arms which provides good, reasonably priced food. Also recommended at the other end of the spectrum is Kenwards – described by Tére and Tony as the 'jewel in Lewes's gastronomic crown'.

Easily Accessible: Lewes is an interesting town dating back to the Norman Conquest with steep narrow streets and a mixture of Georgian and older buildings including antique shops, a ruined castle, museums and a house which once belonged to Anne of Cleves. The surrounding countryside is very pretty, with the South Downs attracting many walkers. Stroll along the disused railway line from Lewes to Uckfield and around the Seven Sisters Country Park where you can enjoy the coastal scene. Opera buffs will enjoy the summer season at Glyndebourne, 3 miles away. Bloomsbury enthusiasts can visit Charleston Farmhouse and Monks House, both homes to the Bloomsbury set. Alfriston is a very pretty village with a children's zoo. The popular seaside resort of Brighton with its flamboyant Royal Pavilion is 8 miles away.

Barn House
Rodmell
Lewes
East Sussex
BN7 3HF

Sorry, no pets
Bed and Breakfast only

☎ Brighton (0273) 477 865

Ian and Bernadette Fraser

Off A275 Lewes/Newhaven road

This very charming beamed house is in fact an 18th-century converted barn. It has a pretty stone-walled mature garden with lovely views of the surrounding farmland, downs and the four acres of grounds and orchards. There are seven guest bedrooms, all with private or en suite facilities, colour TV, and a comfortable guest lounge. One of the bedrooms has a four-poster bed and a Victorian bathroom. All the rooms are individually and very attractively designed (Bernadette herself has a keen interest in interior design).

An evening meal is not provided but there are numerous local pubs and restaurants in Lewes, just over 2 miles away.

Easily Accessible: Rodmell is situated on the South Downs Way, so the immediate area is excellent for downland walks, and the River Ouse provides a variety of scenery and wildlife. For local attractions please see the entry on Millers.

Local Activities: walks, horse-riding, bird-watching.

Blacklands House
Blacklands
East Malling
Kent
ME19 6DS

Bed and Breakfast only
Chauffeuring – short distances

☎ West Malling (0732) 844274

Ann and Vernon Leonard

Off M20 exit 4 to A20, direction Maidstone.

This is a fine listed Georgian building standing in half an acre of grounds with a stream – once famous for driving the greatest concentration of water mills in Great Britain. A man-made millpond with a splashing waterfall can be seen and heard from the rear rooms.

Ann and Vernon have decorated and furnished Blacklands in a comfortable and homely style, and have succeeded in retaining the original ambience of the house. Pictures and documents about Robert Tassell, the original owner of Blacklands, who was twice Mayor of Maidstone, hang on the walls of the comfortable TV lounge. There are five bedrooms all tastefully furnished in a style reflecting the relaxed, 'old world' grace that permeates the house.

Dinner is not usually available but there are several pubs and restaurants within walking distance. They vary considerably in price range from the 'upmarket' Wealden Hall which serves French and Italian food, to the locally renowned Indian restaurant, the Gandhi Tandoori.

Easily Accessible: Blacklands is surrounded by the fine countryside of the heart of Kent with its hopfields and oast houses. Close by is the picturesque village of West Malling with its high street of protected buildings, scheduled as places of architectural interest. There are numerous walks; directly from Blacklands you can follow the East Malling stream which runs through its garden, through the East Malling village conservation area, and leads right to the source of the stream in the pretty hamlet of West Stree; you can also join the Pilgrims Way, the medieval route from Winchester to Canterbury which can be reached 2 miles away. There are a profusion of historic buildings to visit; within half an hour's drive you can visit Penshurst Place, a Tudor manor house; Chartwell, once the home of Sir Winston Churchill; Hever Castle, once the home of Anne Boleyn, and Leeds Castle. Brands Hatch, the famous racing circuit, is a fifteen-minute drive away.

Local Activities: walks, golf, horse-riding, wind-surfing, gliding.

Huggetts Furnace Farm
Stonehurst Lane
Five Ashes
Nr Mayfield
East Sussex
TN20 6LL

Closed January for lambing
Sorry, no pets
No smoking in bedrooms

☎ Hadlow Down (082585) 220/722

Gillian and John Mulcare

Phone for directions

This house dating back to medieval times stands in tranquillity at the end of a long drive. It has a lovely garden with a heated swimming pool and very fine views of fields and the River Uck – its 'new' extension is Tudor. Inside there are old beams, inglenook fireplaces, oriental carpets and a warm and friendly ambience. Gillian Mulcare is often very busy breeding Charolais sheep and growing vegetables, but despite this she is always on hand to assist her guests. There are three bedrooms which are off their own landing and so are very private. The prettiest bedroom has oak beams and original wide floor boards. The sitting room has a colour TV, open fire, and lots of books and games.

Dinner makes excellent use of fresh locally grown and home produce; fresh eggs, fruit and meat all feature. Packed lunches can be provided by arrangement.

Easily Accessible: There are many footpaths around the farm. A short drive will take you to the Downs and Ashdown Forest. A 20-minute drive will take you to Tunbridge Wells, a spa town (you can still sample the waters) with excellent modern shops and some beautiful Georgian architecture, seen particularly in the Pantiles. Wakehurst Place is a beautiful Elizabethan mansion known primarily for its exotic gardens. The old locomotives of the Bluebell railway will take you through woods and green fields on a round trip starting from Sheffield Park. Hever Castle, an impressive Tudor mansion, once the home of the Boleyn family, has a maze, a walled Italian garden, a moat and drawbridge. The popular sea-side resort of Brighton is 40 minutes away.

Local Activities: heated swimming pool (Huggetts – bring your own swimming towel), walks, bird-watching.

Weavers
Warwick Wold
Merstham
Surrey
RH1 3DG

Sorry, no pets
Bed and Breakfast only
A 'no smoking' home

☎ Merstham (07374) 5491
(from mid 1990 (0737) 645491)

The Rayner Family

1 mile from Merstham village; 16 minutes from Gatwick

Nestling on the southern slopes of the Downs, this 16th-century house (once two cottages) is reached by way of a long drive. From the moment you step inside, the surroundings are impressive, a heavy oak door leads into a beamed hall, with a slate floor and two staircases at opposite ends of the room. There is a comfortable sitting room, with beams and an inglenook fireplace with bricks worn down by centuries of knife sharpening. The four guest bedrooms are later additions, and constitute a separate 'wing' with their own entrance.

The garden is very pretty, with foxgloves, daffodils and primroses, a lawn enclosed by conifers, willows and ornamental cherry trees, and a pond with water lilies. Growing along the side of the house, is a vine producing a lesser known wine, 'Chateau Weaver'!

There is an excellent three-course English breakfast. No dinner is offered but there are several local pubs and restaurants, including the pub The Feathers situated just one mile from Weavers, which has its own restaurant.

Easily Accessible: Merstham is convenient for Gatwick airport and London is just over half an hour away by train. There are several pretty and interesting villages to explore including Outwood, where you can see one of England's few remaining watermills. There are numerous gardens to enjoy: Wilsey, Nymans, Leonards Lee, and Sheffield Park. Of the many castles and stately homes to visit, Chiddingstone, Hever Castle, Penshurst Place, and Hatchlands are all fairly local. The area surrounding Weavers is criss-crossed with many bridlepaths and footpaths, including the Old Pilgrims Way, a path running from Winchester to Canterbury, which starts just 200 yards from the house and runs along the top of the Downs. Sandown Park, Worcester Park and Epsom racecourses and Brands Hatch motor racing circuit are all within half an hour's drive.

Local Activities: walks, horse-riding, golf, sailing, wind-surfing.

Mizzards Farm

Rogate
Petersfield
Hampshire
GU31 5HS

Award winner
Bed and Breakfast only
Children over 4 welcome
Sorry, no pets
A 'no smoking' house

☎ Rogate (073080) 656
(from May 1990 (0730) 821656)

Mr & Mrs J. C. Francis
Off A272 at church in Rogate Village, then first lane on right after bridge

Set in complete seclusion in thirteen and a half acres of landscaped gardens and fields and surrounded by woodland, Mizzards is an exceptionally attractive 16th-century farmhouse built of brick and stone. In the delightful garden there is a small lake which is being turned into a watergarden with unusual waterside plants. It is altogether a very charming, idyllic setting.

Inside, Mizzards is very prettily decorated; antique furniture, water colours on the walls and Laura Ashley fabrics in the bedrooms. A baby grand piano stands in the drawing room and is often played by guests (not this one unfortunately). The drawing room is an impressive room; a vaulted hall with exposed rafters and a large inglenook fireplace. All three bedrooms are pretty, and have en suite bathroms and colour TV; the main one is particularly luxurious with its large four-poster bed, marble bathroom and fabulous views. In summer, as one would expect, the large covered and heated swimming pool is very popular with guests.

Breakfast is an English affair, with fresh grapefruit, kedgeree, kippers and bacon, eggs and tomatoes. All very delicious and also very filling. An evening meal is not offered but there are many pubs and restaurants of quality in the area.

Easily Accessible: The lovely South Downs Way (which stretches for eighty miles) starts at Petersfield, just 5 miles away. There are numerous shorter walks in the area, which has been designated of outstanding natural beauty, with its landscape of weald hills and wooded, rolling farmland. Petworth House, 10 miles away, is a magnificent 17th-century house with a famous deer park landscaped by Capability Brown. Six miles away at Cowdray you can watch polo, and 8 miles away at Goodwood, you can visit the races. Portsmouth with its historic ships (the *Mary Rose*, *Victory* and *Warrior*) is 15 miles away.

Local Activities: swimming at Mizzards, walks.

Chequers Hotel   Award winner
Church Place
Pulborough
West Sussex
RH20 1AD

☎ Pulborough (07982) 2486

The Searancke Family

This is a very attractive Queen Anne building, situated in a quiet private lane on the outskirts of the pretty village of Pulborough. It has very fine views overlooking the Arun Valley towards the South Downs. John and Ann Searancke have lived at Chequers for nearly twenty years and have continually improved the property – their care and love of the house shows. Today there are eleven bedrooms, all with private bathrooms and colour TV, and individually furnished to a high standard; one has a four-poster bed.

The restaurant is open throughout the year, with a daily change of menu and friendly and helpful staff. The food is freshly cooked using local ingredients.

Easily Accessible: There are several walks beginning directly from the hotel, and the ever popular South Down Way starts within 4 miles. Parham House, an Elizabethan mansion with fine grounds, is only 4 miles away. The Chalk Pits Museum, 6 miles away, is a fascinating industrial heritage centre with demonstrations by craftsmen – blacksmiths, potters, boat builders, and an exhibition of tools, all within the beautiful setting of the Arun Valley. Eight miles away you can visit the magnificent Arundel Castle, which originated in Norman times and was rebuilt by the Duke of Norfolk in the 1870s. Nearby is the Heritage Museum of local history and the Wildfowl Trust bird sanctuary. Twelve miles away at Goodwood, you can visit the racecourse, stately home, and country park. Brighton and Chichester are easily reached for a day trip.

Local Activities: walks, golf, fishing.

Shearings

Rockbourne
Fordingbridge
Hampshire
SP6 3NA

Dinner by arrangement
Children over 12 welcome
Sorry, no pets

☎ Rockbourne (07253) 256

Colin and Rosemary Watts

Off B3078 from Fordingbridge

Shearings, a charming listed, timber-framed, thatched cottage, dates back to 1575 and is, as they say, 'as pretty as a picture'. It lies in a quarter of an acre of secluded garden in the delightful village of Rockbourne. A winter stream runs past and to enter the house, one has to cross a small wooden bridge.

Inside, the oak beams (some of which are 1000 years old), wood panelling and inglenook fireplaces, give one the impression of stepping back in time – although today, with central heating and electric blankets, guests will not experience the full flavour of Tudor life! The three bedrooms are simply but attractively furnished, each with its own bath or shower. The sitting room has a TV, games, and maps to help guests plan their activities. Although a car is really necessary to make the most of your stay, your hosts will meet you at the nearest railway stations and airports.

Before dinner, Colin and Rosemary join their guests for an aperitif, which is taken in the drawing room in winter, and, weather permitting, in the summer months, by the summer house. Dinner is an occasion to be savoured with candlelight, cut glass and fine china. All this, the home-cooking and a complimentary half bottle of wine (per guest) goes down very well with tired walkers.

Easily Accessible: The village of Rockbourne nestles in a hollow in the Downs on the edge of the New Forest and boasts a 13th-century church and a Roman villa. The beautiful medieval cathedral of Salisbury with its famous four-hundred-foot spire (the tallest in England) is 9 miles away. Within a 35-mile radius, you can visit numerous historic places, such as Broadlands, home of the Earl of Mountbatten; Stourhead House and landscaped gardens with fabulous mock Roman temples and eerie grottos; and Longleat House and Safari Park.

Local Activities: walks, golf, horse-riding, fishing.

The Old Vicarage
66 Church Square
Rye
East Sussex
TN31 7HF

Closed for Christmas
Sorry, no pets
Children over 12 welcome
Award winner

☎ Rye (0797) 222119

Julia Lampon and Paul Masters

In town, beside St Mary's Church

The Old Vicarage is a pretty, pink listed building which, despite being four hundred years old, is today mainly Georgian in character. The windows have views over the medieval roofs of the historic and picturesque town of Rye. Henry James was inspired to write *The Spoils of Poynton* whilst living here.

The house is as attractive inside as without. The five bedrooms are charmingly furnished in Laura Ashley fabrics; all have colour TV and private or en suite facilities. Two rooms have four-poster beds. The guest lounge overlooks the pretty garden.

Breakfast is delicious and healthy. Home-made preserves and free-range eggs are used. No dinner is provided but there are numerous pubs, hotels and restaurants within walking distance.

Easily Accessible: The town of Rye is one of the original Cinque Ports. Despite the annual influx of tourists, it has managed to keep its character with medieval, Tudor, Stuart and Georgian houses jostling for space along the cobbled streets. The famous 14th-century church has the oldest turret clock in England and magnificent views from the belfry of the surrounding countryside. You can walk from Rye to the beautiful beach at Camber sands. One and a half miles away at Rye harbour you can visit the Bird Sanctuary. The vicinity is rich in places of historic and architectural interest. Winchelsea, 3 miles away, was created by Edward I and is known as the smallest town in England. At Bateman's, 14 miles away, you can visit Rudyard Kipling's home and see the working watermill. Sissinghurst Castle, 15 miles away, has gardens created by Sir Harold Nicolson and Vita Sackville-West. There are numerous country walks around Rye as well as the Saxon Shore Way, a long-distance path tracing the ancient coastline of Kent for 140 miles.

Local Activities: walks, golf, swimming, sailing, wind-surfing, fishing, bowls, putting, tennis, squash.

The Old Parsonage
West Dean
Seaford
East Sussex
BN25 4AL

Closed Dec-Feb
Sorry, no pets
Children over 12 welcome
Bed and Breakfast only

☎ Alfriston (0323) 870432

Raymond and Angela Woodhams

Off the A259 Newhaven to Eastbourne coast road

In the heart of the Friston forest, in a delightful hamlet, this fabulous building, dating back to 1280, is reputed to be the oldest continually inhabited small medieval house in England. It was built with local greenstone, flint and chalk, by the monks from Wilmington Priory. It retains several distinctive features such as a mighty stone spiral staircase, heavy wooden shutters (which may have doubled as combat shields), a greenstone fireplace, and exposed roof timbers. The old crypt, with its exposed beam ceiling, is now used as a library. To the rear of the house, the lawn surrounded by herbaceous borders leads up to a meadow and copse which is bordered by the northern boundary of the forest.

The house, despite its grand old age, is welcoming and comfortable. There are three bedrooms, each with private facilities; one, in the original hall, has an impressive high timber roof structure, arched latticed windows and a four-poster bed. The drawing room has an open fire and heavy arched doors and on chilly afternoons your hosts will light the fire and offer you complimentary tea and crumpets.

Raymond and Angela bought the Old Parsonage in 1987 after fourteen years of teaching in Mombasa. They are still excited by the house, and enjoy sharing it with their guests. Sea fishing is a particular passion of Raymond's and he will loan tackle and arrange boat trips.

A hearty breakfast is served. Dinner is not offered but there are several excellent local eating places – the most famous being the Hungry Monk at Jevington, where advance booking is essential.

Easily Accessible: The area is very good for walking, through forests, hills or along the coast. The hamlet adjoins the Seven Sisters Country Park where there are some fine coastal and cliff walks, and a shingle beach in the delightful setting of Cuckmere Haven. A ten minute drive will take you to the Seaford Head Nature Reserve with its badgers, foxes and diverse birdlife. There are numerous signposted forest walks through Friston Forest. The South Downs Way passes through the hamlet. Four miles away you can visit the remains of the 13th-century Wilmington Priory and to its south, the extensive hill painting known as 'The Long Man'. The Opera House at Glyndebourne is 7 miles away. Children will love the educational Drussilas Zoo, 4 miles away.

Local Activities: walks, golf, sea fishing, canoeing, rowing, horse-riding.

Culver Lodge Hotel
Culver Road
Shanklin
Isle of Wight
PO37 6ER

☎ Isle of Wight (0983) 863515

Bob and June Ward

Ferry from Portsmouth to Fishbourne, or Lymington to Yarmouth approx 45 mins.

Culver Lodge Hotel is situated in a quiet part of Shanklin but within easy reach of the town centre and beach. It has a distinguished history. It was commissioned for General Gordon (of Khartoum fame) and is mentioned in his diaries as 'this idyllic retirement oasis by the sea'. Unfortunately General Gordon was killed before its completion but his two sisters lived there for forty years. The house was then bought by the island's MP and has seen many worthy visitors in its time – Lord Louis Mountbatten and Douglas Bader, to name but two.

Built in 1884 the house has been modernised but still retains its original charm with a very pretty secluded south-facing garden. Several of the rooms have magnificent sea-views. All are en suite and one, the honeymoon suite, is most attractive with a split level, the bathroom and dressing room on one level, and the bedroom with superb views immediately above.

The Wards are most helpful (they say that running Culver Lodge has restored their faith in human nature as their guests have always been such a pleasure) and are always ready to give advice on places to visit, walks, bus and rail timetables.

The five-course dinner is very good. Vegetables are fresh from the island and herbs come from the kitchen garden. The island's strawberries which are available all year round have a reputation for being particularly delicious.

Easily Accessible: The island is known for its largely unspoilt countryside which ranges from chalk downlands to green fields and from sandy beaches to ancient forest. Much of this land is open to walkers who can use the numerous footpaths and bridleways. The coastal path alone is sixty-five miles long. There are many historic and archaeological sites to visit including Osborne House, owned by the English Heritage, where Queen Victoria spent much time after the death of her beloved Albert. The town of Brading has a Roman villa with fine mosaic floors and a medieval church. You will see many rare plants in the Botanic Gardens at Ventnor, which benefits from a near-Mediterranean climate.

Local Activities: walks, sea-fishing, golf, and of course, Cowes Week.

CENTRAL ENGLAND

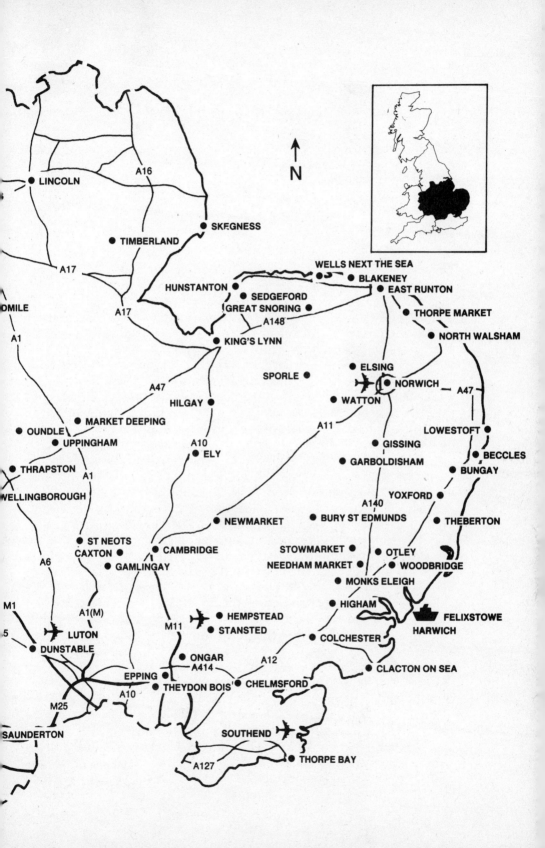

Central England

Covering the counties of: Bedfordshire, Buckinghamshire, Cambridgeshire, Derbyshire, Essex, Gloucestershire, Herefordshire, Hertfordshire, Leicestershire, Lincolnshire, Norfolk, Northamptonshire, Nottinghamshire, Oxfordshire, Shropshire, Staffordshire, Suffolk, Warwickshire, West Midlands, Worcestershire.

This area covers Central England and East Anglia and is so large and varied as to make generalisations quite impossible. However, the four main areas of distinctive countryside are the gentle Cotswold and Malvern hills; the moors, crags and woods of the Peak District National Park; the flat windswept East Anglian Fens, and the thirty miles of navigable waterways known as the Norfolk Broads.

The cities are as varied as the landscape. Oxford and Cambridge boast a wealth of fine architecture, museums, art galleries, and their world-famous universities. In total contrast is Birmingham, a gargantuan sprawl of buildings that was once at the very nub of the coal and iron industries. Indeed, the whole of the West Midlands was deeply affected by the Industrial Revolution – anyone who is interested in this aspect of history can visit the Black Country Museum in Dudley, which recreates a typical working village; and in Shropshire can be seen the very first iron bridge, in its most distinctive arc spanning the River Severn.

Central England also boasts a profusion of great cathedrals: the towering 15th-century spire of Norwich Cathedral is truly inspiring; gracious Ely cathedral, which dominates the surrounding Fens, houses a fabulous stained glass museum; the west face of the triple-towered cathedral of Lincoln is imposing and majestic; and the superb Norman craftsmanship of Southwell Minster in Nottinghamshire is quite outstanding.

Similarly, the stately homes to be found in this area will not disappoint the visitor: the magnificence of the state rooms of Bleinheim Palace in Oxfordshire all but overwhelm; inside the imposing 14th-century stronghold of Warwick Castle, there are fine state rooms and a fascinating Madame Tussaud's exhibition realistically recreating a Victorian royal weekend; and the grand mansion Chatsworth House sits in one of Capability Brown's most delightful settings.

And what of the literary and artistic heritage contained in this area? John Constable regularly painted the quintessentially English landscape of the Stour valley in Suffolk; D.H. Lawrence drew inspiration from the characters and landscape of his home town, Eastwood in Nottinghamshire; and Benjamin Britten so loved the small Suffolk village of

Aldeburgh that he established an annual music and arts festival there. But without a doubt it is Great Britain's most famous son, William Shakespeare, who attracts the most attention: his home town Stratford-upon-Avon is truly a living shrine to the great bard – and it is also, of course, home to the Royal Shakespeare Company.

Regional Tourist Boards:
Heart of England – 2–4 Trinity Street, Worcester, Worcestershire, WR1 2PW
Tel: (0905) 613132
East Midlands – Exchequergate, Lincoln, Lincolnshire LN2 1PZ
Tel: (0522) 531521
Thames & Chilterns – The Mount House, Church Green, Witney, Oxfordshire OX8 6DZ
Tel: (0993) 778800
East Anglia – Toppesfield Hall, Hadleigh, Suffolk IP7 5DN
Tel: (0473) 822922

ASHBOURNE (Swinscoe) DOG AND PARTRIDGE COUNTRY INN
Swinscoe, Ashbourne, Derbyshire DE6 2HS. *Tel*: Ashbourne (0335) 43183.
Hosts: Mary & Martin Stelfox.
Rates: C/D Vouchers accepted.
  17th-century inn with accommodation in motel units. Easy driving access to main restaurant and bars. Spectacular views. 4-poster room available. Bar lounge only. Vegetarian menus daily. Alton Towers, golf, cycle hire and pony-trekking nearby. Pets welcome.

ASHBOURNE THE OLD RECTORY
Blore, Nr Ashbourne, Derbyshire DE6 2BS. *Tel*: Thorpe Cloud (033529) 287.
Hosts: Mr and Mrs Stuart Worthington.
Rates: D Vouchers accepted.
(See page 119 for description)

BANBURY EASINGTON HOUSE
50 Oxford Road, Banbury, Oxfordshire OX16 9AN. *Tel*: Banbury (0295) 259395. *Hosts*: Malcolm & Gwynneth Hearne.
Rates: B/C Vouchers accepted.
(See page 120 for description)

BANBURY (Culworth) FULFORD HOUSE
The Green, Culworth, Nr Banbury, Oxfordshire OX17 2BB. *Tel*: Sulgrave

(029576) 355 and 8304. *Telex*: 83147 G (WILLS). *Hosts*: Stephen & Marypen Wills.
Rates: C   Vouchers accepted.
(See page 121 for description)

BECCLES   RIVERVIEW HOUSE
Ballygate, Beccles, Suffolk NR34 9ND. *Tel*: Beccles (0502) 713519. *Host*: Margaret Shirley.
Rates: B
Large Georgian house in spacious attractive gardens, nicely situated overlooking River Waveney in market town of Beccles. Ideal for exploring Norfolk Broads, coast and countryside. Great Yarmouth 14 miles. Visit Somerleyton House, Fritton Lake and Theme and Wildlife Parks. All rooms colour TV.

BELPER   SHOTTLE HALL FARM
Belper, Derbyshire DE5 2EB. *Tel*: Cowers Lane (077389) 276. *Hosts*: Philip & Phyllis Matthews.
Rates: B   Vouchers accepted.
(See page 122 for description)

BIRMINGHAM   MOXHULL HALL HOTEL
Holly Lane, Wishaw, Sutton Coldfield, Warwickshire B76 9PD. *Tel*: Birmingham (021) 329 2056. *Telex*: 333779. *Fax*: 021 329 2056.
Rates: C/D   Vouchers accepted.
Comfortable and spacious country house hotel with fine carved staircase in 8 acres of gardens and woodlands. 4-poster available. Birmingham 7 miles. National Exhibition Centre 9 miles. Exit 4 off M6 north to Lichfield on A446. Turn at Warmley signpost.

BIRMINGHAM South (Moseley)   WAKE GREEN LODGE HOTEL AND RESTAURANT
20 Wake Green Road, Moseley, Birmingham B13 9EZ. *Tel*: Birmingham (021) 449 4499. *Hosts*: Peter & Sheila Smith.
Rates: A/B   Vouchers accepted.
Attractive, mock–Elizabethan house in residential area with own parking. South of city, 10 mins from centre, near Kings Heath. On B4217, off A34, A38, A45, A435. Easy access M42, M6. Reduced rates 3 nights or more. Sorry, no pets.

BLAKENEY (Nr Holt)   THE BLAKENEY HOTEL
Blakeney, Nr Holt, Norfolk NR25 7NE. *Tel*: Holt (0263) 740797. *Fax*: 0263 740795. *Host*: Mr G. Stannard.
Rates: D

Traditional hotel overlooking NT estuary and marshes. Ideal for touring the north Norfolk coast. All rooms have TV and beverage facilities. Golf, tennis, sailing and bird-watching nearby. 4-poster room. Annexe.

BOURTON-ON-THE-WATER COOMBE HOUSE HOTEL
Rissington Road, Bourton-on-the-Water, Gloucestershire GL54 2DL. *Tel*: Cotswold (0451) 21966. *Hosts*: Michael Young & Jackie Alderton.
Rates: B/C

Bright comfortable Cotswold house with mullioned windows in this attractive 17th-century village known as the 'Venice of the Cotswolds'. Beautiful autumn colours. All rooms en suite. Weekly rate includes dinner. Famous model village nearby. Stratford 25 miles, Bath 50 miles, Cheltenham 17 miles. No smoking in bedrooms. Sorry, no pets.

BRIDGNORTH THE CROFT HOTEL
St Mary's Street, Bridgnorth, Shropshire WV16 4DW. *Tel*: Bridgnorth (07462) 2416. *Hosts*: Gill & John Wilding.
Rates: B/C   Vouchers accepted.
(See page 123 for description)

BROADWAY (Saintbury) CUSACK'S GLEBE
Saintbury, Nr Broadway, Worcestershire WR12 7PX. *Tel*: Broadway (0386) 852210. *Host*: Mme Juliet Carro.
Rates: C   Vouchers accepted.

Lovely 15th-century farmhouse in 5½ acres. Broadway 3 miles. Chipping Campden 2½ miles. Reduced rates 3 nights or more. Rates include bathroom en suite and colour TV. No smoking in bedrooms, 4-poster available. Children over 12 welcome. Sorry, no pets.

BUNGAY (Mettingham) THE RED HOUSE HOTEL
Mettingham, Bungay, Suffolk NR35 1TW. *Tel*: Bungay (0986) 5666. *Hosts*: Elizabeth & Roger Grosvenor.
Rates: C/D

Small, family-run Georgian country house hotel set in 2½ acres of grounds with hard tennis court. On B1062 Beccles to Bungay road (formerly A1116) 2 miles east of Bungay. Home-cooked food. Fishing and bird-watching nearby. Convenient for Norwich, the Broads, Southwold. Sorry, no pets.

BURFORD (Fulbrook) ELM FARM HOUSE
Fulbrook, Burford, Oxfordshire OX8 4BW. *Tel*: Burford (099382) 3611.
Hosts: David & Sue Catlin.
Rates: B/C   Vouchers accepted.

Spacious, comfortable country house in quiet Cotswolds village. Large garden with croquet lawn. Log fires. Children over 10 welcome. No smoking in bedrooms. Cheltenham 20 miles, Oxford 20 miles, Blenheim Palace 15 miles. Off A361 1 mile north of Burford, right at memorial then 100yds on left. Sorry, no pets.

BURY ST EDMUNDS (Rede) PYKARDS HALL
Rede, Bury St Edmunds, Suffolk IP29 4AY. *Tel*: Hawkedon (028489) 229. *Hosts*: Clive & Louise Drayton.
Rates: B

Lovely part-15th-century, comfortable and spacious farmhouse in 300-acre working farm and woodlands. Gardens, ponds. Lovely views. Historic area. Off A143, 4½ miles south-west of Bury St Edmunds. Pubs and restaurants nearby. No smoking in bedrooms. Colour TV all rooms. Sorry, no pets.

BURY ST EDMUNDS (In town) (A 'no smoking' house) OUNCE HOUSE
Northgate Street, Bury St Edmunds, Suffolk IP33 1HP. *Tel*: Bury St Edmunds (0284) 61779. *Hosts*: Simon & Jennifer Pott.
Rates: C/D Vouchers accepted.

Spacious, elegant Victorian merchant's house. Excellent location for touring historic East Anglia. Refurbished and decorated to high standard. All rooms en suite with colour TV and many other facilities. Theatre and restaurant reservations gladly made.

BUXTON THORN HAYES PRIVATE HOTEL
137 London Road, Buxton, Derbyshire SK17 9NW. *Tel*: Buxton (0298) 23539. *Hosts*: Pat & David Green.
Rates: B
(See page 124 for description)

CAMBRIDGE (Little Shelford) (A 'no smoking' house) PURLINS
12 High Street, Little Shelford, Cambridge CB2 5ES. *Tel*: Cambridge (0223) 842643. *Hosts*: Olga & David Hindley.
Rates: B Vouchers accepted.
(See page 124 for description)

CAMBRIDGE (Dry Drayton) (A 'no smoking' house) THE COACH HOUSE
Scotland Road, Dry Drayton, Cambridge CB3 8BX. *Tel*: Crafts Hill (0954) 782439. *Host*: Catherine Child.
Rates: B Vouchers accepted.
(See page 125 for description)

CASTLE DONINGTON PRIEST HOUSE HOTEL
King's Mills, Castle Donington, Derby DE7 2RR. *Tel*: Derby (0332) 810649. *Fax*: 0332 811141 *Host*: Philip Humphries.
Rates: D

Picturesque old mill on banks of river Trent, mentioned in Domesday Book, with cottage accommodation. Within 2 miles Castle Donington off B6540, exit 24 off M1. Derby 10 miles. East Midlands airport 7 miles. Log fires and real ales. Honeymoon specials and 4-poster available. Small meetings welcome.

CASTLE DONINGTON   PARK FARMHOUSE
Melbourne Road, Isley Walton, Castle Donington, Nr Derby DE7 2RN. *Tel*: Derby (0332) 862409. *Hosts*: John & Linda Shields.
Rates: B/C   Vouchers accepted.
 Delightful half-timbered 17th-century farmhouse, overlooking beautiful countryside in private woodlands. Off A453 on Isley Walton to Melbourne road. Log fires. Convenient East Midlands airport and Donington Motor Racing Circuit. Colour TV and direct-dial telephones all rooms. Winter breaks available.

CAXTON (Nr Cambridge)   CAXTON FIELDS HOTEL AND RESTAURANT
Nr Caxton, Cambridgeshire CB3 8PD. *Tel*: Caxton (0954) 719206. *Hosts*: Arnot & Linda Wilson.
Rates: D   Vouchers accepted.
 Modern single-storey hotel in rural area. Small, intimate restaurant with bar specialising in steaks. Excellent access to A1/M11. Near Wimpole Hall. Cambridge, St Neots, Huntingdon, Royston all 8 miles. On A14 north of A14/A45 junction.

CAXTON   DENE HOUSE
96 Ermine Street, Caxton, Cambridge CB3 8PQ. *Tel*: Caxton (09544) 206.
Hosts: Fiona & David Hughes.
Rates: A/B   Vouchers accepted.
(See page 126 for description)

CHARLTON (Nr Banbury)   HOME FARM HOUSE
Charlton, Nr Banbury, Oxfordshire OX17 3DR. *Tel*: Banbury (0295) 811683.
Hosts: Colonel & Mrs Grove-White.
Rates: C   Vouchers accepted.
 Charming house dated 1637 with additional unique accommodation in dovecot adjacent to house. Edge of unspoilt village. Rooms en suite with TV. No smoking in bedrooms except dovecot. Banbury, Bicester, Buckingham within 10 miles. Oxford, Woodstock, Blenheim Palace 20 miles. Stratford, Warwick 30 miles. Phone for directions.

CHELMSFORD   MIAMI MOTEL
Princes Road, Chelmsford, Essex CM2 9AJ. *Tel*: (0245) 264848. *Telex*: 995430.
Host: Colin Newcombe.

: D   Vouchers accepted.

nveniently situated just south of Chelmsford on A12. All hotel facilities
luding 18 bedrooms in main buildings, plus substantial and attractive
motel units. Sauna.

CHELTENHAM   HANNAFORD'S
20 Evesham Rd, Cheltenham, Glos GL52 2AB. *Tel*: Cheltenham (0242) 515181.
Host: Mrs Crowley.
Rates: B
Comfortable Regency house, easy walking distance of town centre. A435
easy access M5 exits 10 and 11. Combines elegance of Cheltenham Spa with
the charm of Cotswold countryside. Most rooms en suite. Colour TVs all
rooms. Home-cooking. Sorry, no pets.

CHELTENHAM   STRETTON LODGE
Western Road, Cheltenham, Gloucestershire GL50 3RN. *Tel*: Cheltenham
(0242) 528724. *Fax*: 0242 528724/570771 *Hosts*: Eric & Kathy Price.
Rates: C   Vouchers accepted.
(See page 127 for description)

CHIPPING CAMPDEN   NOEL ARMS HOTEL
Chipping Campden, Gloucestershire GL55 6AT. *Tel*: Evesham (0386) 840317.
Fax: 0386 841136. *Hosts*: David & Glynis Feasey.
Rates: D   Vouchers accepted.
(See page 128 for description)

CHURCH MINSHULL (Nr Nantwich)   HIGHER ELMS FARM
Minshull Vernon, Crewe, Cheshire CW1 4RG. *Tel*: Church Minshull (027
071) 252. *Hosts*: Brian & Mary Charlesworth.
Rates: A
400-year-old farmhouse on working farm. Oak-beamed comfort
overlooking Shropshire Union canal. Interesting wildlife around. Suppers
only, but 4 pubs within 2 miles. Oulton Park 6 miles, Jodrell Bank 8, Chester
15. From M6 (junc 18) on A530 towards Nantwich.

CHURCH STRETTON   MYND HOUSE HOTEL
Little Stretton, Church Stretton, Shropshire SY6 6RB. *Tel*: Church Stretton
(0694) 722212. *Telex*: 9401 1036 WORD G. *Hosts*: Janet & Robert Hill.
Rates: C   Vouchers accepted.
Small Edwardian house hotel surrounded by beautiful walking country at
the base of the Long Mynd. Restaurant with 4-course table d'hôte or à la carte
dinner. Log fire. 4-poster suite with spa bath now available. Shrewsbury,
Ludlow 13 miles. 200yds off A49 – signed Little Stretton.

CIRENCESTER   RAYDON HOUSE
3 The Avenue, Cirencester, Gloucestershire GL7 1EH. *Tel*: Cirencester (0285)
653485. *Hosts*: Bill & Audrey Peniston.

Rates: B

Victorian house in own grounds, in quiet residential area yet only 3 mins walk to centre of this attractive market town. Near Cotswold Water Park with 1,000 acres lakes for recreational use. Sorry, no pets.

CLACTON-ON-SEA (A 'no smoking' house) LEVERE HOUSE HOTEL
15 Agate Road, Clacton-on-Sea, Essex CO15 1RA. *Tel*: Clacton-on-Sea (0255) 423044. *Host*: Vera Stone.
Rates: B

Warm and comfortable hotel in quiet area. 1 min walk from sandy beaches and from town centre. Children very welcome. Ideal situation for touring Constable country. Limited car park but parking very close. Colour TV all rooms.

COLCHESTER (Aldham) OLD HOUSE
Fordstreet, Aldham, Nr Colchester, Essex CO6 3PH. *Tel*: Colchester (0206) 240456. *Hosts*: Patricia & Richard Mitchell.
Rates: A/B Vouchers accepted.

Friendly 14th-century house, listed as historic building. Exposed beams, log fires, large garden and pond, private parking. 3 pubs with restaurants adjacent. Beauty therapist on premises. On A604 opp Queen's Head, 2 miles from A12 junction. Convenient for Harwich and Felixstowe ferries, East Anglian touring.

CRAVEN ARMS THE OLD RECTORY
Hopesay, Nr Craven Arms, Shropshire SY7 8HD. *Tel*: Little Brampton (05887) 245. *Hosts*: Amy & Graham Spencer.
Rates: C Vouchers accepted.

Wistaria-covered stone Georgian rectory next to village church. Quiet and secluded spot in landscaped gardens in area of outstanding natural beauty. All rooms en suite and with colour TV. Children over 10 welcome. No smoking in bedrooms. Sorry, no children or pets. Please bring own wine. Ludlow 11 miles, Shrewsbury 20. 3 miles off A49 at Craven Arms.

DERBY (Melbourne) (A 'no smoking' house) THE GRANGE
Packhorse Road, Melbourne, Derbyshire DE7 1EG. *Tel*: Derby (0332) 863653.
Hosts: Annette & Mirco Perla.
Rates: B/D
(See page 129 for description)

DUNSTABLE (Eaton Bray) BELLOWS MILL COTTAGE
Bellows Mill, Eaton Bray, Dunstable, Bedfordshire LU6 1QZ. *Tel*: Eaton Bray (0525) 220548/220205. *Hosts*: The Hodge Family.
Rates: B/C Vouchers accepted.
(See page 130 for description)

EAST RUNTON (Nr Cromer) DALKEITH
Lower Common, East Runton, Cromer, Norfolk NR27 9PG. *Tel*: Cromer
(0263) 514803. *Hosts*: Nigel & Jan Slater.
Rates: A
(See page 131 for description)

ELSING (Dereham) CHURCH FARM MOTEL AND
  RESTAURANT
Elsing, Dereham, Norfolk NR20 3EA. *Tel*: Swanton Morley (036 283) 8236.
Hosts: Roy & Pat Stoddart & Roy Brenner.
Rates: B
  Peaceful converted Norfolk farm offers luxury en suite studio apartments,
  one with 4-poster, all colour TV. Set in 4½ acres of meadow and ponds.
  4 miles east E. Dereham.

ELY
31 Egremont Street, Ely, Cambridgeshire CB6 1AE. *Tel*: Ely (0353) 663118.
Hosts: Sheila & Jeremy Friend-Smith.
Rates: A   Vouchers accepted.
(See page 132 for description)

ENSON (Nr Stafford) OAKLEIGH
Salters Lane, Enson, Staffordshire ST18 9TA. *Tel*: Sandon (088 97) 432. *Hosts*:
The Johnson Family.
Rates: B   Vouchers accepted.
  Beautifully converted and appointed annexe to country house in quiet Trent
  Valley location. Meals in the conservatory. Easy access to M6/A34. Alton
  Towers, Shugborough Hall and Wedgewood centre near. Left 1 mile south
  on A34 from A51 junc, 1 mile on right. Sorry, no pets.

EPPING MARSHALL'S FARM
Woodside, Thornwood, Nr Epping, Essex CM16 6LQ. *Tel*: Epping (0378)
74344. *Hosts*: Jack & Doris Potter.
Rates: B
  Lovely 400-year-old farmhouse. 10 acres non-working fields. Facing Epping
  Forest. Historic area. M11, exit 7, 1½ miles to Epping, turn at Blacksmith's
  Arms. London 20 miles. Stansted airport 20 mins. Cambridge 30 mins. Many
  pubs and restaurants nearby. Sorry, no pets.

FIRBECK YEWS FARM
Firbeck, Worksop, Nottinghamshire S81 8JW. *Tel*: Worksop (0909) 731458.
Hosts: John & Catherine Stewart-Smith.
Rates: B/D   Vouchers accepted.
(See page 133 for description)

GAMLINGAY   (A 'no smoking' house) THE EMPLINS
Church Street, Gamlingay, Sandy, Bedfordshire SG19 3ER. *Tel*: Gamlingay
(0767) 50581. *Hosts*: The Gorton Family.
Rates: C   Vouchers accepted.
(See page 134 for description)

GARBOLDISHAM (Near Diss)   INGLENEUK LODGE
Hopton Road, Garboldisham, Diss, Norfolk IP22 2RQ. *Tel*: Garboldisham
(095381) 541. *Hosts*: Connie & Doug Atkins.
Rates: A/B   Vouchers accepted.
   Modern bungalow in 10 acres with wooded riverside walk. All rooms
   colour TV. Home-cooked dinner by arrangement. Cream teas a speciality.
   Reduced short breaks all year. Turn south off A1066 Thetford to Diss road
   onto B1111. 1 mile on right.

GISSING (Nr Diss)   THE OLD RECTORY
Gissing, Diss, Norfolk IP22 3XB. *Tel*: Tivetshall (037 977) 575. *Hosts*: Jill &
Ian Gillam.
Rates: B
(See page 135 for description)

GLOUCESTER (Newent)   OLD COURT
Church Street, Newent, Gloucestershire GL18 1AB. *Tel*: Newent (0531)
820522. *Hosts*: The Reece Family.
Rates: A/C
   Lovely large comfortable William and Mary house in gorgeous mature
   walled gardens. Small historic town in area noted for falconry. Gloucester
   9 miles. Home-cooking, own and local produce. Restaurant. Colour TV all
   rooms. Sorry, no pets.

GREAT SNORING   THE OLD RECTORY
Barsham Road, Great Snoring, Fakenham, Norfolk NR21 OHP. *Tel*:
Walsingham (0328) 820597. *Hosts*: Mr & Mrs W. K. Scoles and Mr & Mrs
R. M. Tooke.
Rates: D
   Peaceful, secluded retreat. Comfortable former manor house, 15th-century
   and architecturally fascinating with stone-mullioned windows, terracotta
   carvings. Easy reach Norwich, King's Lynn. Heritage coast, nature reserves.
   Off A148 3 miles NE of Fakenham. BTA commended. Sorry, no pets.

HEMPSTEAD (Nr Saffron Walden)   YEOMAN COTTAGE
Hempstead, Saffron Walden, Essex CB10 2PH. *Tel*: Radwinter (0799 87) 345.
Hosts: Pat & Peter Thomas.

Rates: A   Vouchers accepted.
Comfortable and welcoming 14th-century cottage with antique furniture. Many historical connections. Edge of Constable country. Twin room with private bathroom. Sorry, no pets. Excellent restaurant 5 min walk. Stables available. Set back from B1053 and marked by a Union Flag. Cambridge, Newmarket, Saffron Walden and Clare all within ½ hour's drive.

HENLEY-ON-THAMES   SHEPHERDS

Rotherfield Greys, Henley on Thames, Oxfordshire RG9 4QL. *Tel*: Rotherfield Greys (04917) 413. *Host*: Sue Fulford-Dobson.
Rates: C   Vouchers accepted.
Pretty period country home with warm welcome, set on edge of peaceful village green. 3 miles Henley. ½hr Heathrow airport and Oxford. Dinner by arrangement. Children over 12 welcome. Reduced rates 3 nights or more. Sorry, no pets.

HENLEY-ON-THAMES   (a 'no smoking' house) HERNES

Henley-on-Thames, Oxfordshire RG9 4NT. *Tel*: Henley (0491) 573245. *Hosts*: Richard & Gillian Ovey.
Rates: D   Vouchers accepted.
Spacious, welcoming home set in an area of outstanding natural beauty. Mature grounds. Easy reach London, Oxford, Windsor, Heathrow, Gatwick, Reading. Rooms en suite or with private bathrooms. Children over 13 welcome. Closed Christmas and New Year. Smoking only in billiards room. Swimming pool, croquet. Dinner by arrangement. Phone for directions. Sorry, no pets.

HEREFORD   CASTLE POOL HOTEL

Castle Street, Hereford HR1 2NR. *Tel*: Hereford (0432) 356321. *Fax*: 0432 356321. *Hosts*: John & Lisa Richardson.
Rates: D
Once a bishop's palace, the hotel is an oasis of quiet, although near the city centre and the cathedral. Charming restaurant leads onto pretty garden featuring the pool, all that remains of the moat that surrounded Hereford's castle. 4-poster available.

HEREFORD (Moreton-on-Lugg)   TALL TREES

Moreton-on-Lugg, Hereford HR4 8AH. *Tel*: Hereford (0432) 760277. *Hosts*: Colin & Mary Riches.
Rates: A/B
Very comfortable and spacious former rectory in 1½ acres of landscaped garden. Easy reach of Wye valley, Malverns, Offa's Dyke. Golf, fishing, riding. Set back from A49, 4 miles north of Hereford. Heated outdoor swimming pool and sun terrace, sauna, hard tennis court, croquet. Children over 7 welcome. Reduced rates for 3 nights or more.

HIGHAM THE BAUBLE
Higham, Nr Colchester, Essex CO7 6LA. *Tel*: Higham (020637) 254. *Hosts*:
Nowell & Penny Watkins.
Rates: B Vouchers accepted.
(See page 136 for description)

HILGAY (Nr Downham Market) CROSSKEYS RIVERSIDE HOTEL
Hilgay, Downham Market, Norfolk PE38 0LN. *Tel*: Downham Market (0366)
387777. *Hosts*: Christine & Alan Bulmer.
Rates: B Vouchers accepted.
Originally a tiny inn in a tiny village beside tranquil River Wissey. Just
off A10, 3 miles south of Downham Market. 4-poster beds. Colour TV all
rooms. Bar/Lounge.

HOPE THE POACHERS ARMS HOTEL
Castleton Road, Hope, Derbyshire S30 2RD. *Tel*: Hope Valley (0433) 20380.
Hosts: G. Bushell and Son.
Rates: C/D
Charming and comfortable country hotel, in the heart of Peak District, close
to Castleton which is renowned for Blue John stone. The Poachers Arms
is proud of its reputation for good food. On A625, Sheffield 14 miles, 40
mins Manchester airport.

HUNSTANTON SUTTON HOUSE HOTEL
24 Northgate, Hunstanton, Norfolk PE36 6AP. *Tel*: Hunstanton (04853) 2552.
Host: Mike Emsden.
Rates: A/C Vouchers accepted.
(See page 137 for description)

KINGHAM (Nr Stow) CONYGREE GATE COUNTRY HOUSE
HOTEL
Church Street, Kingham, Oxfordshire OX7 6YA. *Tel*: Kingham (060871) 389.
Hosts: Brian & Kathryn Sykes.
Rates: B Vouchers accepted.
(See page 137 for description)

KING'S LYNN (A 'no smoking' house) HOMELANDS
79 Sutton Road, Terrington St Clement, King's Lynn, Norfolk PE34 4PJ. *Tel*:
King's Lynn (0553) 828401. *Hosts*: Joan & Doug Smith.
Rates: A/B
Pleasant house set in one acre of attractive gardens in lovely village 2 miles
from A17, 5 miles King's Lynn, 10 miles Sandringham, 14 miles Spalding,
tulip fields. Sorry, no pets.

KINGSTON BAGPUIZE (Southmoor) FALLOWFIELDS
Southmoor, Nr Abingdon, Oxfordshire OX13 5BH. *Tel*: Oxford (0865)

820416. *Telex*: 83388 Kings. T. G. Att. Fallowfields. *Host*: Mrs A. Y. Crowther. *Rates*: C   Vouchers accepted.

Lovely, comfortable country house, once the home of the Begum Aga Khan, in 12 acres gardens. Outdoor swimming pool, croquet lawn. 10 miles south-west of Oxford. Children over 12 welcome. Winter weekend breaks, minimum 4 people, house party. BTA commended. 4-poster available. King-size half-tester. All rooms en suite. Home-cooking. Licensed.

KINGTON   BURTON HOTEL

Mill Street, Kington, Nr Hereford HR5 3BQ. *Tel*: Kington (0544) 230323. *Fax*: 0544 230323. *Hosts*: John & Lisa Richardson.
Rates: C

Attractively modernised authentic coaching inn, in centre of small market town near Welsh border. Beautiful countryside, hills close by. 4-poster available. Ideal for touring and sightseeing. Offa's Dyke long-distance footpath passes through Kington. Highest golf course in the country nearby.

LANGAR   LANGAR HALL

Langar, Nottinghamshire NG13 9HG. *Tel*: Harby (0949) 60559. *Host*: Imogen Skirving.
Rates: B/D   Vouchers accepted.

Lovely country house atmosphere, the Hall (1830) situated behind early English church. Pretty grounds, with views over the Vale of Belvoir and ancient trees in the park. 4-poster available. Off A52 or A46. Nottingham 11 miles.

LEAMINGTON SPA   EATHORPE PARK HOTEL

Fosse Way, Eathorpe, Nr Leamington Spa, Warwickshire CV33 9DQ. *Tel*: Marton (0926) 632245. *Fax*: 0926 632481. *Hosts*: Mrs Delores Deeley.
Rates: C

Spacious country house in 11 acres lawns and woodlands, lovely views. Golf, squash nearby. Royal Leamington Spa 5 miles. National Exhibition Centre 17 miles. National Agricultural Centre (Stoneleigh) 5 miles. On the Fosse, 1 mile south of A423 Coventry/Banbury road.

LEAMINGTON SPA   MILVERTON HOUSE HOTEL

1 Milverton Terrace, Leamington Spa, Warwickshire CV32 5BE. *Tel*: Leamington (0926) 428335. *Hosts*: Leonard & Molly Boyd.
Rates: B/C

Comfortable Victorian house within easy walking distance of lovely Regency town centre, parks, antiques. Warwick Castle 2 miles. Kenilworth medieval castle 4 miles. Agricultural Centre, Stoneleigh; Stratford-on-Avon 10 miles. NEC 15 miles. Edge of Cotswolds. Sorry, no pets.

LEDBURY   GROVE HOUSE

Bromesberrow Heath, Nr Ledbury, Herefordshire HR8 1PE. *Tel*: Bromesberrow (053181) 584. *Host*: Ellen Emerson Ross.

Rates: C/D
Lovely mellow house, spacious and comfortable, surrounded by orchards and fields devoted to horses. Near Stratford, Welsh border, Cotswolds, Malverns, Birmingham, Wye Valley, Forest of Dean. All rooms en suite with colour TV. 4–posters available. Open 8 months in year. Children over 12 welcome. Sorry, no pets. Breaks available. No reductions for dinner for children. Home cooking. Off M50 exit 2.

LEEK (Grindon) THE WHITE HOUSE
Grindon, Nr Leek, Staffordshire ST13 7TP. *Tel*: Onecote (05388) 250. *Hosts*: Philomena & Jack Bunce.
Rates: B Vouchers accepted.
Beautifully decorated, comfortable house (1640) with superb views over valleys and hills. Very quiet. Many NT houses around. Close to potteries. Mid-week dinner at local pub or hosts will book nearby restaurant. Reduced rates 2 or more nights. No smoking in bedrooms. Leek 7 miles, Ashbourne 10 miles.

LEIGHTON BUZZARD THE HUNT HOTEL
Church Road, Linslade, Leighton Buzzard, Bedfordshire LU7 7LR. *Tel*: Leighton Buzzard (0525) 374692. *Fax*: 0525 374692. *Hosts*: David and Janet Naylor.
Rates: D
Once a hunting inn with historical connections, now a family-run hotel overlooking church and parkland in a useful location. M1 exit 13, follow signs to Woburn, then Leighton Buzzard. Aylesbury & Milton Keynes 10 miles. Sorry, no pets.

LEOMINSTER (Eardisland) (A 'no smoking' house) THE ELMS
Eardisland, Nr Leominster, Herefordshire HR6 9BN. *Tel*: Pembridge (05447) 405. *Host*: Mary Johnson.
Rates: A Vouchers accepted.
17th-century farmhouse in 32 acres, set back 100yds off A44. 5 miles west of Leominster in picturesque village. Dinner by arrangement only. Good food at several local pubs. Special terms for Christmas. Children over 10 welcome. Sorry, no pets.

LEOMINSTER WITHENFIELD
South Street, Leominster, Hereford HR6 8JN. *Tel*: Leominster (0568) 2011. *Hosts*: Pam & Jim Cotton.
Rates: C Vouchers accepted.
(See page 138 for description)

LICHFIELD OAKLEIGH HOUSE HOTEL
25 St Chad's Road, Lichfield, Staffordshire WS13 7LZ. *Tel*: Lichfield (0543) 262688. *Hosts*: Pat & Iain McGregor.
Rates: C
(See page 139 for description)

LINCOLN HILLCREST HOTEL
15 Lindum Terrace, Lincoln LN2 5RT. *Tel*: Lincoln (0522) 510182. *Host*:
Jennifer Bennett.
Rates: C   Vouchers accepted.
 Former Victorian rectory with rose garden, terrace and lovely views over
 parklands. Quiet location, close to cathedral and lovely old city. Restaurant
 and bar meals available. Proprietor is proud of reputation for food.

LINCOLN MINSTER LODGE HOTEL
3 Church Lane, Lincoln LN2 1QJ. *Tel*: Lincoln (0522) 513220. *Host*: Ray Brown.
Rates: B/C   Vouchers accepted.
 Warm and friendly small hotel 5 mins walk from the cathedral and
 historic city centre. All rooms with bath and shower, colour TV,
 direct dial phones, bar trays on request. All double-glazed. Car park.
 Sorry, no pets.

LOWESTOFT ROCKVILLE HOUSE
6 Pakefield Road, Lowestoft, Suffolk NR33 0HS. *Tel*: Lowestoft (0502) 581011.
Hosts: Ann & Michael Sims.
Rates: A/B
 Victorian house in residential area in quiet south side of town. Safe sandy
 beaches on Suffolk Heritage coast. Golf, bird and wild life reserves. Broads,
 harbour. Yarmouth 10 miles. Children over 12 welcome. Reduced rates for
 3 or more nights. Sorry, no pets.

LUDLOW
Number 28, Lower Broad Street, Ludlow, Shropshire SY8 1PQ. *Tel*: Ludlow
(0584) 876996. *Hosts*: Patricia & Philip Ross.
Rates: B   Vouchers accepted.
 Elegant Georgian listed house, warm and welcoming, near centre of
 historic Ludlow with castle, antique shops and lanes an easy walk away.
 50yds Ludford Bridge, River Teme. Hosts are proud of their cuisine. En
 suite rooms with TV. Dogs welcome.

LUDLOW (Leintwardine)   (A 'no smoking' house) UPPER BUCKTON
 FARM
Leintwardine, Craven Arms, Shropshire SY7 0JU. *Tel*: Leintwardine (05473)
634. *Hosts*: Hayden & Yvonne Lloyd.
Rates: B
(See page 140 for description)

MALVERN THE COLWALL PARK HOTEL
Colwall, Malvern, Worcestershire WR13 6QG. *Tel*: Colwall (0684)
40206. *Telex*: 335626G. *Fax*: 0684 40847. *Hosts*: Basil & Elizabeth
Frost.
Rates: D   Vouchers accepted.

Family-run hotel, modernised, English menus. Situated on western edge of Malvern hills, on B4218 between Malvern and Ledbury. Between cathedral cities of Worcester, Hereford and Gloucester. Ideal walking, touring and exploring.

MALVERN   ELM BANK

52 Worcester Road, Great Malvern, Worcestershire WR14 4AB. *Tel*: Malvern (0684) 566051. *Hosts*: Helen & Richard Mobbs.
Rates: B   Vouchers accepted.
Elegant late Regency house, comfortably furnished. Fine views of Severn valley. Five mins walk town centre, with priory, park, theatre and shops. Easy access Malvern hills.

MARKET DEEPING (Nr Peterborough)   CAUDLE HOUSE

43 High Street, Market Deeping, Peterborough PE6 8ED. *Tel*: Market Deeping (0778) 347595. *Hosts*: Sue & Chris Boardman.
Rates: C   Vouchers accepted.
Comfortable Georgian listed house in centre of small market town. Excellent position for Burghley House, Rutland Water, Tallington Lakes, Peakirk wildfowl centre. Hosts are proud of their standard of English cooking. Stamford 8 miles, Peterborough 7, Spalding 12.

MARKET DRAYTON   GOLDSTONE HALL

Market Drayton, Shropshire TF9 2NA. *Tel*: Cheswardine (063086) 202. *Hosts*: Helen Ward & John Cushing.
Rates: D
Very comfortable and charming old house (part 16th century) in 5 acres of gardens and paddock. Authentic brass and iron bedsteads and 4-poster available. Proprietors proud of excellent. food. Historic area, potteries and Ironbridge. Off A41 and A529, 3 miles south of Drayton take Goldstone sign.

MATLOCK BATH   SUNNYBANK

Clifton Road, Matlock Bath, Derbyshire DE4 3PW. *Tel*: Matlock (0629) 584621. *Hosts*: Peter & Daphne West.
Rates: B/C   Vouchers accepted.
Comfortable and spacious Victorian house, warm and welcoming, with lovely views in peaceful surroundings. Home-cooking. Nr Chatsworth and many places of interest in the lovely Derbyshire dales and peaks. Reduced rates late autumn and winter.

MATLOCK   ROBERTSWOOD

Farley Hill, Matlock, Derbyshire DE4 3LL. *Tel*: Matlock (0629) 55642. *Fax*: 0629 55642. *Hosts*: John & Sheila Elliott.
Rates: B   Vouchers accepted.
Warm, friendly and elegant Victorian house. Spacious, comfortable accommodation in peaceful surroundings. Home-cooking. Direct dial telephones.

Spectacular views of the dales. Nr Chatsworth and local attractions. Ample parking. 30 mins to M1 (junc 28).

MICKLETON   THREE WAYS HOTEL

Mickleton, Chipping Campden, Gloucestershire GL55 6SB. *Tel*: Mickleton (0386) 438429/438231 *Telex*: 337242. *Fax*: 0386 438118. *Hosts*: Keith and Jean Turner
Rates: D   Vouchers accepted.

Comfortable, friendly and warm hotel in ideal situation on edge of Cotswolds. Shakespeare country. Home-cooked food – puddings a speciality. Vegetarians catered for. Menus include Severn salmon, Cotswold trout and game in season. Comprehensive wine list. On B4632 – Stratford 8 miles, Warwick 15.

MILTON KEYNES   HAVERSHAM GRANGE

Haversham, Nr Milton Keynes, Buckinghamshire MK19 7DX. *Tel*: Milton Keynes (0908) 312389. *Hosts*: Julian & Mafra Smithers.
Rates: B
(See page 141 for description)

MONKS ELEIGH   THE OLD RECTORY

Monks Eleigh, Ipswich, Suffolk. *Tel*: Bildeston (0449) 740811. *Hosts*: The Sharman Family.
Rates: B/C   Vouchers accepted.

Elegant Regency rectory on edge of village in 2 acres of mature gardens with croquet lawn and all-weather tennis court. Spacious bedrooms en suite. Log fires. No smoking in bedrooms. Stables. Closed Dec-Feb. Bury St Edmunds, Cambridge, Constable country, Newmarket and Norwich nearby. Sorry, no pets.

MORETON-IN-MARSH   REDESDALE ARMS

Moreton-in-Marsh, Gloucestershire GL56 0AW. *Tel*: Moreton-in-Marsh (0608) 50308. *Fax*: 0608 51843. *Hosts*: Michael Elvis & Patricia Seedhouse.
Rates: D   Vouchers accepted.

Charming 18th-century coaching inn with 20th-century comforts in heart of Cotswolds. Luxury suites available. Conference facilities. Real ale. Log fires. Award-winning restaurant. Sorry, no pets. Stratford 15 miles, Warwick 18, Cheltenham 22, Oxford 24.

NEEDHAM MARKET   PIPPS FORD

Norwich Road, Needham Market, Suffolk IP6 8LJ. *Tel*: Coddenham (044979) 208. *Hosts*: Raewyn & Anthony Hackett-Jones.
Rates: B/D

Peaceful, very attractive Tudor farmhouse in smallholding. Eight acres gardens and meadows with river frontage. Tiny lane off roundabout at A45 and A140 junction. Home-cooking. Nov-Feb discounts. Disabled persons welcome. No smoking in bedrooms. Annexe. Sorry, no pets.

NEWMARKET (Stetchworth)   LIVE AND LET LIVE GUEST HOUSE

76 High Street, Stetchworth, Newmarket, Suffolk CB8 9TJ. *Tel*: Stetchworth (063 876) 8153. *Hosts*: Dennis & Sylvia Human.
Rates: A/B   Vouchers accepted.
(See page 142 for description)

NORTHLEACH (Hazleton)   WINDRUSH HOUSE

Hazleton, Nr Northleach, Cheltenham, Gloucestershire GL54 4EB. *Tel*: Cotswolds (0451) 60364. *Hosts*: Sydney & Bruce Harrison.
Rates: B   Vouchers accepted.
Modern stone-built house with every comfort in tiny unspoilt Cotswolds hamlet. Between Northleach (4 miles) and Cheltenham (10 miles) 1 mile off A40 on left after church. Touring, golf, riding. Children over 15 welcome. BTA commended. Sorry, no pets.

NORTH WALSHAM (Sloley)   (A 'no smoking' house) CUBITT COTTAGE

Sloley, Norwich NR12 8HD. *Tel*: Swanton Abbott (069269) 295. *Hosts*: The Foulkes Family.
Rates: B   Vouchers accepted.
Homely early 19th-century cottage in one acre mature garden and pond. Off B1150. Norwich 11 miles, North Walsham 5. Three bird reservations, rural Broadland. Local NT and craft centres. Vegetarians catered for. No smoking in bedrooms. Phone for directions. Sorry, no pets.

NORWICH   EARLHAM GUEST HOUSE

147 Earlham Road, Norwich, Norfolk NR2 3RG. *Tel*: Norwich (0603) 54169.
Hosts: Ann & Paul Leeming.
Rates: A   Vouchers accepted.
Conveniently situated house with easy access to Norwich city centre and its many attractions. Many good restaurants nearby. Special breaks available. On B1108 1 mile from city centre between inner and outer ring-roads. Sorry, no pets.

NOTTINGHAM   BESTWOOD LODGE HOTEL

Bestwood Lodge Drive, Arnold, Nottingham NG5 8NF. *Tel*: Nottingham (0602) 203011. *Fax*: 0602 670409. *Hosts*: The Lowe Family.
Rates: C/D
Imposing Victorian/Gothic hunting lodge with minstrels' gallery and historic connections in 70 acres of lovely parkland and woods. Off M1 at junc 26 to A60, only 4 miles city centre. 4-poster available.

OAKAMOOR (Nr Uttoxeter)   OLD FURNACE FARM

Greendale, Oakamoor, Stoke-on-Trent ST10 3AP. *Tel*: Oakamoor (0538) 702442. *Hosts*: The Wheeler Family.
Rates: B   Vouchers accepted.
(See page 143 for description)

ONGAR   STANFORD RIVERS HALL

Stanford Rivers, Ongar, Essex CH5 9QG. *Tel*: Ongar (0277) 362997. *Hosts*: Paul & Jenny Sloan.

Rates: B

Georgian farmhouse in rural surroundings. Oak-beamed lounge. No smoking in bedrooms. Easy access to M25/M11. 10 mins drive to Underground station for London. Good pubs and restaurants near. Entrance behind Stanford Rivers church. Sorry, no pets.

OSWESTRY   PEN-Y-DYFFRYN HALL

Rhydycroesau, Oswestry, Shropshire SY10 7DT. *Tel*: Oswestry (0691) 653700. *Hosts*: Miles & Audrey Hunter.

Rates: C   Vouchers accepted.

(See page 144 for description)

OTLEY   OTLEY HOUSE

Otley, Ipswich, Suffolk IP6 9NR. *Tel*: Helmingham (047339) 253. *Hosts*: Lise & Mike Hilton.

Rates: B/C

(See page 145 for description)

OUNDLE (Aldwincle)   THE MALTINGS

Aldwincle, Kettering, Northants NN14 3EP. *Tel*: Clopton (08015) 233. *Hosts*: Nigel & Margaret Faulkner.

Rates: B   Vouchers accepted.

Lovely 500-year-old farmhouse, inglenooks, beams and antiques. Warm welcome, log fires and 24-hr heating in winter. Large, attractive plant-lovers' garden. Off A604, A605 and A6116. Huntingdon and A1 13 miles. Children over 10 welcome. Sorry, no pets.

OXFORD   THE OLD BLACK HORSE HOTEL

102 St Clements, Oxford OX4 1AR. *Tel*: Oxford (0865) 244691. *Hosts*: Amanda & John Coates.

Rates: D   Vouchers accepted.

Charming 17th-century former coaching inn with panelled restaurant serving traditional English food and wines. Situated just 7 mins walk from the city centre and university, with ample private car parking.

PAINSWICK (Nr Gloucester)   FALCON INN

New Street, Painswick, Gloucestershire GL6 6RN. *Tel*: Gloucester (0452) 812189. *Hosts*: Alan & Pat Kimber.

Rates: C   Vouchers accepted.

Family-run, stone-built (1711) hotel in stone village, 'The Queen of the Cotswolds'. 4-poster available. Guests welcome to bowl on oldest green in Britain. Golf, and Cotswolds Way (walk) nearby. Cheltenham 8 miles, Gloucester 4. On A46 three miles north of Stroud.

READING THE MILL HOUSE
Swallowfield, Nr Reading, Berkshire RG7 1PY. *Tel*: Reading (0734) 883124.
Telex: 847423 ref: M110. *Host*: Graeme Rolfe
Rates: D
Lovely, very comfortable Georgian country house, built on site of
Domesday Book mill. 4-posters available. Peaceful location, with 2 acres
garden on banks of River Lodden. M4 exit 11, 2½ miles. Heathrow 45
mins. Reading 5 miles, Stratford Saye nearby (Iron Duke's house).

REDDITCH THE OLD RECTORY
Ipsley Lane, Ipsley, Redditch, Worcestershire B98 0AP. *Tel*: Redditch (0527)
23000/26739. *Hosts*: Jill, Tony & Martin Moore.
Rates: D   Vouchers accepted.
(See page 146 for description)

REDMILE PEACOCK FARM AND RESTAURANT
Redmile, Nottinghamshire NG13 0GQ. *Tel*: Bottesford (0949) 42475. *Hosts*:
Peter and Marjorie Need.
Rates: A/B   Vouchers accepted.
Within sight of Belvoir Castle, this 250-year-old farmhouse has unbroken
views of wooded hills and villages in the Vale of Belvoir. Area of historic
houses. Off A52. Easy access to A1. Small swimming pool.

ROSS-ON-WYE SUNNYMOUNT HOTEL
Ryefield Road, Ross-on-Wye, Herefordshire HR9 5LU. *Tel*: Ross-on-Wye
(0989) 63880. *Hosts*: Geoff & Peggy Williams.
Rates: A/B   Vouchers accepted.
Quiet, warm and comfortable hotel occupying corner site of residential
road in historic town. The Wye Valley and Forest of Dean are areas
of great beauty with excellent touring facilities. Dinner not available
Wednesdays.

RUGBY AVONDALE GUEST HOUSE
16 Elsee Road, Rugby, Warwickshire CV21 3BA. *Tel*: Rugby (0788) 78639.
Hosts: Carole & Clem Webb.
Rates: B   Vouchers accepted.
Spacious Victorian house, quiet residential cul-de-sac in conservation area.
4 mins walk town centre. Rugby School, Sports Centre and park near. Off
A428. M1 exit 18, M6 exit 1. Leamington/Warwick 14 miles, Stratford and
NEC ½-hour drive. Lounge/dining-room. Own parking.

ST NEOTS ABBOTSLEY (Golf and Squash Club)
Eynesbury Hardwicke, St Neots, Cambridgeshire PE19 4XN. *Tel*:
Huntingdon (0480) 215153/217281. *Host*: Jenny Wisson.
Rates: B/C
Beautiful moated farmhouse in centre of golf course. ¼ mile from
golf and squash clubs, bar and restaurant. Golf breaks available. Vivien

Saunders coaches. Floodlit driving range. Six squash courts. Cambridge 16 miles, Bedford 12 miles, central between A1 and M1. From St Neots, 1 mile towards Abbotsley.

SAUNDERTON (High Wycombe)   ROSE AND CROWN
Wycombe Road. Saunderton, Nr Princes Risborough, Buckinghamshire HP17 9NP. *Tel*: Princes Risborough (08444) 5299. *Hosts*: Robert & John Watson.
Rates: D
Family-run country hotel, well situated on A4010 for industries of High Wycombe or for exploring Chiltern hills (Ridgeway path ½ mile). Many historic sites and buildings nearby. Comfortable bar/lounge, log fires in winter, large garden. Restaurant and bar menus.

SEDGEFORD   SEDGEFORD HALL
Nr Hunstanton, Norfolk PE36 5LT. *Tel*: Heacham (0485) 70902. *Hosts*: Bernard & Susan Campbell.
Rates: C/D   Vouchers accepted.
Spacious, elegantly restored Georgian house in 1200-acre estate bordering Royal Sandringham. Delightful bedrooms – no wash basins but bathrooms nearby. Breakfast overlooking glorious parkland. Guests invited to bring their own wine. Golf, bird sanctuaries near. Tennis, croquet, golf, riding available. Kennels.

SHREWSBURY (Hanwood)   THE WHITE HOUSE
Hanwood, Shrewsbury, Shropshire SY5 8LP. *Tel*: Shrewsbury (0743) 860414. *Hosts*: Mike & Gill Mitchell.
Rates: B
Lovely half-timbered 16th-century beamed country house, with paddock and stables. Off A488, 3½ miles from old market town of Shrewsbury. Near mid-Wales border and famous Ironbridge with museums. Touring, fishing, golf. Short breaks available.

SKEGNESS   THE VINE HOTEL
Vine Road, Seacroft, Skegness, Lincolnshire PE25 3DB. *Tel*: Skegness (0754) 3018. *Hosts*: Hilary & John Martin.
Rates: D
Old 17th-century smuggling inn, now country house hotel on edge of town, where Tennyson stayed as a young man and wrote under the weeping elm. Few minutes walk to sea. Lovely gardens and terrace. Near Gibraltar Point Nature Reserve.

SOUTHWELL   THE OLD FORGE
Burgage Lane, Southwell, Nottinghamshire NG25 0ER. *Tel*: Southwell (0636) 812809. *Hosts*: Hilary & Derek Marston.
Rates: B   Vouchers accepted.
(See page 147 for description)

SOUTHWELL (Uptonfields) UPTONFIELDS HOUSE
Uptonfields, Southwell, Nottinghamshire NG25 OQA. *Tel*: Southwell (0636)
812303. *Hosts*: The Woodhull Family.
Rates: B Vouchers accepted.
Elegant, spacious and unique house, built by a perfectionist in the 1930s.
Solid and inlaid wood everywhere. All rooms en suite. No evening meals
but good food within 1 mile. No smoking in bedrooms. Newark 6 miles;
Mansfield 9; Nottingham 17.

SPORLE (Nr Swaffham) CORFIELD HOUSE
Sporle, Kings Lynn, Norfolk PE32 2DR. *Tel*: Swaffham (0760) 23636. *Hosts*:
Linda & Martin Hickey.
Rates: A/B
Comfortable family-run country guest house in peaceful surroundings 3
miles east of Swaffham. Convenient for coast, Sandringham, Norwich and
many National Trust properties. All rooms have colour TV. The proprietors
are proud of their home-cooking. ½ mile off A47.

STAFFORD BAILEY HOTEL
63 Lichfield Road, Stafford ST17 4LL. *Tel* Stafford (0785) 214133. *Hosts*: Peter
& Jean Ayres.
Rates: A/B Vouchers accepted.
Very pleasant detached corner house, recently completely refurbished and
comfortably furnished, with warm atmosphere. Junction of St Leonards
Avenue on A34 Lichfield Road, 1 mile south of Stafford town centre. Colour
TV all rooms. Ample parking. M6 exit 13 or 14, 10 mins drive.

STANSTED (Thaxted) PIGGOT'S MILL
Watling Lane, Thaxted, Dunmow, Essex CM6 2QY. *Tel*: Thaxted (0371)
830379. *Hosts*: Gillian & Richard Hingston.
Rates: B Vouchers accepted.
Comfortable farmhouse in fine medieval village with many traditional features. Attractive walks. Both rooms en suite with colour TV. Many local
restaurants. No smoking in bedrooms. Children over 12 welcome. Stansted
airport 7 miles. Cambridge 22. M11 12 miles. Sorry, no pets.

STEEPLE ASTON WESTFIELD FARM MOTEL
The Fenway, Steeple Aston, Oxfordshire OX5 3SS. *Tel*: Steeple Aston (0869)
40591. *Hosts*: Graham & Ann Hillier.
Rates: B Vouchers accepted.
Converted stable block with comfortable units. Combined lounge, dining
room and bar. Fringe of Cotswolds, off A423. Banbury 9 miles, Woodstock
5. Riding tuition available. Touring. Colour TV all rooms. Horses stabled.

STOKE-ON-TRENT THE WHITE HOUSE
94 Stone Road, Trent Vale, Stoke-on-Trent ST4 6SP. *Tel*: Stoke (0782) 642460.
Hosts: Philip & Jean Bradbeer.

Rates: B
Warm and friendly detached house on A34, 2 miles city centre. 1 mile from exit 15 on M6. With noise-insulation windows and fresh-air ventilators. Many famous potteries within 5 miles. Alton Towers 15 miles. Annexe. Sorry, no pets.

STOWMARKET (Wetherden)   THE OLD RECTORY
Wetherden, Nr Stowmarket, Suffolk IP14 3RE. *Tel*: Elmswell (0359) 40144. *Host*: Pamela Bowden.
Rates: B
(See page 148 for description)

STRATFORD-ON-AVON   THE COACH HOUSE
17 Warwick Road, Stratford-on-Avon, Warwickshire CV37 6YW. *Tel*: Stratford (0789) 299468. *Hosts*: Geoff & Judy Harden.
Rates: B/D   Vouchers accepted.
Larger than usual spacious Regency-style house and adjacent Waverley rooms of 1850s period. 4-poster available. Cellar restaurant. 7-min walk Royal Shakespeare Theatre. Ideal touring Cotswolds and Warwick Castle. 2 and 3 day breaks. Sorry, no pets.

STRATFORD-ON-AVON   SEQUOIA HOUSE PRIVATE HOTEL
51 Shipston Road, Stratford upon Avon, Warwickshire CV37 7LN. *Tel*: Stratford (0789) 68852. *Fax*: 0789 414559. *Hosts*: Philip & Jean Evans.
Rates: C/D   Vouchers accepted.
(See page 149 for description)

TELFORD (Norton)   THE HUNDRED HOUSE HOTEL
Bridgnorth Road, Norton, Shifnal, Shropshire TF11 9EE. *Tel*: Norton (095 271) 353. *Fax*: 0952 271355. *Hosts*: Henry, David & Sylvia Phillips.
Rates: D   Vouchers accepted.
(See page 150 for description)

TEMPLE GRAFTON (Nr Alcester)   TEMPLAR HOUSE
Temple Grafton, Nr. Alcester, Warwickshire B49 6NS. *Tel*: Bidford on Avon (0789) 490392. *Hosts*: Jean & Gordon Fisher.
Rates: A/B
Pleasant house in large gardens, beautifully situated 6 miles from Stratford-on-Avon near Vale of Evesham. 4-poster bedroom available. Proprietors keen to explain working of arable and beef farm to enthusiasts.

TEWKESBURY   JESSOP HOUSE HOTEL
65 Church Street, Tewkesbury, Gloucestershire GL20 5RZ. *Tel*: Tewkesbury (0684) 292017. *Hosts*: Ron & Sue James.
Rates: D
Georgian town house hotel in attractive small market town on edge of Cotswolds, with magnificent abbey and medieval cottages. 1 mile from M5 (junc 9). Sorry, no pets.

THEBERTON (Nr Leiston)   THEBERTON GRANGE
Theberton, Nr Leiston, Suffolk IP16 4RR. *Tel*: Leiston (0728) 830625. *Hosts*:
Roger & Annette James.
Rates: D
  Beautiful and comfortable Victorian/Tudor farmhouse in 4 acres. Rural
  surroundings. Minsmere bird sanctuary, Aldeburgh Festival, Southwold
  and Heritage Coast within easy reach. Golfing, sailing and riding nearby.
  Phone for directions. Children over 8 welcome. Sorry, no pets.

THEYDON BOIS (A 'no smoking' house)   PARSONAGE FARM HOUSE
Abridge Road, Theydon Bois, Essex CH16 7NN. *Tel*: Theydon Bois (037
881) 4242. *Hosts*: Steve & Marion Dale.
Rates: C   Vouchers accepted.
  Comfortable, spacious 15th-century farmhouse on edge of Epping Forest.
  Sympathetically restored. 2 acres of 'Old English' gardens. Stabling avail-
  able. Central Line Underground station 5 mins walk (20 mins to London).
  Near M25 (exit 26). Sorry, no pets.

THORPE MARKET   ELDERTON LODGE HOTEL
Cromer Road, Thorpe Market, Norwich NR11 8TZ. *Tel*: Southrepps (026
379) 547. *Hosts*: Alistair & Sandie Cameron.
Rates: B/C
  Once a dower house and shooting lodge, pleasant hotel on edge of Gunton
  Park in lovely countryside. North Walsham 4 miles, Cromer 5. Woodland
  walks, fishing on estate, riding, golf, bird-watching, clay pigeon-shooting.
  Nature reserve. Reduced rates for more than 1 night.

THORPE MARKET (Nr Cromer)   GREEN FARM RESTAURANT
  AND HOTEL
North Walsham Road, Thorpe Market, Norwich, Norfolk NR11 8TH. *Tel*:
Southrepps (026 379) 602. *Hosts*: Philip & Susan Lomax.
Rates: D   Vouchers accepted.
  Flint 16th-century farmhouse with comfortable antique beds in all rooms,
  4-poster and half-tester available. Ideal for exploring north Norfolk coast,
  Broads, Norwich. Chef proprietor uses fresh local produce. Fresh flowers
  in rooms. On A149 between Cromer and North Walsham, 18 miles from
  Norwich.

THRAPSTON (Islip)   THE WOOLPACK HOTEL
6 Kettering Road, Islip, Northants NN14 3JU. *Tel*: Thrapston (08012) 2578.
Hosts: The Hollowell Family.
Rates: C
  Completely refurbished 16th-century inn overlooking the River Nene with
  new linked motel. Log fires. New tea-room and Victorian conservatory
  for coffee and cocktails. On A604/605, 10 miles from Kettering, Corby,
  Wellingborough, Oundle and Rushden. A1 15 miles. M1 25 miles.

TIMBERLAND (Nr Lincoln)   THE PENNY FARTHING INN

Timberland, Lincolnshire LN4 3SA. *Tel*: Martin (05267) 359. *Hosts*: Michael Dobson, Anthony & Auzenda Daniel.

Rates: B   Vouchers accepted.

Relaxed 18th-century beamed inn, fully licensed, with comfortable rooms in tiny village near nature reserve. Off A153 at Billingay to B1189. Woodhall Spa 6 miles, Lincoln 14. Golf, boating, riding. Colour TV all rooms.

THORPE BAY   ROSLIN HOTEL

Thorpe Esplanade, Thorpe Bay, Essex SS1 3BG. *Tel*: Southend-on-Sea (0702) 586375. *Fax*: 0702 586663. *Hosts*: Mr K. & Mrs J. Oliver.

Rates: C/D   Vouchers accepted.

In an attractive area with few hotels in this range. Most comfortable hotel with continental-style terrace and Mulberry restaurant overlooking delightful Thames estuary with its ever-changing panorama. Golf, sailing, wind surfing, riding within easy reach. Free entry to Courtlands Park Country Club.

UFFINGTON (Nr Swindon)   THE CRAVEN

Fernham Road, Uffington, Oxfordshire SN7 7RD. *Tel*: Uffington (036 782) 449. *Hosts*: Carol & David Wadsworth.

Rates: B   Vouchers accepted.

Charming thatched (1640) farmhouse. Exposed beams, log fires. 4-poster and half-tester rooms. 2 other rooms without wash-hand-basins. Centre for Cotswolds, antique hunting, walking. In 'Vale of the White Horse', near Avebury stone circle.

UPPINGHAM   RUTLAND HOUSE

61 High Street East, Uppingham, Leicestershire LE15 9PY. *Tel*: Uppingham (0572) 822497. *Host*: Jenny Hitchen.

Rates: B   Vouchers accepted.

Spacious comfortable Victorian house centrally but quietly situated in this pleasant college town off A47. Leicester 18 miles, Oakham, Corby 7. Rutland Water 5. Colour TV all rooms. Ground-floor room available. No lounge. Many pubs and restaurants near.

UPTON-UPON-SEVERN   WHITE LION HOTEL

High Street, Upton-upon-Severn, Worcester WR8 0HJ. *Tel*: Upton-upon-Severn (06846) 2551. *Hosts*: Robert & Bridget Withey.

Rates: D   Vouchers accepted.

(See page 151 for description)

UTTOXETER (Denstone)   STONE HOUSE

College Road, Denstone, Uttoxeter, Staffordshire ST14 5HR. *Tel*: Rocester (0889) 590526. *Fax*: 0889 591 205. *Hosts*: Peter & Diana Moore.

Rates: B   Vouchers accepted.

Mellow, stone-built yeoman cottage (1712) in peaceful village. Comfortable rooms with oak beams. Excellent base for visiting hills and dales, world-famous potteries, stately homes, country pubs, Alton Towers. Some rooms en suite. Dinner by arrangement. Phone for directions. No smoking in bedrooms.

WATTON (Nr Thetford)   CLARENCE HOUSE
78 High Street, Watton, Thetford, Norfolk IP25 6AH. *Tel*: Watton (0953) 884252. *Fax*: 0953 881323. *Hosts*: Peter & Gay Polak.
Rates: C   Vouchers accepted.
   Stylish Victorian house, with many of the original features, in small market town. Central Norfolk area, many historic sites, lovely countryside. Norwich only 21 miles. Proprietors proud of their good food and wines.

WELLINGBOROUGH   THE COLUMBIA HOTEL AND RESTAURANT
19 Northampton Road, Wellingborough, Northamptonshire NN8 3HG. *Tel*: Wellingborough (0933) 229333. *Fax*: 0933 440418. *Hosts*: Barrie & Caroline Fogerty.
Rates: C
   Warm, friendly welcome in a comfortable hotel. Situated ½ mile from centre of thriving market town on tree-lined Northampton Road. Kettering 8 miles, Northampton 10, Bedford, Milton Keynes and Corby within ½ hour.

WELLS-NEXT-THE-SEA   MILL HOUSE
Northfield Lane, Wells-next-the-Sea, Norfolk NR23 1JZ. *Tel*: Fakenham (0328) 710739. *Hosts*: Anna & Andy Fisher.
Rates: A/B
   Former mill owner's house with very attractive garden (croquet, badminton) in this small working seaport. Guests payphone available. Golf, water-sports, lovely sandy beaches, walking, nature reserves, bird-watching, historic houses and museums. Children and pets welcome.

WEM   SOULTON HALL
Near Wem, Shropshire SY4 5RS. *Tel*: Wem (0939) 32786. *Host*: Mrs A. Ashton.
Rates: B/C   Vouchers accepted.
(See page 152 for description)

WINCHCOMBE   POSTLIP HOUSE
Winchcombe, Gloucestershire GL54 5AH. *Tel*: Cheltenham (0242) 602390.
Hosts: Mary & Paul Sparks.
Rates: B   Vouchers accepted.
(See page 153 for description)

WOLVERHAMPTON   THE YORK HOTEL AND RESTAURANT
138-140 Tettenhall Road, Wolverhampton WV6 0BQ. *Tel*: Wolverhampton (0902) 754743/758211/758212. *Hosts*: Maggie & Phil Denton.
Rates: D   Vouchers accepted.
   Victorian house, renovated by enthusiastic proprietors, situated in Royal

Oak country, 1½ m from town centre. New restaurant. Conference room. Off A41 to Whitchurch, easy access M6 exit 10 or M54 exit 3. Birmingham 15 miles and Ludlow, Bridgnorth, Shrewsbury and Ironbridge within 25 miles.

WOODBRIDGE THE OLD RECTORY
Campsea Ashe, Woodbridge, Suffolk IP13 0PU. *Tel*: Wickham Market (0728) 746524. *Host*: Stewart Bassett.
Rates: C
Nice and spacious 17th-century house in 4 acres mature and attractive gardens. Log fires. Off B1078 Wickham Market 2 miles, Woodbridge 5. Golf courses, coast and castle nearby. Food acclaimed in 3 guides. Mid-week breaks available Oct–May. Sorry, no pets.

WORCESTER PARK HOUSE HOTEL
12 Droitwich Rd, Worcester WR3 7LJ. *Tel*: Worcester (0905) 21816. *Hosts*: John and Sheila Smith.
Rates: B Vouchers accepted.
Warm and friendly detached Victorian house, own parking. A38 ½-mile centre. Near river, cathedral and racecourse. Malvern Hills, Cotswolds, NEC and Stratford 30 mins. Easy access M5 exit 5 or 6. Bargain winter and weekend breaks available.

YOXFORD SATIS HOUSE
Yoxford, Saxmundham, Suffolk IP17 3EX. *Tel*: Yoxford (072877) 418. *Hosts*: Chris & Chiu Blackmore.
Rates: C/D
Lovely Georgian country house in 3 acres parkland, very comfortably furnished. Hosts specialise in Malaysian food. Sauna, solarium, whirlpool, gym. Close to Minsmere Bird Sanctuary, Aldeburgh Festival and the Heritage Coast. Near junc A12 and A1120. Ipswich, Lowestoft 20 miles. Half-tester available. Sorry, no pets.

The Old Rectory

Blore
Nr Ashbourne
Derbyshire
DE6 2BS

Closed mid–Dec to mid–Jan
Sorry, no children or pets

☎ Thorpe Cloud (033529) 287

Mr and Mrs Stuart Worthington

Phone for directions

The views of the lovely Derbyshire countryside from this gracious house are wonderful and its location in the tranquil and pretty hamlet of Blore makes it an ideal retreat for the discerning traveller.

There is a double room en suite and two twin rooms with private facilities, all equipped with a television. The spacious elegant drawing room is warmed in winter by a large log fire. Well-travelled Stuart and Geraldine Worthington show considerable flair and sophistication as host and hostess and meals are veritable dinner parties, served by candlelight using the Worthingtons' fine glass and silver ware. Fresh trout, pheasant and venison (when in season) are featured on the menu. If guests prefer to eat out, two well-acclaimed local restaurants, 'Old Beams' and 'Callow Hall' are only a short drive away.

Easily Accessible: The Peak District National Park has much to offer the visitor. The famous and very beautiful areas of Dovedale and Manifold Valley provide many delightful walks, and a little further afield, high up on the moors, near to the source of the Rivers Dove and Manifold in the village of Flash (England's highest village) the only wild walla-bies in England may be seen. Only 4 miles from Blore is the old and very pretty market town of Ashbourne which boasts a cobbled square and magnificent 14th-century church. Alton Towers, 10 miles away, is the largest leisure park in the country and combines a mini-Disneyland with beautiful gardens. Also well worth a visit are the famous potteries of Royal Dalton and Wedgewood. In summer the arts festival at Buxton is a popular attraction.

Local Activities: walks, golf, horse-riding, fishing (day passes available), cycling (cycle hire locally), squash, swimming, pony-trekking.

Easington House   Bed and Breakfast only
50 Oxford Road   Spanish and French spoken
Banbury
Oxfordshire
OX16 9AN

☎ Banbury (0295) 259395

Malcom and Gwynneth Hearne

The estate of this house dates back to 650 AD when it belonged to the Bishop of Dorchester who was later canonised as Saint Birinius. The house itself is, not surprisingly, a little younger and dates back to the 16th century when it was owned by the great-great-aunt of President George Washington.

Today it is the home of Malcom and Gwynneth Hearne who have carried out extensive restoration work. There is a pleasant Victorian conservatory leading into a pretty garden, a fine mahogany furnished dining room and a comfortable guest lounge. Each of the eleven bedrooms (all with colour TV) is decorated in a unique style, one has beams, another antique pine furniture, all have charm and character.

Breakfast is excellent (croissants and petit pain are imported directly from France) but no dinner is offered. There are many pubs and restaurants nearby – The Easington, ½ mile away, serves good pub food and the Duke of Cumberland's Head which specialises in French cuisine, to name but two.

Easily Accessible: Banbury lies on the edge of the Cotswolds and is therefore ideally situated for walking, but it is probably best known for both the nursery rhyme 'Ride a cock horse to Banbury Cross, To see a fine lady, upon a white horse' and for its special cakes made from a 300-year old recipe. It is less well known, probably, that Banbury has been a trade centre since Viking times, and the design of the town still bears witness to this. Banbury also had the oldest brewery in the country. Among the historic houses are Broughton Castle, originally a 14th-century castle, later changed into a country house; Wroxham Abbey, a 17th-century gabled house; and Hidcote Manor, famous for its unusual garden.

Fulford House
The Green
Culworth
Nr Banbury
Oxfordshire
OX17 2BB

Chauffeuring available
No smoking in bedrooms
Children welcome

☎ Sulgrave (029576) 355/8304

Stephen and Marypen Wills

Phone for directions

This is a lovely 17th-century country home with beams, sloping walls, a priest hole and lots of character. It has sixteen acres of pasture and an acre of most attractive and interesting gardens laid out on three levels – the top layer has very fine views across a valley over miles of rolling farmland, and amongst its beautiful trees it boasts a 'Parrotia Persica Pendula', twenty feet high and ninety feet round.

Stephen and Marypen bought Fulford House for their family of three, and in particular their daughter Antonia needed land and stabling for her riding career – the horses are always a centre of interest for visitors. When their children moved away, the house seemed empty and so with some trepidation Stephen and Marypen began to take in guests, their intention being that every guest should be 'entertained as a friend'. They are both friendly and helpful and take an interest in their guests itineraries making sure that everyone makes the most of their stay.

The three bedrooms are of a high standard, furnished elegantly with antiques, each with its own sitting area, private bathroom and colour TV. Evening meals are by prior arrangement only, and generally Marypen likes to cook for her guests three times a week. She and her husband eat en famille with their guests at a circular Georgian, candlelit table. On non-cooking nights there are a variety of local pubs and restaurants to choose from.

Easily Accessible: Culworth is an ancient settlement, standing on a prehistoric trade-route and mentioned in the Domesday Book. It has a beautiful 13th-century church and a fine manor house, Sulgrave, also mentioned in the Domesday Book and once the home of George Washington's ancestors. Within half an hour's drive from Fulford you can walk on the Cotswolds, or more immediately there are numerous footpaths and country lanes around the village. Banbury, 7 miles away, was founded as a Saxon settlement and today is a busy market town. Seventeen miles away in the Rollrights you can examine a mysterious circle of early Bronze Age stones. Twenty-three miles away at Warwick, you can visit one of the most magnificent of English castles.

Oxford with its splendid college buildings, theatres and museums is 30 miles to the south.

Local Activities: walks, golf, horse-riding.

Shottle Hall Farm   Award winner
Belper
Derbyshire
DE5 2EB

☎ Cowers Lane (077389) 276

Philip and Phyllis Matthews

Phone for directions

Shottle Hall is an attractive mid-19th-century farmhouse set in acres and acres of farmland and a large colourful garden in the picturesque valley of Ecclesbourne. The area is noted as much for its natural beauty as for its industrial history – it was here, in the lush valleys of Derbyshire that the first stirrings of the Industrial Revolution were felt and today working mills and factory shops testify to this heritage.

Inside, Shottle Hall is spacious and comfortable. Each bedroom has distinctive features and outlook. The lounge has an adjoining bar for guests to enjoy conversation in a relaxing atmosphere, and in a separate room a game of snooker can be enjoyed and TV viewed.

The four-course dinner is home-cooked. Rolls and bread are home-baked and the delicious sweets are home-made. Vegetarian meals are available but please order in advance.

Easily Accessible: The countryside is stunning. The Sett Valley Trail will take you along paths created from disused railway lines, past unspoilt villages and through areas of fascinating wildlife. This trail is open to walkers, cyclists and horse-riders. More rugged landscape can be found in the Peak District National Park to the north-west. Belper itself is an interesting town with echoes of its grand industrial past seen in the iron-framed North Mill, and the forbidding old Victorian poorhouse, now a modern hospital. There are many historic houses in the area including Kedleston Hall, built in 1759 and regarded as Robert Adam's finest work; and Wingfield Manor, a romantic ruined manor where Mary Queen of Scots was once imprisoned.

Local Activities: walks, cycling (cycle hire locally), horse-riding, golf, course-fishing.

The Croft Hotel
St Mary's Street
Bridgnorth
Shropshire
WV16 4DW

☎ Bridgnorth (07462) 2416

Gill and John Wilding

This attractive four-hundred-year-old listed building situated in a con-servation area in the old town of Bridgnorth was once a Temperance hostel. Today after much restoration work by its proprietors, Gill and John Wilding, it is a warm, intimate and happily intemperate hotel with exposed beams and inglenook fireplaces adding considerable character. All twelve bedrooms are carefully colour co-ordinated and have en suite facilities and a colour TV. There is a pleasant rear garden. In a converted stable and bath-house, self-catering accommodation is offered.

There are two dinner menus to choose from (a three-course or four-course meal) and food is fresh and well prepared. Your genial hosts will recommend several excellent local restaurants. Special diets are catered for with advance notice.

Easily Accessible: Bridgnorth is a pretty and ancient town, dating back to the 10th century, with a good level of conservation and with the unusual feature of being divided by a river – the Severn. It offers a theatre, sports facilities (listed below), some fine churches and an open market on Saturdays. The county of Shropshire in the Marches has some beautiful and varied scenery. Walkers will enjoy the Brown and Clee hills, 11 miles away – where on a clear day one can see eleven counties; and 20 miles away, the Stretton Hills. Take a trip on the Severn Valley Steam Railway which runs through 14 miles of the Wyre Forest. The UNESCO World Heritage site of the Ironbridge Gorge marks the birth place of the Industrial Revolution. The Lawns at Broseley, the home of John Wilkinson who built the first iron bridge, now houses a large impressive collection of English pottery and porcelain.

Local Activities: walks, bowls, tennis, leisure centre, golf.

Thorn Hayes
No dinner on Thursdays

137 London Road
Buxton
Derbyshire
SK17 9NW

☎ Buxton (0298) 3539

Pat and David Green

Thorn Hayes is a comfortable Victorian house situated in the Victorian spa town of Buxton, with a mature, well-kept garden which is much enjoyed by guests. There are seven bedrooms, all en suite, a dining room with separate tables and a relaxing lounge bar. There is a full choice of evening meal, including a vegetarian dish. Pat makes all her own patés, sauces and desserts, as well as the breakfast marmalade. Local produce is used.

   Pat and David have known each other since they were eight years old and astonishingly they say they always knew they would marry! Both are very well acquainted with the area, but David is particularly knowledgable, having lived in Buxton all his life.

Easily Accessible: Buxton was discovered by the Romans who named it rather poetically 'the spa of the Blue Waters'. It is an interesting town with several historical buildings including the Old Hall, where Mary Queen of Scots once stayed, and a wealth of fine Georgian architecture seen at its best in the famous Crescent. Poole's Cavern in the Buxton Country Park is a very impressive natural cave and the source of the river Wye. Buxton is host to an annual summer arts festival. The surrounding countryside of the Peak District National Park is very beautiful and to the north of Buxton, the Goyt Valley affords some excellent walks. Lyme Park has 1323 acres of land with red deer and superb views of the Peak District, Pennines and the Cheshire Plain. The Hall is a very fine Elizabethan mansion with a fine collection of tapestries.

Local Activities: golf, swimming pool (containing spa water), country park.

Purlins
12 High St
Little Shelford
Cambridge
CB2 5ES

Closed Christmas to 1 Feb
A 'no smoking' home
Sorry, no children or pets
Bed and Breakfast only,
   closed to guests from
   10.30am to 5pm.

☎ Cambridge (0223) 842643

Olga and David Hindley

4 miles south of Cambridge M11 exits 10 or 11.

Purlins is the highly original dream house of Olga and David Hindley, located in a pretty, tranquil Cambridgeshire village. With its galleried dining hall lying off the octagonal entrance hall, one sees echoes (intentionally) of a medieval manor house. It is elegantly furnished with antiques. The guests' lounge in the conservatory is very comfortable, and is home to a variety of plants including a 10-foot Kentie. It opens onto two acres of gardens and woodland. Olga and David have planted over two hundred trees which supplement those existing before the house. There are three attractive bedrooms, all with en suite facilities and colour TV.

David and Olga are both retired from Cambridge University where David was a principal lecturer and member of the music faculty and where Olga was a music librarian. They stress that as Purlins is run on a bed and breakfast basis, it is normally closed from 10.30am to 5pm every day. However, given prior notice, they will accommodate guests' needs. No dinner is offered but there are many and varied eating establishments within a short drive.

A chauffeuring service is offered using a dashing S-type Jaguar.

Easily Accessible: Little Shelford is an ancient village with thatched-roof houses and a flint church mentioned in the Domesday Book. You can take a 12-mile or 20-mile circular walk around the village. Cambridge is only 4 miles away with a wealth of beautiful architecture; amongst other treasures, the excellent Fitzwilliam Museum and the University Botanic Garden. The choirs of King's and St John's are renowned for the beauty of their singing. In summer you can enjoy punting along the river Cam, and the Cambridge Festival of music, drama and film. Fifteen miles north of Cambridge is the splendid Romanesque cathedral at Ely. Nine miles away, Audley End House was once the Royal residence of Charles II and has a fine park landscaped by Capability Brown. Three miles south the Imperial War Museum has an exciting collection of military and civil aircraft at Duxford airfield. A 30-minute drive will take you to Newmarket, home of English horse-racing, where you can watch the horses being exercised on the heath. Wimpole Hall, 8 miles south west of Cambridge is a spectacular 18th-century mansion with a 350-acre park and a farm dedicated to rare breeds of animals.

The Coach House
Scotland Road
Dry Drayton
Cambridge
CB3 8BX

A 'no smoking' home
Sorry, no children or pets
Closed mid Dec-mid March
Bed and Breakfast only

☎ Crafts Hill (0954) 782439

Catherine Child

Between A604 and A45, north-west of Cambridge

This gracious 18th-century converted coach house is situated in the small and peaceful village of Dry Drayton, five miles north-west of Cambridge. It stands in two acres of landscaped garden which was once a paddock for horses, and has a delightful lily pond and a revolving Victorian summer house.

The Coach House originally provided stabling for a wealthy rector who lived next door. Inside it retains an old forge, providing winter visitors with a truly warm welcome. Catherine has considerable interest in interior design and the Coach House is attractively decorated throughout; each room (all face south) has its own mood and character and one has a four-poster bed. Half-way up the handsome pine staircase that Catherine installed, a collection of locally bought antiques is displayed for guests to purchase. There is an elegant conference room and a comfortable lounge with a TV.

Breakfast is taken in the large dining room with mahogany tables with home-made marmalades and preserves, and locally made honey is offered. Packed lunches are provided on request. No dinner is offered, but there are many well-recommended pubs and restaurants in the area including The Plough at Coton, 2 miles away, which gives excellent value for money, and is open seven days a week for lunch and evening meals.

Easily Accessible: (see Purlins, p.125)

Dene House

96 Ermine Street
Caxton
Cambridge
CB3 8PQ

Children over 7 welcome
Sorry, no pets

☎ Caxton (09544) 206

Fiona and David Hughes

Phone for directions

Dene House is an elegant ivy-covered Victorian residence which rests in peace and tranquillity amidst lovely gardens. The bedrooms are warm and comfortable and are equipped with colour TVs. Fiona Hughes, a trained cordon bleu cook, makes good use of fresh produce from the large kitchen garden. If guests wish to eat out, there are several pubs including the Caxton Gibbet Inn.

Easily Accessible: Dene House is a perfect base for touring East Anglia and visiting Cambridge. Four miles away is Wimpole Hall, a 17th-century mansion which has a farm for rare breeds. At Duxford airfield you can see the Imperial War Museum's collection of military and civil aircraft. Anglesey Abbey, an Elizabethan manor house, has splendid gardens.

Stretton Lodge

No smoking in bedrooms

Western Road
Cheltenham
Gloucestershire
GL50 3RN

☎ Cheltenham (0242) 528724

Eric and Kathy Price

10 minutes from city centre. Phone for directions

Kathy and Eric Price run this small hotel as an 'extended home' which should give you a good idea as to its all pervading atmosphere of warmth and hospitality. It is elegantly furnished in light, pleasant colours. A crystal chandelier hangs in the lounge and the marble fireplace has a newly acquired 'dancing horseshoe' Victorian grate. There are high ceilings, tall windows, moulded cornices and a splendid original staircase with a mahogany handrail sweeping down into a carved lion's head. The pretty walled garden shelters a patio. The nine bedrooms are decorated with charm and character, some with pretty flower fabrics and pine furnishings, others more grandly with extravagant drapes and period furniture. All have en suite facilities, a mini-bar and colour TV. One bedroom at garden level has direct access to the patio.

A set evening meal is offered (by arrangement) of traditional English cooking. For guests wishing to sample some of Cheltenham's many restaurants, Kathy and Eric will recommend one to suit your tastes, be it vegetarian, Italian, a steak house, or gourmet cuisine.

Easily Accessible: Cheltenham is one of the most elegant and complete of all our Regency towns with excellent antique shops, theatres, and colourful gardens. Its flower-decked balconies have won it the 'Britain in Bloom' award. It is ideally placed for exploring the Cotswolds, which are dotted with beautiful old towns and villages famed for their warm golden limestone buildings – Bourton-on-the-Water, Stow-on-the-Wold, Chipping Campden and Broadway are all a delight to stroll through.

y Castle, built by the Normans in 1117, is still the home of the
ley family who gave their name to Berkeley Square in London.
dworth Roman villa, 8 miles south-east from Cheltenham, has some
onderfully preserved mosaics and a water shrine fed from an ancient
spring. Sudeley Castle, the palace of Henry VIII's sixth wife Katherine
Parr, has some gruesome dungeons; a less macabre attraction are the
displays given by the resident falconer. Bath, Bristol, Stratford-upon-
Avon, Oxford and the Forest of Dean are all easily reached for day trips.

Noel Arms Hotel
Chipping Campden
Gloucestershire
GL55 6AT

Sorry, no pets

☎ Evesham (0386) 840317

David and Glynis Feasey

This was a 14th-century coaching inn (the oldest inn in Campden)
where, apparently, King Charles II stayed during the battle of Worcester
in 1651. The whole house is laden with interesting antiques, such as a
fabulous collection of armour, muskets and swords. There are eighteen
bedrooms; each is individually furnished, and has private facilities and
a colour TV. Two of the bedrooms have magnificent four-poster beds.
The bar is warm and cosy, with an open fire and oak beams.

The lovely oak-panelled dining room seats up to sixty guests, and
offers a very traditional English menu, which includes a number of
vegetarian dishes. Obviously, as it is situated near to the famous Vale
of Evesham, the market garden of England, the produce is excellent.

Easily Accessible: Chipping Campden was mentioned in the Domesday
Book, and is lined with picturesque 13th-century houses, including the
old market hall, almshouses and St John's parish church. There are many
walks in the vicinity, the most popular being the Cotswold Way, which
starts here, and finishes in Bath. If you climb Dovers Hill, you can see
the wonderful views across the Vale of Evesham to the Malvern Hills.
Three miles from Chipping Campden are the National Trust gardens
at Hidcote Manor. The beautiful Cotswold town of Broadway is just
5 miles away. Stratford-upon-Avon, home to the Royal Shakespeare
Theatre, is just 12 miles away. At Beckford, on the southern slopes of
Bredon Hill, you can visit Beckford Silk Centre and view the processes
involved in the dyeing and printing of their unusual silks, and make
purchases at the adjacent store.

Local Activities: walks, horse-riding, golf.

The Grange

Packhorse Road
Melbourne
Derbyshire
DE7 1EG

A 'no smoking' home
Sorry, no pets
Will collect guests from
  airport

☎ Derby (0332) 863653

Annette and Mirco Perla

M1 and M52, 6 miles. Phone for directions

The oldest part of this spacious house dates back to 1720, with two wings added later. The rooms are high-ceilinged but warm colours, myriad plants and dried flowers, patchwork and three purring ginger cats create a cosy atmosphere. The two guest bedrooms have private bathrooms and colour TVs.

Mirco is Czech and Annette is half-French so you can expect some creative cuisine here. Dinner is taken at a large pine table in the breakfast room or in the dining room at a rather grand table, polished and adorned with the best china, silver-ware and of course, candles. Annette makes the bread, jams, jellies, marmalade, soups and desserts and Mirco enjoys experimenting with the likes of poppy seeds and curd cheese. Herbs and vegetables come from the garden as do the pre-prandial hazelnuts.

Easily Accessible: The surrounding countryside is very pleasant. From the Grange you can walk to Calke Park where deer and sheep wander in magnificent surroundings. Twenty-five miles away lies the entrance to the Peak National Park where there are many waymarked walks. Melbourne has a fine Norman church and at Melbourne Hall there are delightful formal gardens of terraced lawns, a lake and avenues of limes to amble through. The small town of Ashby-de-la-Zouch was named after a Breton nobleman and has a castle where in 1569 Mary Queen of Scots was imprisoned. In a different vein, a half-hour drive will take you to the gardens and leisure park at Alton Towers. Eight miles north of Melbourne lies Derby where you can visit the interesting part-18th century and part-modern cathedral.

Bellows Mill Cottage   Sorry, no pets
Bellows Mill
Eaton Bray
Dunstable
Bedfordshire
LU6 1QZ

☎ Eaton Bray (0525) 220548 / 220205

The Hodge Family

M1 exit 9 off B489

Hodges have lived here for eight generations but Rachel Hodge is relaxed about most things her guests do – even the Czechoslovakian guests who played tennis on her court in brown walking shoes and underwear! The house, which was a working mill until 1955, has twenty-one acres of grounds which encompass a wood, three lakes and an all-weather tennis court. Accommodation is provided in the pretty, converted stables that surround the courtyard. The bedrooms are attractively decorated with chintzy materials and antiques and have mini-bars and TVs. There is a small kitchenette available for use at any time by guests who wish to make tea or coffee, a small dining room, and a patio.

Dinner is offered, but if guests wish to eat out, there are several local pubs and restaurants recommended by Rachel. These include The Bell at Aston Clinton and The Kings Head at Ivinghoe.

Easily Accessible: Bellows Mill is situated on the edge of the villages of Eaton Bray and Edlesborough. The surrounding countryside is very pretty and there are numerous walks, many of which start a couple of miles from the house. These include Ivinghoe Beacon, the Ridgeway long- distance footpath and Two Ridges Link. Whipsnade Zoo is only 2 miles away. Woburn Abbey, a beautiful 18th-century mansion with a fine art collection and 3000-acre deer park, is 10 miles away. St Albans with its Verulamium, ruined abbey and rose gardens is 15 miles away. Hatfield House, a very fine Jacobean House with gardens and park, is 20 miles away.

Local Activities: fly fishing – (£9 per day), all-weather tennis court, table tennis (at Bellows Mill), walks, horse-riding, clay pigeon shooting, hot-air ballooning, squash (locally).

Dalkeith   No smoking in bedrooms

Lower Common
East Runton
Cromer
Norfolk
NR27 9PG

☎ Cromer (0263) 514803

Nigel and Jan Slater

From Cromer 1 mile on A149, left opp Fishing Boat pub, 50 yds

Overlooking the village green, in a pretty conservation village, this
fine Victorian house has a half-acre garden, two greenhouses (one has a
vine that produces heaps of succulent black grapes), a sunken-terraced
garden with lily pond and an affectionate three-legged cat.

The panelled dining room and lounge (with TV) are sun-lit in the
morning (in cooler weather the dining room glows with a log fire),
and the four comfortable spacious bedrooms are light and airy and
attractively furnished in period furniture and antiques.

On arrival guests are treated to a cup of tea or coffee by the
charming Jan Slater. Dinner is offered (with advance warning) and
meals are produced from organically grown fresh and local produce –
eggs come from your hosts' free-range hens. The home-made bread,
pies and puddings are a speciality. Vegetarians are catered for.

Easily Accessible: East Runton is a pretty Norfolk fishing village with
(apart from some basic stores) two good pubs (both serving food) and
a Greek restaurant. Just a few minutes will take you to a sandy beach. Half
an hour's car journey will take you to Norwich and the Broads. There
are several National Trust properties nearby including: Sheringham
Park, a beautiful landscaped garden with exciting views; and Blickling
Hall, a 17th-century mansion with a park open for riding and walking,
and magnificent state rooms. There are numerous walks directly from
East Runton – footpaths and bridleways lead out into the lovely gentle
countryside and unspoilt coast.

Local Activities: walks, bird-watching, golf, sailing, horse-riding, sandy
beaches.

ont Street

Bed and Breakfast only
No lounge
Children over 12 welcome

shire

1AE

☎ Ely (0353) 663118

Sheila and Jeremy Friend-Smith

This delightful 17th-century house has wistaria and roses crawling up its south wall and a walled garden laden with beautiful trees and shrubs – a ginkgo, mulberry, tulip tree and several varieties of magnolia to name but a few. The ageing orchard is full of spring bulbs and old fruit trees. The kitchen garden has a large conservatory with an old vine and cucumber frames straight out of Beatrix Potter. There is also a grass tennis court which guests are welcome to use. The south-facing house is situated in one of the oldest streets in Ely and boasts superb views of the medieval cathedral. There are two spacious bedrooms furnished as bed-sitting-rooms with arm-chairs, table and colour TV. Throughout the house there are interesting antiques, clocks, paintings, and lovely oak beams.

The house is run on a bed and breakfast basis by the Friend-Smiths – an encouraging name! Breakfast, served in the dining room at a large Victorian mahogany table, is prepared to order with locally baked wholemeal bread, farm eggs and home-made marmalade. Dinner is not provided but there are nearly thirty restaurants and pubs in Ely.

Jeremy is a maths teacher and Sheila, who now runs the business, was once a history teacher which accounts for her detailed knowledge of the area – a great help to any visitor.

Easily Accessible: Ely is an ancient market town famous for its magnificent medieval cathedral and stained glass museum. It is full of narrow winding streets and beautiful Tudor buildings and has an attractive waterfront. There are many pretty walks in the area, along the banks of the River Ouse, the Hereward Way, a 110-mile long-distance footpath which passes through Ely, and the medieval track known as Bishops Way which traces the 12-mile route used by the Bishops of Ely from their palace in Ely to their country residence in Little Downham. Ten miles away the Welney Wildfowl Refuge is famous for its floodlit sessions at dusk when a multitude of birds return to feed. Newmarket race course and the National Horseracing Museum are 12 miles away. Cambridge is 16 miles away.

Local Activities: walks, boating, fishing, golf.

Yews Farm

Firbeck
Worksop
Nottinghamshire
S81 8JW

☎ Worksop (0909) 731458

John and Catherine Stewart-Smith

5 miles to M1, M18 and A1

Unlicensed, guests welcome
to bring own wine
Will collect guests from station
Sorry, no pets

This attractive country home dates back to the 16th century when it was once a farm labourer's cottage. It is set in a garden and fields which look south towards a fresh stream and woodland beyond. Across the courtyard lies an Elizabethan building, believed to be the original farmhouse. Much has been added to the house over the years and today, with its elegant 18th-century front rooms, there is little to remind one of its humble beginnings. There is a restful green drawing room with a log fire, piano and colour TV. The dining room is rakishly decked out in Regency stripes with deep red walls. There are two comfortable bedrooms with en suite bathrooms.

Dinner is offered by prior arrangement. The food is home-cooked using fresh ingredients, and vegetables and herbs from the kitchen garden.

Easily Accessible: There are several local walks which start directly from the house, taking in the village (one mile from Yew Farm) and the surrounding woods and fields. Sherwood Forest Country Park, once the haunt of Robin Hood, has numerous waymarked walks among its famous glades and great oaks. Two and a half miles away, you can visit Roche Abbey, a Cistercian monastery. Chatsworth, the splendid stately home of the Duke and Duchess of Devonshire, with its marvellous painted walls, woodcarvings, tapestry and paintings, and Capability Brown's landscaped park, is within an hour's drive. Conisbrough Castle, 7 miles away, has an unusual keep and is the setting for Sir Walter Scott's *Ivanhoe*. Three miles away at Doncaster, you can enjoy the famous race-meetings and horse sales. The cathedral cities of York and Lincoln are both within an hour's drive.

Local Activities: walks, golf, horse-riding.

The Emplins
Church Street
Gamlingay
Sandy
Bedfordshire
SG19 3ER

A 'no smoking' house

☎ Gamlingay (0767) 50581

The Gorton Family

This delightful timber-framed listed building was once the medieval home of six priests, and then became a rectory, which it remained until 1840. In all this time it has only ever had three owners. When Rosalind and Philip first moved in, it was in a pretty parlous condition, with, amongst other nightmares, an elder tree with its roots in the great hall and its branches spreading in through the windows. Today, renovated and furnished with family antiques and oriental rugs, it is on show, not only to guests, but to the general public. Many fine original features remain, the oak beams, the 16th-century wall paintings, and in the great hall, a huge fireplace which can take thirty-inch logs.

The garden too has been saved from neglect. It has pretty herbaceous borders and an attractive paved herb garden, where on fine mornings breakfast is served.

Rosalind bakes her own bread and croissants and will prepare an evening meal with advance notice. Fresh herbs and vegetables come from the garden. If guests wish to eat out, there are several local pubs in the village, and 16 miles away, in Cambridge, there are numerous excellent eating establishments.

Easily Accessible: Emplins is situated in a conservation area in the village of Gamlingay, which among its attractions boasts a vineyard producing white wine, Hayley Wood, a naturalists' paradise. There are many local walks including the long-distance Greenlands walk which starts from the village and finishes at Dunstable. A twenty-five minute drive will take you to the races at Newmarket. Seven miles away, the National Trust property of Wimpole Hall is a fine house, with lovely grounds and a collection of 'rare breed' animals. A very pleasant day trip can be spent journeying through the pretty Suffolk villages of Little Cavendish and Long Melford, and the medieval town of Lavenham where a delicious meal is to be had at the Swan.

Local Activities: golf, fishing, horse-riding.

The Old Rectory

Gissing
Diss
Norfolk
IP22 3XB

No smoking in bedrooms
Pick-up service from local
   station
Fax/photocopying
No smoking in bedrooms

☎ Tivetshall (037977) 575

Jill and Ian Gillam

4 miles north of Diss, 2 miles from A140, phone for directions

The red-brick Victorian rectory, commissioned by the Bishop of Norwich, is reached by way of a sweeping gravel drive. It stands in three acres of garden, woodland and paddock in the delightful village of Gissing. Inside, high ceilings, plaster cornices, marble fireplaces and a pine staircase contribute to its air of grandeur. The large sash windows open up to embrace the beautiful surrounding countryside. There are three bedrooms, one with an en suite shower room, all decorated very prettily with floral prints. The comfortable drawing room has a TV and a log fire.

A four-course dinner is available, by prior arrangement. The cuisine is traditional English using good quality fresh and local ingredients. Low fat and vegetarian diets and packed lunches can be provided if adequate notice is given. A house wine is on offer, or you can bring your own. Occasionally dinner is not offered, in which case there are several excellent local restaurants and pubs including the gourmet but expensive Fox and Goose at Fressingfield and the Ram, which serves good pub food.

Easily Accessible: There are many walks immediately around Diss and Harleston and along Marriotts Way, a path following an old railway line. Diss itself is an interesting part-Tudor town, built around a 6 acre lake. Eight miles away at the Bressingham gardens, you can see the famous perennials, steam engines and garden shop. At the Otter Trust in Earsham, 15 miles away, you can revel at the sight of the world's largest gathering of otters. The fine medieval city of Norwich, 17 miles away, has a cathedral, castle and market. Thirty miles away, Wroxham Barns has a collection of traditional 18th-century working barns set in ten acres of parkland. The unspoilt coastline with its pretty resorts such as the harbour town of Southwold, is only 25 miles away. Bury St Edmunds, Cambridge, Ely and the Broads are all easily reached for a day trip.

Local Activities: walks, golf, swimming pool, horse-riding.

The Bauble

Higham
Nr Colchester
Essex
CO7 6LA

Bed and Breakfast only
Children over 12 welcome
Sorry, no pets

☎ Higham (020637) 254

Nowell and Penny Watkins

Phone for directions

Nowell, a solicitor, and his wife Penny have taken thirty years to develop the lovely garden at Baubles which now boasts ornamental and wildlife ponds and a wide variety of trees, shrubs, a tennis court and a swimming pool. The house has been renovated and modernised but retains beams, an inglenook fireplace and a lot of character. There is a charming drawing room and dining room furnished with antiques. Five guests can be accommodated and each bedroom is furnished in a 'country house' style and equipped with, amongst other things, a sewing kit and a radio or TV.

Dinner is not available but a full English breakfast is offered. Within a five mile radius there are several pubs and restaurants. Nowell and Penny recommend the Angel in Stoke-by-Nayland which they say has become a favourite with visitors, and the Terrace Restaurant which provides a sophisticated atmosphere.

Easily Accessible: The rivers Brett and Stour, closely associated with the painter John Constable, lie within walking distance. There are interesting walks in the countryside surrounding the medieval towns of Lavenham, Long Melford and Sudbury, once centres of the Suffolk wool trade. Sudbury remains a bustling market town and is still rightly proud of its famous son, Thomas Gainsborough, whose house is open to the public. Lavenham and Long Melford have many interesting buildings, the former in particular retains its medieval character. The Suffolk Coastal Path passes through areas designated 'of outstanding natural beauty'. Eight miles from the Bauble lies the historic town of Colchester, an ancient town dating back to the 1st century BC with Roman remains, a ruined Norman castle, a 15th-century abbey, museums and excellent shopping facilities.

Local Activities: swimming and tennis at the Bauble, walks, Higham point-to-point with four meetings a year, golf, walks, squash, sailing, fishing.

Sutton House Hotel

24 Northgate
Hunstanton
Norfolk
PE36 6AP

☎ Hunstanton (04853) 2552
(will change 1990)

Mike Emsden

This is a comfortable Edwardian house, whose rather ordinary exterior completely belies its unusual and attractive interior. It is conveniently situated close to the town centre and the sea, which can be seen from several of the the rooms. Its eight comfortable bedrooms are tastefully decorated and furnished, five have full en suite facilities, and all have colour TV. There is an à la carte dinner menu of traditional English food home-cooked using fresh vegetables. Bar meals are also on offer until late.

Easily Accessible: There are miles and miles of sandy beaches and dramatic cliff-top scenery to enjoy. The coastal path, Peddars Way, and Thetford Forest provide many interesting walks. Three miles away at Heacham you can visit the only lavender farm in England and 5 miles away, at Park Farm in Snettisham, children can enjoy special guided tours and nature trails around this working farm. Sandringham House, the Queen's country residence, is 7 miles away. Little Walsingham, 15 miles from Hunstanton, is a beautiful village with a collection of medieval buildings including the most complete remains of any Franciscan friary in Britain. Fifteen miles away, you can visit Houghton Hall, home of the Marquess of Cholmondeley, where on summer weekends the British Army's regimental bands perform the ancient ceremony of 'Beating the Retreat'. There are RSPB reserves at Snettisham Beach and Titchwell, both 5 miles away. The beautiful city of Norwich, and Peterborough with its cathedral and excellent shops, are both within 50 miles.

Local Activities: walks, golf, wind-surfing, water-skiing, sandy beach.

Conygree Gate

Church Street
Kingham
Oxfordshire
OX7 6YA

Closed January
Will collect guests from
 station

☎ Kingham (060871) 389

Brian and Kathryn Sykes

Off A436 between Stow-on-the-Wold and Chipping Norton

This solid-looking house is built of Cotswold stone and dates from around 1648. It was once a farmhouse, and now the outbuildings are being converted into self-catering accommodation. There are pretty front and back gardens, roses growing round the front entrance, and inside, lots of exposed beams. Kathryn Sykes has run a pottery, and worked for many years as a window dresser and she has used her sense of style and colour to decorate each room individually. Most of the eight bedrooms are en suite and have colour TV. The lounge is comfortable and has an open fire in winter.

Kathyrn cooks a traditionally English meal every evening using fresh local produce and vegetables. If guests wish to eat out two local pubs, The Kings Head in Bledington and the Chequers Inn at Churchill, are recommended.

Easily Accessible: There is a large number of footpaths and bridleways in the area, and two long-distance paths, the Oxford Way and the Cotswold Way, pass within a few miles of the hotel. The Cotswold Wild Life Park is home to many exotic species of animals ranging from big cats to tarantulas. Nearby is the very attractive town of Burford, built of rich golden Cotswold stone. Bibury, 8 miles north-east of Cirenester, is generally held to be the most attractive of all the Cotswold towns and has a trout farm you can visit. Nearby at Arlington Mill museum you can see a display of rural crafts many of which are no longer practised. Cirencester has some excellent Roman remains and a museum. A visit to the Westonbirt Arboretum with its 13,000 trees and shrubs is always a sight for sore eyes. Oxford, Cheltenham and Bath are all within easy reach for day trips.

Local Activities: walks, golf.

Withenfield
South Street
Leominster
Hereford
HR6 8JN

Sorry, no pets
Will collect guests from
    station

☎ Leominster (0586) 2011

Jim and Pam Cotton

On edge of town

In this impressive Georgian house guests can use the original internal bell system, once used by the ruling classes, to call room service! The house is elegant, furnished with antiques, and has some fine features such as the marble fireplace in the drawing room, and a conservatory with Italian terrazzo flooring. All the bedrooms are en suite, and are equipped with colour TV, one has a four-poster bed, and the spacious master bedroom has a luxurious bathroom with a corner bath. There is a pretty half-acre garden where guests can enjoy afternoon tea or a pre-prandial drink.

Snacks, salads, and a four- or five-course dinner using fresh and local produce and home-grown herbs and vegetables are provided. Wye salmon, local trout and lamb, and Hereford beef, are regular features. If guests wish to eat out, your friendly and welcoming proprietors, Jim and Pam, will recommend local restaurants and pubs.

Easily Accessible: Leominster is an attractive market town with a weekly antiques sale, some fine timber buildings, and a Norman church which features a ducking stool (last used in 1809) and a beautiful 14th-century chalice. The surrounding countryside is largely unspoilt and is dotted with picturesque villages (such as the thatched and timbered Brampton Bryan, and Eardisley, with its 30-ft wide oak) and cider orchards. There are many local walks, including Offa's Dyke (with its 168 miles of rugged footpath), and in a gentler vein, the 170 acres of the wooded Queenswood Country Park. A few miles north of Leominster, Berrington Hall is an 18th-century house with gardens designed by the father-in-law of Capability Brown. Croft Castle, 5 miles north-east of Leominster, is a 14th-century fortified mansion with extensive grounds and magnificent views of the Welsh borders. The attractive town of Hereford is only 12 miles away, and Worcester is 20 miles.

Local Activities: walks, golf, fishing, leisure centre.

Oakleigh House Hotel   No dinner on Sun or Mon
25 St Chad's Road
Lichfield
Staffordshire
WS13 7LZ

☎ Lichfield (0543) 262688

Pat and Iain McGregor

In city, 600 yards from cathedral

This is an attractive Edwardian house with a delightful garden (which overlooks Stowe Pool with its water sports facilities), and a large conservatory. Its proprietor was a sea captain from 1953 to 1986, when he went into partnership with friends and bought Oakleigh House; he bought his partners out in April 1988. There are ten bedrooms, each with colour TV, and a lounge with a bar. The restaurant has a very imaginative à la carte menu which includes such culinary delights as 'Halibut with Lobster Mousse', 'Smoked Goose Breast served with Orange and Pink Peppercorn Salad'. Sounds delicious!

Easily Accessible: Lichfield is famous for being the home town of Samuel Johnson, and his birthplace, now a museum, is open to the public. Incidentally, Dr Johnson believed that here (in Lichfield) was 'genuine civilised life in an English provincial town'. Its spectacular cathedral has three spires known as the 'Ladies of the Vale'. Altogether a most attractive and unspoilt city, it has some pretty medieval streets, some of which are pedestrianised. The city is also host to annual arts, jazz and folk festivals. Eight miles outside the city, the Drayton Manor Park is a 60-acre leisure park with a zoo and some breathtaking fun rides. The Walsall Arboretum, also 8 miles away, has over two hundred varieties of trees and shrubs in 33 acres of land. Ten miles away, you can visit the Castle Ring Iron Age hill fort at Cannock Chase. Nearby is Tamworth Castle, one of the country's few remaining Norman shell-keeps, which is reputedly haunted. Its grounds have picnic areas, river boats, swimming pools and playgrounds.

Local Activities: fishing, sailing, sports centre with swimming, sauna and fitness room, tennis, bowls, miniature golf course.

Upper Buckton Farm
Leintwardine
Craven Arms
Shropshire
SY7 0JU

Closed Dec–Jan.
Dogs only in outhouse accom.
A 'no smoking' house
Unlicensed, guests welcome to
   bring own wine

☎ Leintwardine (05473) 634

Hayden and Yvonne Lloyd

A 4113 from Ludlow to Knighton, turn right past A 4110.

Well off the main road, Upper Buckton, a gracious Georgian farmhouse, nestles in the remote and tranquil hamlet of Buckton and overlooks the river Teme. The house is large, white and elegantly proportioned with a south-facing porch equipped with comfortable chairs for guests to relax on. The garden slopes down to a peaceful mill stream. It is a truly delightful place to stay.

Whilst the three hundred acre farm is run by Hayden Lloyd, his wife, Yvonne, takes great pleasure in looking after the guests. The house is beautifully decorated with antique furniture, paintings and honey-coloured natural pine woodwork. Children and adults can enjoy the recreation room with snooker, table tennis and darts facilities as well as the croquet lawn outside. There is a guest dining room and drawing room with colour TV.

The food is delicious. Dinner is a four-course meal and menus vary from traditional roasts to imaginative cordon bleu dishes. Hayden and Yvonne enjoy meeting their guests and their tradition of taking after-dinner coffee en famille in the sitting room has led to many new friendships.

Easily Accessible: There are several gentle walks along the banks of the Teme. Further away you can reach Offa's Dyke, Radnor Forest and the Stretton Hills. Ten miles away at Ludlow you are bound to be impressed by its looming castle, the delightful mixture of Georgian and medieval architecture and the interesting museum of local history. Here you can also see National Hunt horse racing. At Church Stretton the Acton Scott working farm museum demonstrates 19th-century farming methods and here you can see butter being churned and traditional crafts being practised. Burford House Gardens have extensive lawns and a large collection of rare plants. The history and natural beauty of the Welsh borders is easily reached.

Local Activities: walks, golf, horse-riding, pony-trekking, bird-watching.

Haversham Grange
Haversham
Nr Milton Keynes
Buckinghamshire
MK19 7DX

☎ Milton Keynes (0908) 312389

Julian and Mafra Smithers

Phone for directions

Bed and Breakfast only
No smoking in bedrooms

The oldest part of this charming listed house dates back to 1387. Two later additions, one in 1528, and one in the 1750s, complete its distinctive 'E' shape. It was originally the farm to a nearby monastery. The garden is pretty and looks out onto six acres of fields and a copse, and contains a tennis court which guests are welcome to use. There are three comfortable bedrooms filled with family 'bit and pieces'. Two have private facilities, all have colour TV.

A full English breakfast is served, and jams and marmalades are home-made. No dinner is offered but there are numerous local pubs and restaurants to choose from.

Easily Accessible: Haversham Grange is situated in a small tranquil village with an attractive church, a post office and a pub. The magnificent stately home of Woburn is only 12 miles away. The two university towns of Cambridge and Oxford are within an hour's driving distance. Walkers will enjoy the Swan's Way, which passes within ½ mile of the house. It starts in the south of Buckinghamshire and ends 6 miles north of the Grange. There is also some pleasant walking along the banks of the river Ouse, and around the lakes at the back of the house.

Local Activities: walks, golf.

Live and Let Live
76 High Street
Stetchworth
Newmarket
Suffolk
CB8 9TJ

No smoking in bedrooms
Sorry, no pets
Unlicensed

☎ Stetchworth (063876) 8153

Dennis and Sylvia Human

This is an attractive 18th-century building which was originally a village inn. It is conveniently situated in the high street of Stetchworth, just outside Newmarket, in Suffolk. It has a large garden with fruit trees and a splendid mature walnut tree. There are seven comfortable bedrooms, a beamed lounge with a TV and a dining room. The proprietors are happy to provide dinner with prior notice or to direct you to any of the many pubs and restaurants within a three-mile radius.

Easily Accessible: The surrounding countryside is very gentle and peaceful. There are numerous footpaths including Devil's Ditch, a long defensive fortification dating from 500AD, which runs from the woodlands south of Stetchworth, northwards to the Fens, and the Icknield Way. Newmarket, the famous horse-racing centre, home of the National Stud and the National Horseracing Museum, is just 3 miles away. Anglesey Abbey, 6 miles away, was originally an Augustinian priory, and was later transformed into a fine Elizabethan manor house with gardens. Cambridge is just 12 miles away. There are many pretty villages nearby, one of the most picturesque is Lavenham, situated between Bury St Edmunds and Sudbury. Lavenham is widely regarded as the most complete example of a medieval town with its superb timber-framed houses, medieval street pattern and market place. Altogether it has three hundred buildings listed as being of architectural and historical interest. There is also a very pretty walk here, along the old railway line to another picturesque village, Little Melford.

Local Activities: walks, golf.

Old Furnace Farm

Greendale
Oakamoor
Stoke-on-Trent
ST10 3AP

Sorry, no pets
Local chauffeuring

☎ Oakamoor (0538) 702442

The Wheeler Family

1 mile off B5032, turn opp Highwayman Inn at Threapwood.

This pretty Victorian farmhouse set in the hills of Staffordshire has beautiful views from all aspects overlooking a peaceful valley. The farm itself consists of forty acres grazed by sheep and pedigree Charolais cattle. The pretty garden has its own trout lake.

Maggie Wheeler makes her guests feel entirely at home and certainly it is very easy to relax in this 'no rules' atmosphere, where you can enjoy meeting the other guests around the kitchen table in an informal atmosphere with Maggie taking the time to help you plan your itinerary.

The house is furnished with antiques and memorabilia. All bedrooms have full en suite bathrooms. The charming honeymoon suite has its own gallery and a large double Victorian brass bed. There is a television in the comfortable lounge.

Dinner is home-made English fare using, whenever possible, fresh local produce. Maggie recommends several restaurants and pubs within a five-mile radius of the farm – the Admiral Jervis Inn, the Bulls Head Inn, Old Beams Restaurant, and the Jervis Arms.

There are self-catering holidays available in a cottage and a chalet.

Easily Accessible: The nearest bus stop is 1 mile away and the nearest train station is in Stoke-on-Trent, 12 miles away. There are many walks (from 3 to 40 miles) starting directly from the farm which will take you through woods, valleys and hills. The farm is actually situated on the Staffordshire Way (an old Roman route) and nearby is the Hawkesmoor Nature Reserve where wildlife is abundant. The Peak National Park is only 8 miles away. Alton Towers, the large leisure park with gardens, is only 2 miles away. The pretty market town of Ashbourne with its antique centre is only 9 miles away. Take a ride on the Foxfield Steam Railway which can be joined 4 miles away. The Wedgewood and Royal Dalton potteries are within a 12-mile radius.

Local Activities: walks, golf, leisure centre, cycling, horse-riding, pony-trekking.

Pen-y-Dyffryn Hall
Rhydycroesau
Oswestry
Shropshire
SY10 7DT

☎ Oswestry (0691) 653700

Miles and Audrey Hunter

On B4580 west of Oswestry

Pen-y-Dyffryn Hall (the name is Welsh for 'The Head of the Valley'), lies in a remote hamlet in a fairy-tale landscape of verdant valleys, gently rolling hills, and pastures dotted with white sheep. Your hosts, Miles and Audrey Hunter, came to this spot to escape the rat-race – and they could not have chosen more perfectly.

The hall is a beautiful listed Georgian rectory, built of local stone. It is elegantly and comfortably furnished. The bedrooms are south-facing (including the honeymoon suite with four-poster bed) and have panoramic views of the neighbouring Welsh hills. All are en suite and have colour TV. The south-facing terrace is perfect for enjoying early morning coffee, evening cocktails or just admiring the scenery.

The food is imaginative British cuisine and breakast, lunch and dinner are all available. Vegetarians are catered for. Whenever possible, organic and free-range produce is served. Puddings, however, are definitely 'naughty (but nice)', spotted dick and jam roly-poly being two of the naughtiest!

Easily Accessible: Many short walks from the hotel take in standing stones, old wells and disused mines. Offa's Dyke, one of the country's finest long-distance footpaths with views into both England and Wales, can be reached under 1 mile from the hotel and is dotted with ancient fortifications. Snowdonia National Park is just a short drive away. Wales' highest waterfall, Pistyll Rhaeder, is 10 miles away. There are numerous castles, including Chirk Castle which dates back to the 14th century and has some lovely formal gardens, and a little further away, Powis Castle, built in the 15th century but altered through the years and now very much a stately home with a large deer park.

Local Activities: walks, fishing (access to private trout lake), golf, canoeing, mountain-biking, hill walking, pony-trekking.

Otley House
Otley
Ipswich
Sufolk
IP6 9NR

'No smoking' areas
Sorry, no pets
Children over 12 welcome
Closed Dec 16 to 14 Feb
Award winner

☎ Helmingham (047339) 253

Lise and Mike Hilton

This is a beautiful elegant Georgian house with ivy-clad stone walls, fine proportions and a very pleasing aspect. It looks onto a pretty ordered garden with a small lake, large terrace, and summer pavilion. Inside there is parquet flooring, a splendid Queen Anne staircase and fine antique furniture. The drawing room has French doors leading out into the garden, and the dining room replete with Regency furniture and crystal chandelier and grand piano is a treat. The bedrooms are furnished to a very high standard, all are en suite, one has a four-poster bed, another a half-tester. There is also a sumptuous leather-chaired billiard room.

Lise is not a trained cook, but has a wealth of valuable experience which began with helping her mother in a small hotel in Copenhagen. Thus the delicious Scandinavian dishes that frequently crop up among the traditional English farmhouse cuisine are no surprise in the menu. Guests eat together around an elegantly decorated table and the atmosphere is very much that of a dinner party between friends.

Easily Accessible: Otley is just 6 miles from the pretty Elizabethan market town of Woodbridge which overlooks the Sutton Hoo burial mounds and possesses the only surviving tide mill in the country. Half an hour's drive away, Bury St Edmunds is a beautiful ancient town with an abbey and clock museum. Cambridge and Norwich can be reached within an hour's drive. Between Norwich and the coast there are over thirty Broads – if you feel like a trip you can hire a boat at Oulton Broad. There are many beautiful walks nearby, along the coast, the Deben River, and through forests. Much of the look and feel of the scenery will be familiar, as it has been brilliantly captured by the artist John Constable in his many paintings of the area. Ipswich, 7 miles south, has been a settlement since the Stone Age, with interesting historical buildings and good modern amenities including a large shopping centre and leisure complex.

Local Activities: walks, golf, horse-riding, bird-watching.

The Old Rectory
Ipsley Lane
Ipsley
Redditch
Worcestershire
B98 0AP

☎ Redditch (0527) 23000

Jill, Tony and Martin Moore

Phone for directions

No smoking in dining room
Sorry, no pets

The foundations and frame of this gracious building have existed since the days of the Domesday Book but the interior was redesigned by Sir Christopher Wren's great grandson in 1812. There is a pretty conservatory where meals are served, a large, colourful garden and several interesting outbuildings such as the 17th-century half-timbered stable block which has been converted to provide four bedrooms, and the cellar, bread oven and fishpond dug by the monks from Bordesley Abbey. In the house the rooms range from a beamed attic style to the Chapel Room with its fine barrel ceiling. All the bedrooms have en suite or private bathrooms.

Tony, Jill and their son, Martin, have lived at the Old Rectory for twenty years and it is very much their home – as your hosts they will bring early morning tea (if requested), and arrange numerous activities. Good home cooking is served and fresh local and garden produce are used. Specialities are the home-baked bread and delicious mulberry ice-cream made with fruit from the ancient mulbèrrry tree in the garden (when in season).

Easily Accessible: One hundred yards from the house lies the Arraw Valley

Park which follows the course of the River Arraw and is ideal for walkers, but also has bridleways and a lake for boating. Eleven miles away lies the Lickey Hills Country Park which is linked to the North Worcestershire Way (20 miles long). Walkers will also enjoy the Malvern Hills, the Wyre Forest and the Cotswold Way, all of which are within a 25-mile radius. The ruined Cistercian Abbey of Bordesley is just 3 miles away. Hanberry Hall, 15 miles away, is a splendid Palladian mansion. Four miles away at Caughton Court the wives of the Gunpowder plotters awaited news of the plot. Warwick Castle 16 miles away is one of the finest castles in England. Stratford-upon-Avon is just 12 miles away. Eighteen miles away at Worcester you can visit the beautiful cathedral with its Norman crypt.

Local Activities: walks, golf, fishing, cycling, horse-riding, boating, health centre with swimming, snooker, squash.

The Old Forge
Burgage Lane
Southwell
Nottinghamshire
NG25 0ER

Bed and Breakfast only
No smoking in bedrooms

☎ Southwell (0636) 812809

Hilary and Derek Marston

The Old Forge is an attractive Victorian house situated in the peaceful town of Southwell in the Trent valley. It was once a working forge and today brims with character and antiques. The colour scheme is delicate and pleasing and most of the rooms have a view of the Minster. The dining room adjoins a conservatory and in summer, weather permitting, with the French windows open, guests can enjoy breakfast in the fresh air. No dinner is provided but there are numerous pubs and restaurants within walking distance.

Your hosts Derek and Hilary Marston take the ups and downs of running a guest house in their stride. Only once Hilary admits to being seriously rattled. A stern and rather humourless vicar's wife angrily rejected the offer of morning newspapers, admonishing the bemused Hilary with 'I only read the psalms at breakfast' – there were angry looks all round.

Easily Accessible: Southwell is dominated by the impressive Norman Minster (incidentally the most rural minster in Great Britain) and is a quiet, pretty town, famous for the beautiful foliage carvings in the Chapter House. Nearby Newark is a picturesque market town with a

d square overlooked by buildings of architectural interest. The
ding countryside is lush and fertile and much is given over to
agricultural use. There are numerous country parks with nature trails,
including the Sherwood Forest Country Park with its Robin Hood exhibition. Newstead Abbey was once the home of Lord Byron and now
contains a museum dedicated to the poet. Nottingham is an ancient city
with a Norman castle and an excellent variety of shops, theatre and other
modern amenities.

Local Activities: walks, leisure centre, water sports, golf.

The Old Rectory   Bed and Breakfast only
Wetherden   Children over 12 welcome
Nr Stowmarket   Sorry, no pets
Suffolk
IP14 3RE

☎ Elmswell (0359) 40144

Pamela Bowden

Situated off A45 between Stowmarket and Bury St Edmunds.

This airy square Georgian building with thirteen acres of garden, parkland and trees, stands on a hill overlooking the village of Wetherden in
rural Suffolk. The rooms are high-ceilinged and spacious and attractively
furnished. There is a dining room (with a beautiful Italian monks' table
dating from the early 18th century which interestingly has been lowered
a few inches – the monks ate standing up), three bedrooms individually
decorated, a comfortable study-cum-television room with a log-burning
stove – and for bookworms, over 3,000 books.
   No dinner is provided but Pamela Bowden serves a hearty breakfast
which includes a choice of a wide variety of cereals and traditional
English cooked dishes. For lunch and the evening meal there are several
recommended local pubs and restaurants.

Easily Accessible: Situated a mile from the A45 and near to the M11 and
A12, it is ideally placed for touring East Anglia. The countryside is fairly
flat but a day trip to the coast provides some interest for walkers. Also,
the Stour Valley, on the border of Suffolk and Essex, made famous by
the painter John Constable, is well-loved by walkers and bird-watchers.
Bury St Edmunds is a picturesque historical town with many interesting
buildings including the remains of an abbey founded in 945 and Moyse's
Hall, a 12th-century mansion now a museum of local history. In May
you can visit its arts festival, and in September, it plays host to a famous

antiques fair. Nearby Ickworth House, built in the late 18th century, has fine state rooms and a deer park and formal gardens. Newmarket, famous for its horse-racing, and Lavenham, a very pretty town lined with half-timbered buildings, are within a short drive. Cambridge has a wealth of beautiful architecture, museums, and punting on the river.

Sequoia House Private Hotel

51 Shipston Road
Stratford-upon-Avon
Warwickshire
CV37 7LN

Bed and Breakfast only
Sorry, no pets
5-bedroom cottage annexe

☎ Stratford (0789) 68852

Philip and Jean Evans

Off A34 near Clopton Bridge

Just a few minutes from the Royal Shakespeare Theatre (the car park is just 500 yards away), this typically Victorian house takes its name from the sequoia tree that graces the pretty lawned gardens. The spacious rooms have large bay windows and cast-iron fireplaces with marble surrounds, and are furnished in Laura Ashley fabrics and antiques. The lounge has an open fire and bar. Of the twenty-one bedrooms, seventeen are spacious with private facilities, and the remaining four are attic rooms with shared bathrooms.

Tasty snacks, traditional afternoon teas, lunches and suppers with wine are all offered. For a full-blown meal Stratford has numerous pubs and restaurants to choose from – 600 yards from the hotel is the excellent Shepherds Restaurant and 100 yards from the garden gate lies The Water Rat, a highly acclaimed café-brasserie.

Easily Accessible: If you are not keen on Shakespeare, Stratford may not be the place for you – nearly everywhere you go you will be reminded that this was his birthplace. Indeed you can visit the house where he was born, see one of his plays at the Royal Shakespeare Theatre, or a contemporary performance at the Swan Theatre, see an exhibition of his life and times at the Shakespeare Centre and visit the picturesque home of his wife, Anne Hathaway. If you want to escape the Great Bard for a while, take a day trip to the beautiful Cotswolds to nose around its idyllic villages and walk in the beautiful scenery. Blenheim Palace, the magnificently grand birthplace of Winston Churchill, with 2,000 acres of grounds landscaped by Capability Brown, is 35 miles away. Warwick Castle, only 10 miles away, is a splendid 14th-century stronghold with

Madame Tussaud's waxworks inside. Coventry and its controversial cathedral is 20 miles away.

Nearby Activities: boating, golf, swimming pool,squash, sauna, solarium.

The Hundred House Hotel

Bridgnorth Road
Norton
Shifnal
Shropshire
TF11 9EE

☎ Norton (095271) 353

Henry, David and Sylvia Phillips

On A442 (Kidderminster Rd) 3 miles from M54 (exit 4)

A wealth of fascinating history lies within the very name of the Hundred House Hotel which refers to the ancient subdivisions of the shires of England into areas known as 'hundreds'. In the courtyard, a 14th-century half-timbered and thatched roof building was for many centuries the local courthouse where justice was meted out. The remains of stocks and the whipping post serve as uncomfortable reminders of the not so good old days.

The main building is Georgian with very attractive exposed brick-work, beamed ceilings and oak panelling. The décor is very pretty; period furniture, lots of wood, patchwork and brass – everything one feels a country inn should be. The cosy dining room has a lovely Jacobean fireplace, and a separate bar is decorated with an array of dried herbs grown in the herb garden. The ten bedrooms are beautifully furnished, some have half-tester beds and all have en suite bathrooms and colour TVs.

The restaurant is open for breakfast, lunch and dinner. The food is traditional English with some French cuisine. Herbs come from the garden; game, meat and fish are locally produced.

Easily Accessible: The area affords many beautiful walks: a couple of miles from the hotel is the Severn Valley walk along the track of an old railway from Bridgnorth to Coalport and Ironbridge. Further afield are the Malvern and Clee Hills, Wenlock Edge with numerous paths and trails and the Wrekin, a famous local landmark with panoramic views and an Iron Age Fort. At Ironbridge, 7 miles away, you can see the World Heritage Site. In the interesting town of Bridgnorth, also 7 miles away, you can take a ride on the Severn Valley Railway. Twenty-five miles away is Shrewsbury, an ancient town with many historical buildings, where you can visit the castle, Rowley's House Museum with Roman remains, and Clive House, an 18th-century residence which houses an interesting collection of local paintings and porcelain.

Local Activities: walks, golf, swimming, ice-skating, tennis, squash, fishing.

White Lion Hotel
High Street
Upton-upon-Severn
Worcester
WR8 0HJ

Conference room available

☎ Upton–upon Severn (06846) 2551

Robert and Bridget Withey

Five minutes drive from M5/M50

The elegant Georgian facade of this small hotel hides its earlier origins as a Tudor coaching inn. The building dates back to 1510 and, whilst it has been sympathetically modernised, it retains much of its original character. It was the Inn of Fielding's *Tom Jones*, and the 'Wild Goose Room' and 'Rose Room' referred to in the novel have been preserved. The bedrooms are attractive and have been individually designed, with specific themes in mind, such as the Tudor Room, the Georgian Room and the Chinese Room, using fabrics, furnishings and paintings to create just the right style. One bedroom has an original four-poster bed; all have private bathrooms and colour TV. There is a comfortable beamed bar lounge where snacks are served.

The beamed Burgundy Restaurant offers a table d'hôte and à la carte menu using fresh local produce. A house speciality is the Royal Double Gloucester omelette filled with smoked salmon.

Easily Accessible: Upton-upon-Severn is a very pretty town, nestling at the foot of the Malvern Hills, beside the River Severn. Its history goes back to Saxon times, and it contains several interesting historical buildings, and a peaceful marina, from which you can take a river cruise. There are numerous walks on the ancient Malvern Hills (the oldest rock in England), and many are fairly easy and suitable for a family outing, yet yield superb panoramic views. The historic town of Great Malvern, 7 miles away, came into prominence through its spa waters in the 18th and 19th centuries, although its origins as several disconnected villages are much earlier; indeed its beautiful priory church was completed by craftsmen in 1460. There are further walks to be enjoyed in the Cotswolds, 20 miles away, and the Forest of Dean, 25 miles away. Cheltenham, Worcester and Hereford racecourses are all within easy reach. Worcester, 10 miles away, has a splendid Norman cathedral, some attractive Tudor buildings, a carnival in July and an arts festival in August.

Local Activities: walks, coarse-fishing, golf, river cruises.

Soulton Hall   No smoking in bedrooms
Nr Wem
Shropshire
SY4 5RS

☎ Wem (0939) 32786

Mrs A. Ashton

On B5065, two miles from Wem.

As one approaches this house one cannot fail to find it incredibly impressive – a large mansion, constructed of Tudor brick. One half expects a ruffled, doubleted figure to emerge from its grand doorway. It is not surprising to learn that the 'Manor of Suleton' is listed in the Domesday Book. You can see the moated site of the castle from the present hall. The interior has beams, panelled walls, and inglenook fireplaces. All the rooms are carefully furnished in keeping with the rest of the house. present hall. The interior has beams, panelled walls, and inglenook fireplaces. All the rooms are carefully furnished in keeping with the rest of the house. The four bedrooms are equipped with colour TV. There is an attractive walled garden, fifty acres of tranquil woods, farmland, and over a mile of brook and riverside for guests to enjoy at their leisure.

Dinner is provided as long as it is requested the morning of the day you dine. A full five courses are served, and good use is made of fresh local and home-grown produce.

Easily Accessible: Wem is a small market town with a 14th-century church and a castle mound. William Hazlitt, the essayist, grew up here. The border with North Wales is only 5 miles away. There are many local walks, including the Hawkestone Hills, just 2 miles away. The boundry of the estate itself constitutes an eight mile walk. At the nearby village of Weston, you can see the old stocks. Hodnet Hall has sixty acres of gardens. Its village is most attractive, with mostly black and white buildings. Shrewsbury, 12 miles away, is a medieval town once built on its wool trade, and peppered with Tudor, Georgian and Queen Anne architecture.

Local Activities: walks, golf, fishing, horse-riding, boating, swimming, bird-watching.

Postlip House

Winchcombe
Gloucestershire
GL54 5AH

Children over 12 welcome
Sorry, no pets

☎ Cheltenham (0242) 602390

Mary and Paul Sparks

In Cotswold countryside, 7 miles from Cheltenham

On the outskirts of the 1000-year-old village of Winchcombe, Postlip House, a 19th-century stone manor house, stands in eight acres of wooded grounds surrounded by the beautiful Cotswolds. The views are outstanding. The main house has two bedrooms with bathrooms en suite, a lounge with TV, a large mullioned windowed kitchen where breakfast is taken, and an elegant dining room with views of the garden. The outbuildings, once stables and tack rooms, have been converted into superior self-catering cottages with a meal service from the main house if required.

Your hosts have a wealth of experience in catering and the evening meal is prepared to a very high standard making good use of fresh vegetables, fruit and herbs from the garden. Jams, chutneys and marmalade are home-made.

Easily Accessible: Winchcombe is a charming town with many 16th-century buildings and a fine church containing an altar cloth embroidered by Catherine of Aragon. Two miles away lies Sudley Castle where Henry VIII's widow, Catherine Parr, once lived; she was buried in the castle chapel. Cheltenham Spa, a fine Regency town, lies 6 miles to the south and is enjoyable for its shops, architecture and nearby racecourse. There are famous horse trials at Badminton, 38 miles away. Take a day trip to Bath, Stratford, Oxford or Winchester. Walkers will enjoy the Cotswold Way, which runs for 102 miles from Chipping Campden to Bath and which passes through Winchcombe. There are many places of interest *en route* including the picturesque and much-visited village

THE NORTH

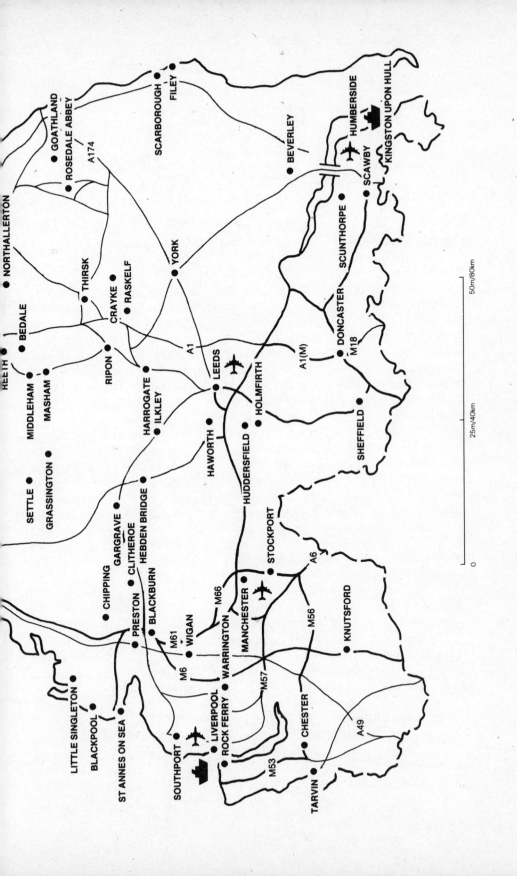

The North

Covering the counties of: Cheshire, Cleveland, Cumbria, Durham, Humberside, Lancashire, Greater Manchester, Merseyside, Northumberland, Tyne & Wear and Yorkshire.

The North of England boasts some of the most magnificent scenery in the whole of Great Britain. Its *pièce de résistance* must be the Lake District National Park in Cumbria – the largest National Park in Great Britain. It is an impressive landscape of high mountains encircling quiet lakes, of green hills latticed with crumbling stone walls, and of high mountain passes with breathtaking views and ancient routes. The Yorkshire Dales and moors come a close second – the former with their limestone hills, remote farms and waterfalls; the latter, a landscape of heather-clad undulations cut by ribbon streams. Both the east and west coasts are blessed with miles and miles of sandy beaches. Blackpool on the north-west coast is the main resort: a lively town, it literally dazzles every autumn when its illuminations are switched on. Its piers, tram-cars, donkey rides and tower (once the tallest building in Great Britain) are famous (or maybe infamous!).

Many of the North's major cities are immediately associated with heavy industry. However, to imagine that this is the whole story is completely wrong. For some, like York and Durham, are steeped in history and remain largely unaltered by recent events. Both are fascinating, picturesque cities, with equally magnificent cathedrals. York Minster is a gracious medieval building; Durham Cathedral is a grand building of Norman origin standing on a high rock over the River Wear, and it dominates the skyline.

The North East is particularly rich in grand historic houses, castles, and ruined abbeys. In North Yorkshire, there are the romantic and eerie ruins of the abbeys of Rievaulx, Fountains, and Jervaulx; the magnificent Robert Adam rooms of Harewood House in West Yorkshire are outstanding; and Castle Howard in North Yorkshire must be one of the most palatial stately homes in the country. The North West, too, has its fair share of great houses, including Houghton Tower in Lancashire, a 16th-century battlemented house; and Norton Priory in Cheshire, a ruined Augustinian priory which originated in the 13th century.

And what of the artistic and literary heritage of the North? The Brontë family lived austerely in the remote West Yorkshire village of Haworth (house open to the public); Wordsworth, Ruskin and Beatrix Potter lived in and loved the Lake District; the composer, Frederick

Delius, hailed from Cumbria; and in a very different vein, one of the most popular groups of all time, the Beatles, emerged from the lively musical scene in Liverpool. Leaving behind the arts, one of the North's most famous sons, Captain Cook, was born in Cleveland. This great seafarer discovered Australia and his ship, the *Endeavour*, was built in Whitby harbour.

Of all Great Britain's Roman remains, the North lays claim to the finest – Hadrian's Wall. This defensive fortification, built by the Romans to guard the northern frontier of their empire, once stretched for 73 miles across the width of northern England. Today, although broken in many places, it still has the power to enthral and amaze.

Regional Tourist Boards:
Cumbria – Ashleigh, Holly Road, Windermere, Cumbria LA23 2AQ
Tel: (09662) 4444
Northumbria – Aykley Heads, Durham DH1 5UX
Tel: (091 38) 46905
North West – The Last Drop Village, Bromley Cross, Bolton, Lancashire BL7 9PZ
Tel: (0204) 591511
Yorkshire & Humberside – 312 Tadcaster Road, York YO2 2HF
Tel: (0904) 707961

ALLENDALE   THORNLEY HOUSE
Thornley Gate, Allendale, Nr Hexham, Northumberland NE47 9NH. *Tel*: Allendale (0434) 683255. *Host*: Eileen Finn.
Rates: A/B   Vouchers accepted.
  Cosy house in spacious grounds, 1 mile from picturesque Allendale. In Northumberland's National Park. Lovely views. Steinway grand piano. Golf course and riding school nearby. Historic area, castles and Hadrian's Wall. Welcome to bring own wine. Christmas breaks available.

ALNMOUTH   BLUE DOLPHINS
11 Riverside Road, Alnmouth, Northumberland NE66 2SD. *Tel*: Alnwick (0665) 830893. *Hosts*: Jack & Joan Davidson.
Rates: B
(See page 175 for description)

AMBLESIDE   KENT HOUSE
Lake Road, Ambleside, Cumbria LA22 0AD. *Tel*: Ambleside (0966) 33279.
Hosts: John & Betty Heaver.

Rates: A/B   Vouchers accepted.
Pleasant Victorian house occupying commanding position off main road, overlooking quaint and unspoilt village. Few mins walk village centre and Lake Windermere with all watersports and lake steamer. Fell walking, golf, riding, tennis.

AMBLESIDE   RIVERSIDE LODGE COUNTRY HOUSE
Rothay Bridge, Ambleside, Cumbria LA22 0EH. *Tel*: Ambleside (05394) 34208. *Hosts*: Alan & Gillian Rhone.
Rates: B/C
Small family-run Georgian country house hotel in idyllic riverside setting. Historic associations with Bonnie Prince Charlie. Near Ambleside –'Heart of the English Lake District'. Children over 10 welcome. Sorry, no pets. No smoking in bedrooms.

APPLEBY   THE ROYAL OAK INN
Bongate, Appleby-in-Westmorland, Cumbria CA16 6UN. *Tel*: Appleby (07683) 51463. *Hosts*: Hilary & Colin Cheyne.
Rates: C
Old black-and-white coaching inn on south approach to Appleby from A66. Proprietors proud of their interesting food, attractive rooms and welcoming atmosphere. Golf, fishing, walking. Dogs welcome. Scotch Corner 38 miles. Penrith 14. M6 exit 38, 14 miles.

BEDALE (Arrathorne)   ELMFIELD COUNTRY HOUSE
Arrathorne, Bedale, North Yorkshire DL8 1NE. *Tel*: Bedale (0677) 50558. *Hosts*: Edith & Jim Lillie.
Rates: B   Vouchers accepted.
(See page 176 for description)

BELLINGHAM (Nr Hexham)   RIVERDALE HALL HOTEL
Bellingham, Hexham, Northumberland NE48 2JT. *Tel*: Bellingham (0660) 20254. *Hosts*: The Cocker Family.
Rates: C/D   Vouchers accepted.
Country house hotel in 5 acres with river frontage. Indoor heated pool, sauna, picturesque cricket pitch. Salmon and trout fishing. Golf. On Pennine Way, near Hadrian's Wall, 8 miles Kielder Water with wide range watersports. 18 miles Hexham on B6320 off A68 or A69. Four 4-posters available.

BELLINGHAM   (A 'no smoking' house)   WESTFIELD HOUSE
Bellingham, Nr Hexham, Northumberland NE48 2DP. *Tel*: Hexham (0434) 220340. *Hosts*: David & June Minchin.
Rates: A/B   Vouchers accepted.
Warm, spacious and friendly house in a quiet town surrounded by woods, moorland and forests. Stately homes, Hadrian's Wall and forts, Kielder Water

and Northumberland National Park nearby. On edge of village on Hexham Road. Reduced rates Nov-Mar.

BEVERLEY NUMBER ONE
1 Woodlands, Beverley, East Yorkshire HU17 8BT. *Tel*: Hull (0482) 862752. *Hosts*: Neil & Sarah King.
Rates: A Vouchers accepted.
  Interesting Victorian house in quiet conservation area, yet only 2 mins walk from centre of charming historic market town. Hull 7 miles, Humber Bridge 9. Easy run York 30 miles. Home-cooking. Wine cellar. Library.

BLACKBURN (Whalley) MYTTON FOLD FARM HOTEL
Langho, Whalley, Lancashire BB6 8AB. *Tel*: Blackburn (0254) 240662. *Fax*: 0254 248119. *Hosts*: Frank & Lilian Hargreaves.
Rates: C/D
  Family-owned and run farm hotel set in 100 acres of farmland yet conveni-ent for Preston, Burnley, Accrington and Clitheroe. Proprietors are proud of their reputation for a warm welcome and excellent food. Two 4-poster rooms available.

BLACKPOOL THE BRABYNS HOTEL
Shaftesbury Avenue, North Shore, Blackpool, Lancashire FY2 9QQ. *Tel*: Blackpool (0253) 54263/52163. *Hosts*: Cedric & Maureen Barker.
Rates: C/D Vouchers accepted.
  Friendly, family-operated hotel, just off the promenade close to the cliffs in quiet residential North Shore area. Restaurant with 'old world' charm, varied menu incl vegetarian dishes. Easy access to M55 3 miles. Ideal touring centre for rural Fylde, Lakeland and Yorkshire Dales. Own parking.

BLACKPOOL SUNRAY HOTEL
42 Knowle Avenue, Blackpool, Lancashire FY2 9TQ. *Tel*: Blackpool (0253) 51937. *Hosts*: Jean & John Dodgson.
Rates: B/C
(See page 177 for description)

BRAMPTON OAKWOOD PARK HOTEL
Longtown Road, Brampton, Cumbria CA8 2AP. *Tel*: Brampton Cumbria (06977) 2436. *Hosts*: Wendy & Ian Phillips.
Rates: B
  Spacious and comfortable Victorian residence in 10 acres grounds up long drive. Hard tennis court. ½ mile from town on Longtown road A6071. 1 mile Hadrian's Wall. Bargain breaks all year. Cottage annexe.

CALDBECK HIGH GREENRIGG HOUSE
Caldbeck, Wigton, Cumbria CA7 8HD. *Tel*: Caldbeck (06998) 430. *Hosts*: Fran & Robin Jacobs.

Rates: B   Vouchers accepted.
(See page 177 for description)

CARLISLE (Heads Nook)   CROFTLANDS
Heads Nook, Carlisle, Cumbria CA4 9AF. *Tel*: Carlisle (0228) 60437. *Hosts*:
Hugh & Ann Lawson.
Rates: B
>Comfortable stone house on edge of village. Hadrian's Wall, Eden Valley,
the fells all nearby. All rooms en suite or with private bathroom. Electric
blankets. Children over 7 welcome. Billiards room. Log fires. Kennels and
stabling available. Phone for directions. M6 and Carlisle 4 miles.

CARLISLE (Rockcliffe)   DEMESNE HOUSE
Rockcliffe, Carlisle, Cumbria CA6 4BW. *Tel*: Rockcliffe (022874) 280. *Host*:
Peggy Rowcliffe.
Rates: B   Vouchers accepted.
(See page 178 for description)

CHESTER   BROOKSIDE HOTEL
Brook Lane, Chester, Cheshire CH2 2AN. *Tel*: Chester (0244) 381943. *Hosts*:
William, Ian and Betty McConnell.
Rates: C
>Attractive and comfortable family-run hotel in residential area. Exceptional
value, being only 7 mins walk to city centre with its ancient walls. Off Liver-
pool Road, nr Northgate Arena. Sauna, solarium. Garden award winner.

CHESTERFIELD (Spinkhill)   PARK HALL HOTEL AND UPLANDS
MANOR RESTAURANT
Spinkhill, Sheffield S31 9YD. *Tel*: Eckington (0246) 434897. *Fax*: 0246 436282.
Hosts: The Clarke Family
Rates: C/D   Vouchers accepted.
>Delightful 16th-century manor house in extensive grounds. Comfortable
and friendly atmosphere. 4-poster available. Squash, golf nearby. 1 mile
from M1 (junc 30). 7 miles from A1. Chesterfield 7 miles, Sheffield 8. Phone
for directions. Children welcome. Sorry, no pets.

CHIPPING (Nr Longridge)   GIBBON BRIDGE COUNTRY HOUSE
AND RESTAURANT
Gibbon Bridge, Chipping, Lancashire PR3 2TQ. *Tel*: Chipping (0995) 61456.
Fax: 0995 61277 *Hosts*: Janet & Margaret Simpson.
Rates: D
>Lovely comfortable modern conversion of large barn, set in very attractive
garden with stream. Fine views over Pendle and Jeffrey hills. 4-poster
available. Golf, museums, 'Relax & Be Driven'. M6 exit 32 to Longridge.
'Britain in Bloom' award. BTA commended. Sorry, no pets.

CLITHEROE (Harrop Fold)   HARROP FOLD COUNTRY
FARMHOUSE HOTEL
Bolton-by-Bowland, Clitheroe, Lancashire RB7 4PJ. *Tel*: Bolton-by-Bowland

(02007) 600. *Hosts*: Peter, Victoria & Andrew Wood.
Rates: C   Vouchers accepted.
(See page 179 for description)

COCKERMOUTH   SUNDAWN GUEST HOUSE

Carlisle Road, Bridekirk, Cockermouth, Cumbria CA13 0PA. *Tel*:
Cockermouth (0900) 822384. *Hosts*: Bob & Pauline Hodge.
Rates: A   Vouchers accepted.
   Spacious early Victorian family home with garden and paddock. Beautiful
   panoramic views over lakeland, fells and historic market town. Walking,
   fishing, touring centre. Wordsworth country. Off A595 to Carlisle 25 miles.
   Home-cooking. Sun lounge and lounge/dining room.

CORBRIDGE   THE RIVERSIDE HOTEL

Main Street, Corbridge, Northumberland NE45 5LE. *Tel*: Corbridge (043471)
2942. *Hosts*: Harry & Judy Fawcett.
Rates: B/C
(See page 180 for description)

CORNHILL-ON-TWEED   THE COACH HOUSE

Crookham, Cornhill-on-Tweed, Northumberland TD12 4TD. *Tel*:
Crookham (089 082) 293. *Hosts*: Jamie & Lynne Anderson.
Rates: B/C   Vouchers accepted.
(See page 181 for description)

CRAYKE (Nr York)   CRAYKE CASTLE

Crayke, York YO6 4TA. *Tel*: Easingwold (0347) 22285. *Hosts*: Peter & Belle
Hepworth.
Rates: D   Vouchers accepted.
(See page 182 for description)

DONCASTER (Skellow)   (A 'no smoking' house)   CANDA

Hampole Balk Lane, Skellow, Doncaster DN6 8LF. *Tel*: Doncaster (0302)
724028. *Hosts*: Kath & Wally Norton.
Rates: B
   Warm and comfortable modern house adjacent to A1 (access north and
   south). Ideal for halfway stop London/Scotland, 10 mins Doncaster centre.
   Sheffield and Leeds 15 miles. No evening meals but excellent pubs nearby.
   Good parking. Sauna.

ENNERDALE BRIDGE   THE SHEPHERD'S ARMS HOTEL

Ennerdale Bridge, Nr Cockermouth, Cumbria CA23 3AR. *Tel*: Lamplugh
(0946) 861249. *Hosts*: David & Dorothy Whitfield Bott.
Rates: B   Vouchers accepted.
   Old, traditional Lakeland house, unspoilt village in Ennerdale valley. Lake,
   river, trout and salmon fishing. A66 to Cockermouth (10 miles), turn left

to A5086. After Lamplugh turn left at signpost. Home-cooking; local fish and game. Winter breaks available.

FILEY ABBOT'S LEIGH

7 Rutland Street, Filey, North Yorkshire YO14 9JA. *Tel*: Scarborough (0723) 513334. *Hosts*: Mike & Pat Carter.

Rates: A Vouchers accepted.

Friendly, comfortable, warm house in a quiet street 200 yards from sea and cliffs. Sailing, walking and bird watching nearby. Ground-floor room available. All rooms with bathroom en suite. Home-grown produce. 5-course dinners. Castle Howard and North Yorks moors within easy reach. Sorry, no pets.

GARGRAVE ESHTON GRANGE

Gargrave, Nr Skipton, North Yorkshire BD23 3QE. *Tel*: Gargrave (0756) 749383. *Hosts*: Terry & Judy Shelmerdine.

Rates: A/B

18th-century farmhouse, attractive garden, open log fires and antiques in 20 acres of beautiful Dales National Park. Shetland pony stud and sheep. Healthy appetites catered for. Lovely views and walks. Phone for directions. Dinner by arrangement only. Sorry, no pets.

GOATHLAND WHITFIELD HOUSE HOTEL

Darnholm, Goathland, Whitby, North Yorkshire YO22 5LA. *Tel*: Whitby (0947) 86215. *Hosts*: John & Pauline Lusher.

Rates: A/B Vouchers accepted.

(See page 183 for description)

GRASMERE OAK BANK HOTEL

Broadgate, Grasmere, Cumbria LA22 9TA. *Tel*: Grasmere (09665) 217. *Hosts*: Sharon & Attilio Savasi and Pat Smith.

Rates: D Vouchers accepted.

(See page 184 for description)

GRASSINGTON GREENWAYS

Wharfeside Avenue, Threshfield, Grassington, Skipton, North Yorkshire BD23 5BS. *Tel*: Grassington (0756) 752598. *Hosts*: Mike & Jill Popplewell.

Rates: B Vouchers accepted.

(See page 185 for description)

GREENHEAD HOLMHEAD

Hadrian's Wall, Greenhead, via Carlisle CA6 7HY. *Tel*: Gilsland (06972) 402 (will change during 1990 to (06977) 47402). *Hosts*: Brian & Pauline Staff.

Rates: A/B Vouchers accepted.

Modernised farmhouse on the most spectacular part of Hadrian's Wall and on the Pennine Way. Providing home-cooking and friendly service. Hadrian's Wall information service for guests and guided tours. The longest breakfast menu in the world. Reduced rates for 2 nights or more. Sorry, no pets.

GREENLAW   PURVES HALL HOTEL
Greenlaw, Berwickshire TD10 6UJ. *Tel*: Leitholm (089 084) 558. *Hosts*: Sheila
& Brian Everett.
Rates: C/D
   Friendly, elegant small Edwardian hotel in 10 acres of park and woodlands.
   Heated outdoor swimming pool, tennis court, putting green, croquet
   lawn. Log fires. Stabling available. Fishing and many golf courses nearby.
   Edinburgh 1 hr, Berwick ½ hr.

HAMSTERLEY   (A 'no smoking' house)   GROVE HOUSE
Hamsterley Forest, Redford, Nr Bishop Auckland, Co Durham DL13 3NL.
Tel: Witton-le-Wear (038888) 203. *Hosts*: Helene & Russell Close.
Rates: B   Vouchers accepted.
(See page 186 for description)

HARROGATE   STONEY LEA
13 Spring Grove, Springfield Ave, Harrogate, North Yorkshire HG1 2HS.
Tel: Harrogate (0423) 501524. *Hosts*: Geoff & Barbara Cargill.
Rates: B
   Attractive Victorian house situated at the end of a quiet cul-de-sac, in the
   centre of town within 4 mins walk of Conference Centre, theatre, gardens
   and local amenities. Located directly behind Hotel Majestic. Evening meal
   by arrangement. Sorry, no pets.

HARROGATE   THE WHITE HOUSE HOTEL
Park Parade, Harrogate, North Yorkshire HG1 5AH. *Tel*: (0423) 501388.
Hosts: Anne & Edward Bamforth.
Rates: C/D
   Delightful small hotel, overlooking the famous 'Stray', extensive parkland
   in picturesque and quiet area. The Grade II listed building is a charming 19th-
   century copy of a Venetian villa. Harrogate is an exhibition and conference
   town near beautiful Brontë country. 4-poster available.

HAWES   COCKETT'S HOTEL
Market Place, Hawes, North Yorkshire DL8 3RD. *Tel*: Hawes (09697) 312.
Hosts: John Oddi & Jacquie Bryan.
Rates: B/C   Vouchers accepted.
   Listed 17th-century stone-built house with original beams, in old market
   town in 'Herriot' country. Dale walks, pony-trekking, fishing. Two 4-poster
   beds available. English and French cuisine, extensive wine list. Colour TV
   all rooms.

HAWES   ROOKHURST GEORGIAN COUNTRY HOUSE
Gaye, Hawes, Wensleydale, North Yorkshire DL8 3RT. *Tel*: Hawes (0969)
667312. *Host*: Mrs Van Der Steen.
Rates: D
   Tranquil, award-winning country house, magnificent Dales National Park.
   Superb cuisine, fine wines. Relax in Wensleydale's most beautiful bedrooms.

All bedrooms en suite. Licensed. Antique 4-posters and half-testers available. No smoking in bedrooms. Winter breaks available. Home-cooking. Sorry, no children or pets. Brochure available.

HAWORTH   MOORFIELD GUEST HOUSE

80 West Lane, Haworth, Keighley BD22 8EN. *Tel*: Haworth (0535) 43689. *Hosts*: Pat & Barry Hargreaves. *Rates*: A   Vouchers accepted.

Detached Victorian residence situated between Haworth village and the moors. Splendid views to front and rear. Within walking distance of the Brontë Parsonage and the famous Main Street. Colour TV all rooms, bar, car park.

HAYDON BRIDGE   THE ANCHOR HOTEL

Haydon Bridge, Hexham, Northumberland NE47 6AB. *Tel*: Haydon Bridge (043484) 227. *Hosts*: John & Vivienne Dees. *Rates*: C

Old coaching inn on river bank, dating back to 1422. Just off A69. Hexham 7 miles and midway between Newcastle and Carlisle. Hadrian's Wall Roman camps 4 miles. On edge of Northumberland National Park. Convenient for Kielder Water.

HEBDEN BRIDGE   HEBDEN LODGE HOTEL

New Road, Hebden Bridge, West Yorkshire HX7 8AD. *Tel*: Halifax (0422) 845272. *Hosts*: Mr & Mrs Nicholas. *Rates*: C/D   Vouchers accepted.

Victorian house with good modern facilities overlooking Rochdale Canal and new marina in 'The Pennine Centre' in historic weaving town. Halifax 7 miles, Todmorden 5. M62 exit 21 or 22, then A646. Vegetarians and vegans catered for. Sorry, no pets.

HELTON (Nr Penrith)   BECKFOOT HOUSE

Helton, Nr Penrith, Cumbria CA10 2QB. *Tel*: Bampton (09313) 241. *Hosts*: Lesley & David White. *Rates*: B   Vouchers accepted.

Spacious, comfortable country house in 3 acres of grounds in peaceful and tranquil Lake District National Park. From south M6, exit 39, to Shap, then through Bampton, before Helton. From north, M6, exit 40.

HOLMFIRTH   (A 'no smoking' house)   HOLME CASTLE COUNTRY HOTEL

Holme Village, Nr Holmfirth, West Yorkshire HD7 1QG. *Tel*: Holmfirth (0484) 686764. *Hosts*: Jill Hayfield & John Sandford. *Rates*: B/C   Vouchers accepted.

(See page 187 for description)

HUDDERSFIELD   (A 'no smoking' house)   ELM CREST GUEST HOUSE

2 Queen's Road, Edgerton, Huddersfield HD2 2AG. *Tel*: Huddersfield (0484)

530990. *Hosts*: Derek & Margaret Gee.

Rates: B/C

Spacious, large Victorian property overlooking Clayton Fields, Floodlit car park, 10 mins walk town centre. Off A629 Halifax Road, 1½ miles M62 exit 24, M1 exit 38. Reduced rates for children. Interesting historic town, handy for touring Yorkshire. Sorry, no pets.

HUDDERSFIELD WELLFIELD HOUSE HOTEL
33 New Hey Road, Marsh, Huddersfield HD3 4AL. *Tel*: Huddersfield (0484) 25776. *Hosts*: John & Paulaine Whitehead.
Rates: C   Vouchers accepted.
(See page 188 for description)

ILKLEY MOORVIEW HOUSE HOTEL
104 Skipton Road, Ilkley, West Yorkshire LS29 9HE. *Tel*: Ilkley (0943) 600156.
Hosts: Jean & David Cockburn.
Rates: B/C   Vouchers accepted.

Comfortable Victorian villa overlooking River Wharfe and moors. Convenient for Brontë country, Bolton Abbey and walking on the lovely Dales Way. Wonderful views. Golf, fishing, boating, tennis, bowling. Sorry, no pets.

INGLEBY GREENHOW MANOR HOUSE FARM
Ingleby Greenhow, Great Ayton, North Yorkshire TS9 6RB. *Tel*: Gt Ayton (0642) 722384. *Hosts*: Margaret & Martin Bloom.
Rates: C (incl dinner)   Vouchers accepted.
(See page 189 for description)

KESWICK THE QUEEN'S HOTEL
Main Street, Keswick, Cumbria CA12 5JF. *Tel*: Keswick (07687) 73333. *Fax*: 07687 71144 *Hosts*: The Williams Family.
Rates: D   Vouchers accepted.

Originally an old posting house in centre of attractive Lakeland market town, surrounded by beautiful countryside. Central for Penrith, Carlisle, Workington, Whitehaven and Windermere. Sorry, no pets.

KIRKBY LONSDALE THE COURTYARD
Fairbank, Kirkby Lonsdale, Cumbria LA6 2AZ. *Tel*: Kirkby Lonsdale (05242) 71613. *Hosts*: Gill & Timothy Grey.
Rates: B/C   Vouchers accepted.
(See page 190 for description)

KIRKOSWALD (Nr Penrith) PROSPECT HILL HOTEL
Kirkoswald, Penrith, Cumbria CA10 1ER. *Tel*: Lazonby (076 883) 500. *Hosts*: John & Isa Henderson.
Rates: B/C   Vouchers accepted.

Most appealing 18th-century converted farm-building complex; panoramic views of unspoilt valley. 9 miles north of Penrith off M6 and A6 to B6413,

13 miles Hadrian's Wall. At Kirkoswald, take Armathwaite road for 1 mile. Sorry, no pets (kennel available).

KNUTSFORD LONGVIEW HOTEL
51-55, Manchester Road, Knutsford, Cheshire WA16 0LX. *Tel*: Knutsford (0565) 2119. *Hosts*: Pauline & Stephen West.
Rates: B
Warm and comfortable Victorian houses in this historic market town with cobbled streets overlooking Knutsford Common. Traditional décor with antiques. Full dinner or supper available. Cellar bar. Ample car parking. Easy reach M6 (junc 19).

LANCASTER (Capernwray) NEW CAPERNWRAY FARM
Capernwray, Carnforth, Lancashire LA6 1AD. *Tel*: Carnforth (0524) 734284.
Hosts: Sally & Peter Townend.
Rates: C   Vouchers accepted.
(See page 191 for description)

LANCASTER (Melling) MELLING HALL HOTEL
Melling, via Carnforth, Nr Lancaster LA6 2RA. *Tel*: Hornby (05242) 21298.
Hosts: Jim & Christine Ross.
Rates: C   Vouchers accepted.
Comfortable and attractive 17th-century inn with views over picturesque Lune valley. Ideal for touring Yorkshire Dales, Lake District and the Trough of Bowland, M6 exit 34 to A683. Lancaster 8 miles, Kirkby Lonsdale 4.

LEEDS PINEWOOD HOTEL
78 Potternewton Lane, Leeds, West Yorkshire LS7 3LW. *Tel*: Leeds (0532) 622561. *Hosts*: Vic & Liz Heffer.
Rates: B
Comfortable detached Victorian house with warm, friendly atmosphere, set well back in residential area 2 miles north of city centre. Close to bus routes. Off A61 Harrogate Road. 8 miles Leeds/Bradford airport. No dinner at weekends. Sorry, no pets.

LITTLE SINGLETON (Nr Blackpool) MAINS HALL COUNTRY HOTEL
Mains Lane, Little Singleton, Nr Blackpool, Lancashire FY6 7LE. *Tel*: Poulton-le-Fylde (0253) 885130. *Hosts*: Robert & Beryl Owen.
Rates: B/C
(See page 192 for description)

MANCHESTER NEW CENTRAL HOTEL
144-146 Heywood Street, Manchester M8 7PD. *Tel*: Manchester (061) 205 2169. *Host*: Alan Mills.
Rates: B
Selected for its important location, a double-fronted house with friendly relaxed atmosphere in residential area 1 mile city centre and Victoria station.

Opposite gardens. Airport 9 miles. Mon–Thurs, grills only. Children over 5 welcome. Sorry, no pets.

MANCHESTER (Salford) HAZELDEAN HOTEL
467 Bury New Road, Kersal, Salford, Manchester M7 ONX. *Tel*: Manchester (061) 792 6667. *Fax*: 061 792 6668. *Host*: I.D.Whittle.
Rates: D Vouchers accepted.
   Nicely renovated Victorian mansion in slightly elevated position, residential area of Salford. Off A56 2½ miles city centre, 9 miles Manchester airport. M62, exit 17, 2 miles towards central Manchester.

MASHAM BANK VILLA
Masham, Ripon, North Yorkshire HG4 4DB. *Tel*: Ripon (0765) 89605. *Hosts*: Anton van der Horst & Philip Gill.
Rates: B
   Comfortable stone-built Georgian house in ¾-acre terraced gardens overlooking River Ure. On A6108, 9 miles north of Ripon in lower Wensleydale. Dinner by arrangment only. Imaginative home-cooking, own and local produce. BTA commended.

MIDDLEHAM GREYSTONES
Market Place, Middleham, North Yorkshire DL8 4NR. *Tel*: Wensleydale (0969) 22016. *Hosts*: Keith & Frances Greenwood.
Rates: B Vouchers accepted.
(See page 193 for description)

MOSEDALE (A 'no smoking' house) SWINESIDE
Swineside, Mosedale, Nr Penrith, Cumbria CA11 0XQ. *Tel*: Threlkeld (059 683) 702. *Hosts*: Roy & Melanie Johnson.
Rates: C
   Warm and comfortable 17th-century stone farmhouse in National Park. Peace and tranquillity in lovely Mosedale valley surrounded by the fells. All rooms with private bathroom. Children over 7 welcome. Please bring own wine. Phone for directions. Penrith 13 miles, Keswick 11.

MUNGRISDALE THE MILL HOTEL
Mungrisdale, Penrith, Cumbria CA11 0XR. *Tel*: Threlkeld (059683) 659. *Hosts*: Richard & Eleanor Quinlan.
Rates: B/C
(See page 194 for description)

NEWBROUGH (Nr Hexham) THE STANEGATE AND RESTAURANT
Newbrough, Hexham, Northumberland NE47 5AR. *Tel*: Newbrough (043474) 241. *Hosts*: Ann & Lu Fenton.
Rates: C Vouchers accepted.
   Stone-built, modernised house with large attractive garden and views over adjoining farm parkland. Hadrian's Wall 5 mins' drive. Off A69 on

Stanegate Roman Road. Proprietors proud of 'enviable growing reputation for excellent food'. No smoking in bedrooms. Sorry, no pets.

NEWBY BRIDGE   SWAN HOTEL
Newby Bridge, Ulverston. Cumbria LA12 8NB. *Tel*: Newby Bridge (05395) 31681. *Telex*: 65108. *Fax*: 053 95 31917. *Hosts*: James & Jill Bertlin.
Rates: D   Vouchers accepted.
Delightfully situated at water's edge of River Leven, south Lake Windermere. Originally 17th-century coaching inn. By A590 16 miles M6 (exit 36). Boat moorings, private fishing. Sorry, no pets. Half-tester in suite.

NORTHALLERTON   (A 'no smoking' house)   PORCH HOUSE
High Street, Northallerton, North Yorkshire DL7 8EG. *Tel*: Northallerton (0609) 779831. *Hosts*: Peter & Shirley Thompson.
Rates: B/C   Vouchers accepted.
Charming family house in centre of this busy and picturesque market town. Many interesting historical connections. Beamed ceilings. Ample parking. Dinner by arrangement. York, Durham and Newcastle all within 1 hour's drive.

PORTINSCALE (Nr Keswick)   RICKERBY GRANGE
Portinscale, Keswick, Cumbria CA12 5RH. *Tel*: Keswick (0596) 72344. *Hosts*: Rodney & Margaret Roper.
Rates: B/C. Vouchers accepted.
An attractive home in this pretty little village of Portinscale in the Lake District. Off A66 road, mile west of Keswick. Find lane marked 'Footpath to Ullock and Swinside'. Two ground-floor bedrooms have patio doors. Home-cooking.

PRESTON   BRIARFIELD GUEST HOUSE
147 Watling Street Road, Fulwood, Preston, Lancashire PR2 4AE. *Tel*: Preston (0772) 700917. *Hosts*: Joe & Ruth Southward.
Rates: B
Very comfortable large Edwardian house in residential area, 3 miles town centre. Off M6, exit 32, take A6 to Preston. Turn left at third traffic lights, continue 1 mile. Colour TV all rooms. Will recommend nearby restaurants. Sorry, no pets.

PRESTON   TULKETH HOTEL
209 Tulketh Road, Ashton, Preston, Lancashire PR2 1ES. *Tel*: Preston (0772) 726250. *Hosts*: The Hardwick Family.
Rates: B/C
Impressive detached Edwardian hotel situated in quiet residential area under 2 miles from city centre. Cosy bar lounge. Varied dinner menus. 10 mins from M6 (junc 31) and M55 (junc l) towards Blackpool, left turn after second rail bridge. Sorry, no pets.

RASKELF   OLD FARMHOUSE COUNTRY HOTEL
Raskelf, York, North Yorkshire YO6 3LF. *Tel*: Easingwold (0347) 21971.
Hosts: Bill & Jenny Frost.
Rates: B
(See page 195 for description)

RAVENSTONEDALE (Nr Kirkby Stephen)   THE FAT LAMB
Crossbank, Ravenstonedale, Kirkby Stephen, Cumbria CA17 4LL. *Tel*:
Newbiggin on Lune (05873) 242. *Hosts*: Paul & Helen Bonsall.
Rates: B/C   Vouchers accepted.
(See page 196 for description)

REETH (Nr Richmond)   BURGOYNE HOTEL
Reeth, Richmond, North Yorkshire DL11 6SN. *Tel*: Richmond (0748) 84292.
Hosts: Steve & Pat Foster.
Rates: B   Vouchers accepted.
(See page 197 for description)

RICHMOND   WHASHTON SPRINGS FARM
Whashton, Richmond, North Yorkshire DL11 7JS. *Tel*: Richmond (0748)
2884. *Hosts*: Fairlie & Gordon Turnbull.
Rates: A/B
(See page 198 for description)

RIPON   BRIDGE HOTEL
Magdalen Road, Ripon, North Yorkshire HG4 1HX. *Tel*: Ripon (0765) 3687.
Hosts: Jean & Allan Reinhard.
Rates: C/D
Victorian hotel refurbished with charm and elegance. Log fires. Fine antiques
in every room. Ground floor rooms. Intimate dining room with excellent
reputation uses fresh, local produce. Special diets. Walking distance from
cathedral and countryside. Near moors and dales, Harrogate, Ripley Castle.

ROCK FERRY (Nr Liverpool)   THE YEW TREE
58 Rock Lane West, Rock Ferry, Wirrall, Merseyside L42 4PA. *Tel*: Liverpool
(051) 645 4112. *Hosts*: Ray & Dilly Arnold.
Rates: B/C
Georgian house in residential area 4 miles central Liverpool. From south,
follow A41 until roundabout with sign to New Ferry B5136, left at second
traffic lights. Home-cooking. Lock-up car park. Convenient Liverpool and
Chester trains. Reduced rates at weekend. Sorry, no pets.

ROSEDALE ABBEY   MILBURN ARMS HOTEL
Rosedale Abbey, Pickering, North Yorkshire YO18 8RA. *Tel*: Lastingham
(07515) 312. *Hosts*: Stephen & Frances Colling.
Rates: C/D
Comfortable 17th-century beamed country inn, heart of North Yorkshire
Moors National Park. Proprietors proud of their reputation for food and

wine. 4–poster available. Breaks all year. Claim Guestaccom rates when booking and confirm on arrival.

SCARBOROUGH   (A 'no smoking' house)   CHALFONT HOUSE
64 Filey Road, South Cliff, Scarborough, North Yorkshire YO11 3AY. *Tel*:
Scarborough (0723) 375757. *Host*: Mrs B. Lewis.
Rates: B

Charming and elegant guest house in residential area. Within walking distance of town centre. Esplanade and Italian gardens. Bowls, golf, sports centre complex. Couples only. Colour TV all rooms. Sorry, no pets.

SCARBOROUGH (East Ayton)   EAST AYTON LODGE HOTEL
AND RESTAURANT
Moor Lane, East Ayton, Scarborough, North Yorkshire YO13 9EW. *Tel*:
Scarborough (0723) 864227. *Hosts*: Brian & Paola Gardner.
Rates: C   Vouchers accepted.

Attractive, early 19th-century country house in tranquil and idyllic setting. Three acres gardens and lawns in National Park, near River Derwent. Specialising English and French cuisine, home grown produce in season. Children and pets welcome. Off A170, Scarborough 5 miles. Lounge/bar. 4–poster available. Closed 11 Jan-13 Feb.

SCAWBY, Nr Scunthorpe   OLIVER'S OF SCAWBY
Church Street, Scawby, Brigg, South Humberside DN20 9AM. *Tel*: Brigg
(0652) 650446. *Hosts*: Hazel & Derek Oliver.
Rates: B   Vouchers accepted.

Comfortable 17th-century cottage, once the Post Office, in attractive village off A15. Lincoln 20 miles. York 35. Humber Bridge and airport 8 miles. A1(M) link to M180, exit 4. Colour TV all rooms. Dinner by arrangement. Children over 10 welcome. Sorry, no pets.

SCOTCH CORNER (Nr Richmond)   (A 'no smoking' house)   BROOK
HOUSE
Middleton Tyas, Richmond, North Yorkshire DL10 6RP. *Tel*: Barton (032577)
713. *Hosts*: John & Eleanor Harrop.
Rates: C

Comfortable and elegant Georgian farmhouse overlooking garden and wooded pastures. Convenient for Dales, York, Durham and on way to Scotland. All rooms en suite. Log fires. French and English country cooking. Dinner by arrangement only. Phone for directions.

SCUNTHORPE   THE PORTLAND HOTEL
80 Oswald Road, Scunthorpe, South Humberside DN15 7PG. *Tel*: Scunthorpe
(0724) 280755. *Hosts*: Derek & Hazel Oliver.
Rates: D

Comfortable Victorian house in residential area ½ mile from the centre of this industrial garden town. Ample parking. 1½ miles from M180, exit 3. Humber bridge 8 miles. Children over 10 welcome. Sorry, no pets.

SETTLE (Wigglesworth)   TEENLEY COUNTRY HOUSE
Wigglesworth, Nr Skipton, North Yorkshire BD23 4RJ. *Tel*: Long Preston
(07294) 599. *Hosts*: Richard Phillips & Lyndsey Greer.
Rates: B   Vouchers accepted.
    Beautiful 17th-century renovated farmhouse overlooking Ribble valley.
Malham Cove, Forest of Bowland, Settle-Carlisle railway nearby. No
smoking in bedrooms. Special diets catered for. 2 night breaks available.
Settle 5 miles, Skipton 16. Phone for directions. Sorry, no pets.

SHEFFIELD   RUTLAND HOTEL
452 Glossop Road, Sheffield S10 2PY. *Tel*: Sheffield (0742) 665215. *Telex*:
547500. *Fax*: 0742 670348. *Host*: Robert Harwood.
Rates: D
    Graceful Victorian houses, cleverly linked with modern additions. In
residential area of Broomhill, 5 mins drive from centre of England's fourth
largest city. Easy access, excellent facilities. Hair-dryers in rooms. M1, exit
33, follow A57 to Glossop, then Hallamshire Hospital. Annexe.

SILLOTH   THE QUEENS HOTEL
Park Terrace, Silloth, Nr Carlisle, Cumbria CA5 4QF. *Tel*: Silloth (06973)
31373. *Hosts*: John & Sandra Morgan.
Rates: C   Vouchers accepted.
    Nicely situated overlooking promenade and rose garden, with uninterrupted
views of Solway Firth and Scottish fells, in area of outstanding natural beauty.
Bird sanctuary. Miles of sandy beaches. Golf at Silloth Championship course.
Tennis, bowling, wild carp fishing.

SOUTHPORT   CRIMOND HOTEL
28 Knowsley Rd, Southport, Merseyside PR9 0HN. *Tel*: Southport (0704)
36456. *Hosts*: Geoff & Pat Randle.
Rates: C   Vouchers accepted.
    Comfortable and friendly family-run hotel. Large car park, 5 mins walk
to the promenade and Lord Street's famous shops. Six golf courses within
5 min drive. Heated swimming pool, sauna, solarium and jacuzzi. 4-poster
and half-tester available.

SPENNYMOOR   THE GABLES
South View, Middlestone Moor, Spennymoor, Co Durham DL16 7DF. *Tel*:
Spennymoor (0388) 817544. *Hosts*: David & Daphne Mullins.
Rates: A/B   Vouchers accepted.
    Spacious Victorian detached house, comfortable rooms with colour TV and
welcome trays. A1(M) 5 miles, Durham City 7. Gateshead Garden Festival
& Metro Centre 30 mins. Ideal touring centre for Hadrian's Wall, Yorkshire
Moors, Weardale, Teesdale.

ST ANNES-ON-SEA   BEDFORD HOTEL
307-311 Clifton Drive South, St Annes-on- Sea, Lancashire FY8 1HN. *Tel*: St
Annes (0253) 724636. *Fax*: 0253 729244. *Hosts*: Jim & Terri Baker.

Rates: C   Vouchers accepted.

Elegant and comfortable family-run hotel. Some ground-floor rooms. Lift. 3 mins from shops and beach. Four golf courses within 5 mins drive. Solarium. 4-poster bedroom. Valet service. Coffee shop. From M55 follow St Annes signs, then turn left off St Annes Road East.

STANHOPE   STANHOPE OLD HALL
Stanhope, Bishop Auckland, Co Durham DL13 2PF. *Tel*: Weardale (0388) 528451. *Fax*: 0388 527795. *Hosts*: Phyllis & Keith Robson.
Rates: C/D
(See page 199 for description)

STOCKPORT (Marple)   SHIRE COTTAGE
Benches Lane, Ernocroft Farm, Marple Bridge, Stockport, Cheshire SK6 5NT. *Tel*: Daytime, Manchester (061427) 2377 (before 10am and after 4pm Marple (0457) 866536). *Hosts*: The Sidebottom Family.
Rates: A/B   Vouchers accepted.
(See page 200 for description)

SUNDERLAND   GELT HOUSE
23 St Bedes Terrace, Sunderland, Tyne & Wear SR2 8HS. *Tel*: Sunderland (091) 567-2990. *Hosts*: Jim & Moraig Mercer.
Rates: C

Friendly and comfortable small hotel in tree-lined terrace. Perfect location for business/pleasure in Sunderland area. Bar and restaurant. Durham 12 miles, Newcastle 15. Half mile from city centre off Mowbray Park.

TARVIN (Nr Chester)   STAPLEFORD HALL
Tarvin, Nr Chester CH3 8HH. *Tel*: Tarvin (0829) 40202. *Hosts*: The Winward Family.
Rates: B

Beautiful Georgian farmhouse of historic and architectural interest, set in peaceful countryside with large garden, tennis, croquet. In 250-acre dairy farm. Log fires. Restaurants nearby. Off A51 Nantwich Road 6 miles from Chester. Phone for directions. Annexe.

THIRSK (Sowerby)   SHEPPARD'S CHURCH FARM AND RESTAURANT
Sowerby, Thirsk, North Yorkshire YO7 1JF. *Tel*: Thirsk (0845) 23655 (will change during 1990). *Hosts*: Olga & Roy Sheppard.
Rates: B/C   Vouchers accepted.

300-year-old farmhouse and converted stable block with courtyard. Opposite church on village green. 'Herriott' country, golf, fishing, hang-gliding, riding. Area of historic castles and abbeys. TV all rooms. Restaurant listed in major guides. Children over 10 welcome. Sorry, no pets.

WARRINGTON   THE PADDINGTON HOUSE HOTEL AND ALBAN RESTAURANT
514 Manchester Road, Paddington, Nr. Warrington WA1 3TZ. *Tel*: Padgate

(0925) 816767. *Host*: Alban Stirrup.
Rates: D   Vouchers accepted.
A fine example of 'Old Warrington' in own peaceful grounds with sweeping, tree-lined lawns and gardens. Lift to all floors. Just off A57, 1½ miles M6. Warrington 2 miles. Proprietor claims his Alban Restaurant is second to none. 4-poster available.

WIGAN   AALTON COURT PRIVATE HOTEL
23 Upper Dicconson Street, Wigan, Lancashire WN1 2AG. *Tel*: Wigan (0942) 322220. *Hosts*: Susan & Malcolm Ellison.
Rates: B
Victorian terraced house, professionally modernised by the owner, in quiet residential tree-lined area. 5 mins walk shops. Museum and Heritage Centre. 4 miles from M6 and M61. Sorry, no pets.

WINDERMERE   BRAEMOUNT HOUSE
Sunny Bank Road, Windermere, Cumbria LA23 2EN. *Tel*: Windermere (09662) 5967. *Hosts*: Tony & Mary Eley.
Rates: B/C
(See page 201 for description)

WINDERMERE   CEDAR MANOR HOTEL
Ambleside Road, Windermere, Cumbria LA23 1AX. *Tel*: Windermere (09662) 3192. *Hosts*: Lynn & Martin Hadley.
Rates: C/D   Vouchers accepted.
Relaxing, friendly atmosphere in handsome 18th-century manor house with spectacular views of fells. Candlelit dining room. 4-poster bedroom. Golf, sailing and walking nearby. Easy access from M6. Kendal 8 miles, Coniston 12.

WITHERSLACK   THE OLD VICARAGE
Church Road, Witherslack, Grange-over-Sands, Cumbria LA11 6RS. *Tel*: Witherslack (044852) 381. *Telex*. 668230. *Fax*: 044852 373. *Hosts*: Stanley & Irene Reeve, Roger & Jill Brown.
Rates: C
Small, elegant Georgian country house in idyllic setting near Windermere. Proprietors are proud of their 5-course, set gourmet dinner, featuring traditional specialities and excellent wine list. M6 exit 36, A590 towards Barrow, watch for 'Witherslack' sign. BTA commended, Red Stars and Merit Award winners.

WOOLER   THE RYECROFT HOTEL
Wooler, Northumberland NE71 6AB. *Tel*: Wooler (0668) 81459. *Hosts*: Pat & David McKechnie.
Rates: C
Warm, friendly hotel, log fires and real ales. All rooms with bathroom en

suite. Outskirts of Wooler, just off A697 - popular scenic route to Edinburgh. Central for peaceful hills. Border and lovely coast. Hosts proud that guests return repeatedly. Food award. Reduced rates all year for 2 nights or more.

YORK   THE HILL HOTEL
60 York Road, Acomb, York Y02 5LW. *Tel*: York (0904) 790777. *Telex*: 57567 (Att. HH). *Host*: Mr P. J. Blackburn.
Rates: D
> Gracious Georgian hotel in 1 acre of attractive gardens, only 1½ m from centre of cathedral city. Off A59 on B1224. Two rooms with 4-poster beds. Sorry, no pets. BTA commended.

YORK   WHITE DOVES
20 Claremont Terrace (off Gillygate), York YO3 7EJ. *Tel*: York (0904) 625957.
Hosts: Espie Bleasdale.
Rates: A/B   Vouchers accepted.
(See page 202 for description)

YORK (Appleton Roebuck)   THE DUKE OF CONNAUGHT
Copmanthorpe Grange, Copmanthorpe, York YO2 3TN. *Tel*: York (0904) 84318. *Hosts*: The Hughes Family.
Rates: B   Vouchers accepted.
> Not a pub, but an unusual conversion of a stud farm, in open countryside 6 miles south of York. Turn off A64 AT GARAGE to Appleton Roebuck. Then, through village a further 1½ miles towards York. Hotel next turning on left by large wood up long drive. Must book dinner. Rates include bathroom en suite. Stable annexe.

YORK (Barmby Moor)   BARMBY MOOR COUNTRY HOTEL AND RESTAURANT
Hull Road, Barmby Moor, York YO4 5EZ. *Tel*: Pocklington (0759) 302700.
Hosts: Peter & Pat Otterburn.
Rates: C   Vouchers accepted.
> Delightful Georgian ex-coaching house with flagstone floors and attractive courtyard. Outdoor heated swimming pool. 10 miles east of York, set back off A1079. All rooms en suite with colour TV and direct-dial telephones. Sorry, no pets.

YORK (Thorganby)   JEFFERSON ARMS
Thorganby, York YO4 6DB. *Tel*: Wheldrake (090 489) 316. *Host*: Robert Mason.
Rates: C/D   Vouchers accepted.
(See page 203 for description)

Blue Dolphins
11 Riverside Road
Alnmouth
Northumberland
NE66 2SD

Bed and Breakfast only
Dogs welcome only with own
  beds
Unlicensed
Will collect guests from
  station

☎ Alnwick(0665) 830893

Jack and Joan Davidson

This lovely Victorian house is quite blissfully situated amongst a cluster of houses, in the village of Alnmouth, right on the banks of the river estuary, with only a small garden and a 'no through' road between it and the beach – it is brilliant for tumbling out of bed and enjoying a long walk on almost deserted sands. There are five comfortable bedrooms, each individually decorated, with en suite facilities and a colour TV.

Joan and Jack enjoy meeting their guests and many breakfasts stretch into the mid-morning as new friendships are made. No evening meal is offered but there are several pubs in the village. Within four miles there is an even greater choice – such as the Carribe Northumbria at Shilbottle, and Blackmore's at Alnwick which are run by chef/owners.

Easily Accessible: The village is small, unspoilt and well serviced. It is one of the few places (in this book) where a car is not an absolute necessity: Alnmouth is on the main London- Edinburgh rail line and the village has an excellent local bus service. The village has an ancient history dating back to Roman times(the remains of a Roman wall testify to this). Once Alnmouth was a busy corn port but today the estuary is used solely for pleasure activities such as wind-surfing and sailing. North of Alnmouth and accessible by boat lie the Farne Islands famous for their seal colonies. Near to them is Lindisfarne or Holy Isle which can only be reached by way of a causeway at low tide. Holy Isle was the site of one of the oldest Christian communities in Britain and is now a nature reserve. If you take a small step inland from Alnmouth, you can enjoy the stunning countryside of north Northumberland and the National Park.

Local Activities: walks, golf, fishing, wind-surfing, sailing, bird-watching.

Elmfield Country House
Arrathorne
Bedale
North Yorkshire
DL8 1NE

2 ground-floor rooms fully
equipped for disabled guests

☎ Bedale (0677) 50558

Edith and Jim Lillie

The proprieters of Elmfield House, Jim and Edith Lillie, were initially a little apprehensive about opening their much restored and much-cared for home to the public – but they soon came to appreciate the friendship and interest given to them by their visitors from all over the world. Edith finds the cooking a cinch. She is a local farmer's daughter and was quite used to cooking for her six brothers and one sister.

The house is set back from the main road and has wonderful views of the surrounding farmland. Inside, it is very comfortable and spacious and has a well-kept garden with a large illuminated pond with waterfall. There are nine double bedrooms, all with private facilities and colour TV. Two ground-floor bedrooms have been designed to accommodate disabled guests. There is also a games room and a solarium, available for guests to use for a small charge.

Dinner is home-cooked traditional English fare, the favourite dish being roast beef and Yorkshire pudding. There are plenty of fresh vegetables and sweets, and soups are home-made.

Easily Accessible: There are numerous walks around the moors and dales. Public transport is pretty thin on the ground so it is advisable to have your own. There are several fascinating castles and abbeys in the vicinity including: Richmond Castle, 6 miles away, which was built in 1071 as protection against the Saxons, and Bolton Castle, 12 miles away, where Mary Queen of Scots was imprisoned, and the ruins of the once magnificent Abbeys of Easby, Jervaulx and Coverham. York, 40 miles away, and Durham, 30 miles away, are both beautiful historical cities. There is horse-racing 5 miles away at Catterick.

Local Activities: walks, fishing, gliding, hang-gliding, golf, swimming, indoor skiing, sailing, squash, tennis, bowls, horse-riding.

Sunray Hotel

42 Knowle Avenue
Blackpool
Lancashire
FY2 9TQ

Award winner
Unlicensed

☎ Blackpool (0253) 51937

Jean and John Dodgson

300 yards off Queens Promenade

In a town with over 200,000 holiday beds, this small unprepossessing semi-detached house lying in a quiet residential area has a reputation for being special – in fact for being one of the best small hotels in the resort. What makes it so is the extraordinary care and attention given to every guest by its owner, Jean Dodgson. No one escapes from her warm welcome. The nine bedrooms have en suite facilities and colour TV. There is a comfortable lounge. Jean provides a very good five-course evening meal and will cater for special diets on request. There is a small front garden with a swing chair, deck chairs and parasols.

Easily Accessible: Blackpool is the archetypal British seaside resort, probably most famous for its tower, three piers, spectacular illuminations which shine through September and October, and its tram cars – the last in the country. Its pleasure beach is the largest in Europe and one of the country's top attractions.

During the summer season, Blackpool plays host to many events, sports championships (bowls, water polo), vintage car run and, more improbably, 'the best bus driver of the year' competition. Lesser known are its beautiful gardens in Stanley Park. Lytham St Annes, a short distance to the south, has sandy beaches and several excellent golf courses. Using the M55 and M6, the beautiful countryside, historic houses, ruined abbeys, and picturesque villages of the Yorkshire Dales and the Lake District can be easily visited for a day trip.

High Greenrigg House

Caldbeck
Wigton
Cumbria
CA7 8HD

Closed Nov-Feb

☎ Caldbeck (06998) 430

Fran and Robin Jacobs

Off B5299 Carlisle 15 miles: phone for directions

This carefully restored farmhouse with original beams, a stone-flagged floor and open fire is located just three miles outside the small lakeland village of Caldbeck. It is very simply furnished with pine used throughout. There are three lounges to choose from; one has a colour TV, one an open fire, and the third, a bar with table-tennis and snooker tables and a darts board. The eight bedrooms are very comfortable, many have en suite facilities.

Food is taken seriously – with all the walking done every day, Fran and Robin Jacobs believe a good breakfast and dinner to be of the utmost importance. The four-course evening meal is home-cooked using fresh ingredients. Bread, soups and ice-cream are all home-made. The cuisine is a mix of American, traditional English, Cumbrian and vegetarian. Packed lunches are available.

Easily Accessible: Greenrigg Hotel is situated at the foot of the Caldbeck Fells and only a mile from the Cumbrian Way in the more northern and in summer, less crowded area of the Lake District. The Jacobs have produced their own booklet on walks from the house which encompass fells (including Scafell, the highest peak in the National Park), lakes, waterfalls, woods and farmland. Caldbeck is a pretty village with several attractions, including a spinning workshop and John Peel's grave. The neighbouring town of Hesket New Market has a delightful pub with its own brewed beer. Within a radius of 15 miles, you can visit Keswick, a Victorian town, at the heart of the district; Carlisle with its castle and cathedral, museum and art gallery; Cockermouth, the birthplace of Wordsworth; and the Solway, a bird-watchers' delight.

Local Activities: walks, golf, wind-surfing, fishing.

Demesne House   Unlicensed
Rockcliffe
Carlisle
Cumbria
CA6 4BW

☎ Rockliffe (022874) 280

Peggy Rowcliffe

5 miles north of Carlisle. Phone for directions

Over 200 years old, this lovely farmhouse stands in a garden on the banks of the River Eden. It was once a coaching house, standing on the main road between England and Scotland (all that remains today of this road is a grass track). Rumours abound; it is said that Bonnie Prince Charlie stayed here after his defeat in 1745, and it is also suggested that the house was a centre of smuggling as it stands a mere hundred yards from the head of the Solway Firth.

Peggy Rockcliffe has worked hard to achieve its present high degree of comfort, adding bathrooms, a dining room and turning a barn into a spacious sitting room. All three bedrooms have private bathrooms. An excellent home-cooked three-course dinner is served. If Peggy cannot offer dinner she will direct you to local pubs and restaurants.

Easily Accessible: There are many fine local walks particularly in the upper reaches of the River Eden. Dumfries is now a tourist centre. It was once the home of Robert Burns and has a museum in his name. At the wildlife sanctuary in Caerlaverock you can see natterjack toads, and in winter flocks of geese arrive. The ruins of Caerlaverock Castle are prominent against the flat marshes of the Solway Firth. You can take a day trip to the Esk Valley, famous for its tweed and knitwear mills (where you can purchase goods at mill prices) and where you can enjoy the stunning countryside.

Local Activities: walks, fishing, golf, pony-trekking.

Harrop Fold Country Farmhouse Hotel
Bolton-by-Bowland   Award winner
Clitheroe
Lancashire
RB7 4PJ

☎ Bolton-by-Bowland (02007) 600

The Wood Family

Phone for directions

This typical Pennine longhouse with thick stone walls, Viking timbers and mullioned windows was built in the 17th century in a style originated by the Norsemen. Situated in the tranquil hamlet of Harrop Fold, it is smoothly run by the welcoming Wood family, consisting of Peter and Victoria, their son, Andrew, and his wife, Anna.

The house is comfortable and tastefully furnished with antiques and period pieces. Peter runs a small well-stocked bar and encourages evening conversation in the cosy lounge. All six bedrooms, carefully colour co-ordinated by Victoria, are en suite and stocked with lots of toiletries and a colour television – not to mention a complimentary bottle of wine on arrival. For honeymooners a bottle of champagne, a basket of

flowers and a heart-shaped sachet are offered at a charge. Throughout
the house there are interesting knick-knacks – in particular a collection
of maritime memorabilia put together by Victoria who is proud of her
sea-faring ancestors.

The table d'hôte menu is prepared by Andrew (a trained chef) using
fresh local produce with a vegetarian choice. Andrew's home-made
bread is excellent.

There is entertainment on your doorstep; Andrew has created
a fairway on the farm for guests to practise their golf and
they are also invited to take a planned walk around the
280-acre farm.

Easily Accessible: Walks on the local fells and in the Ribble Valley, and
further afield in the Yorkshire Dales and the Lake District. There are
numerous historic sites to visit, including Skipton with its castle, its
church with fascinating family tombs, and the local history museum,
and Gawthorpe Hall, a mid-19th-century stately home with an interesting textile collection. You can take the Settle to Carlisle Railway
with an exciting trip over the Ribblehead Viaduct. York, Manchester,
Liverpool, and Lancaster are all within easy reach for day trips.

Local Activities: walks, golf, horse-riding.

The Riverside Hotel   Closed Christmas–New Year
Main Street
Corbridge
Northumberland
NE45 5LE

☎ Corbridge (0434) 632942

Harry and Judy Fawcett

This pleasant hotel, built in 1760 from local stone, is situated in
the pretty village of Corbridge. With Victorian, Edwardian and later
additions, it has a small bar, comfortable sitting room and very pretty
Laura Ashley decorated bedrooms most of which are en suite. All are
equipped with a TV.

The three-course dinner is served daily from a table d'hôte menu and
is cooked by Judy Fawcett. Good use is made of fresh vegetables and
herbs from the garden; fresh wholemeal bread from the village baker and
salmon and trout from the river Tyne (which runs behind the house).
Vegetarian dishes and other special diets are no problem for Judy and
snacks and light lunches will be provided on request.

Harry and Judy will collect guests from the station (there is also an excellent local taxi service) and will advise on places to visit and lend maps to walkers.

Easily Accessible: Several walks taking you through unspoilt countryside begin near the hotel. The National Park is a short drive away. Corbridge itself has a 17th-century bridge, and the excavated site of the Roman town of Corstopitum which is open all year. It is surrounded by interesting market towns such as Hexham and Prudhoe which are a pleasure to browse through. Along Hadrian's Wall (which from July to September can be reached by coach from Corbridge) there are a number of interesting historical sites – the Roman Army Museum; Vindolanda (large Roman fort); a Roman hospital and a Roman cavalry fort. Newcastle is just 17 miles away. Day trips within a 50 mile radius include: the Farne Islands (home to seventeen different species of sea-birds and a colony of grey seals), the 16th-century Lindisfarne Castle on Holy Isle (National Trust property), and the historical cathedral city of Durham.

Local Activities: walks, riding, fishing.

The Coach House   Closed Nov–Feb
Crookham   Facilities for disabled
Cornhill-on-Tweed   Award winner
Northumberland
TD12 4TD

☎ Crookham (089082) 293

Jamie and Lynne Anderson

Surrounded by farmland just south of the Scottish border, this house, reputedly the oldest in North Northumberland, is run with panache by Jamie and Lynne – he was a restaurateur, she a singer and actress. Together they saved it from dereliction and have imprinted it with their lively characters. It has a lovely old orchard full of damson trees, a paddock with goats and rare sheep and a sunny terrace. The bedrooms are furnished individually, one with a wall hung with hats, another with bells hung from beams. Those with private bathrooms have fridges. The large high-ceilinged lounge is beamed and in winter is made cosy by a roaring log fire. The dining room is full of character; once a smithy, it has a forge at one end and a quarry-tiled floor. There is a TV and games room.

The food is very wholesome with free-range eggs and lambs, salmon from the River Tweed, local shell fish and pigs once seen roaming the orchard, featuring on the menu. Even the wine is organic. Special diets are catered for.

Easily Accessible: The Coach House lies on the edge of the Ford and Etal estates which consist of 20,000 acres of beautiful countryside, ruined castles, pretty villages and a network of footpaths ideal for walking. Also within the estates is the famous battlefield of Flodden where James IV of Scotland was killed in 1513. Nearby the Pennine Way and Cheviot Hills provide further variety of scenery. The coast is only 15 miles away and has some lovely sandy beaches. Holy Isle and the Farne Islands are ideal for nature lovers – here you may see seals and puffins. Berwick-upon-Tweed is 13 miles away; an interesting town, it has a museum and Tudor fortifications considered the best in Europe.

Local Activities: walks, horse-riding, fishing, golf.

Crayke Castle
Crayke
York
YO6 4TA

Sorry, no pets
No smoking in bedrooms

☎ Easingwold (0347) 22285

Peter and Belle Hepworth

Crayke is 2½ miles from Easingwold off A19

Crayke Castle was built for the Bishop of Durham in 1430. It stands in the pretty hill village of Crayke with magnificent views over the Vale of York, and the Dales. Wandering through the spacious grounds you will come upon what is believed to be the remains of an earlier 12th- century castle visited by five kings of England during the 12th and 13th centuries.

Not surprisingly it was the cost of the restoration that persuaded Peter and Belle to take guests in, to, as they put it, 'let the Castle earn its keep'. Warm, comfortable and elegantly furnished with antiques, there are three individually furnished en suite bedrooms (two are four-posters), each with a colour TV. Dinner is an event; after a pre-prandial drink (included in the price of the meal) is taken in the library or drawing room or on the patio, you are led into the dining room for a candlelit dinner. The menu, a mouth-watering mixture of French and English cuisine, offers a substantial choice for all courses. Coffee and liqueurs are taken in the library. On rare occasions dinner may not be provided but there is a nearby pub recommended by your hosts offering restaurant meals or bar snacks.

Easily Accessible: Crayke's nearest town is Easingwold, a pretty market town set in the Forest of Galtres, a Norman hunting preserve. Walks on the Howardian Hills include a 4-mile one around Byland Abbey, one around the White Horse at Kilburn and another through the forest of Yearsley. Half an hour's drive north will take you to the moors and to the west the dales. York with its famous Gothic Minster and very popular Yorvik Viking Centre, and Castle Howard, John Vanbrugh's 17th-century palatial mansion with a fine collection of paintings and a 1000-acre park, are both 12 miles away. Newby Hall is a famous Adam House with a lovely garden with adventure park for children. Eight miles away at Helmsley is Nunnington Hall, a 17th-century manor house with the Carlisle Collection of twenty-two miniature rooms – each room is one-eighth life size. There are several racecourses nearby suitable for day trips.

Local Activities: walks, golf, gliding, swimming, squash, cycling (bike hire available).

Whitfield House Hotel   Closed mid Nov-mid Jan
Darnholm
Goathland
Whitby
North Yorkshire
YO22 5LA

☎ Whitby (0947) 86215

John and Pauline Lusher

This 17th-century country house in the heart of the North York Moors National Park lies in complete tranquillity at the end of a no-through road where sheep wander. It has been sympathetically modernised and restored whilst retaining beamed ceilings and open fires in the lounge bar and television lounge.

John and Pauline Lusher think of Whitfield House as an old-fashioned residence and are rightly proud of the fact that, with the exception of ice-cream, all food is prepared on the premises. The four-course dinner is wholesome and fresh produce is used whenever possible. Specialities of the house are the traditional roasts and delicious old-fashioned sweets.

Easily Accessible: The nearby village of Goathland (an ancient settlement dating from the 12th century) contains several waterfalls, countless footpaths, and is only a stone's throw from the open moors. The North York Moors Railway (steam) passes through. Three miles away at Wheeldale is a perfectly preserved stretch of Roman road. The coast and Whitby with its harbour, ruined abbey and museum, where you can learn about one of its most famous inhabitants, Captain Cook, is only 9 miles away. A little further along the coast, you can visit the charming fishing villages of Robin Hood's Bay, Runswick Bay and Skinningrove. Fourteen miles away at Pickering is the Beck Island Museum, a castle and church with fascinating wall paintings. The beautiful city of York is 40 miles away.

Local Activities: walks.

Oak Bank Hotel   Closed mid-Nov–mid-Feb
Broadgate   Award winner
Grasmere
Cumbria
LA22 9TA

☎ Grasmere (09665) 217

Sharon and Attilio Savasi and Pat Smith

The views from the ever-changing fells are superb and Wordsworth thought so too. Grasmere was paradise to him and he settled here for several years at Dove cottage (which is open to the public). Oak Bank itself is a beautiful 19th-century house, made of local green slate and furnished in a simple country style, much in keeping with its external character. The dining room looks out onto a mature, secluded garden where the River Rother passes through on its way to Grasemere Lake. There are two lounges ,one has a wood-burning stove, the other a TV and videos on the surrounding area. There are seventeen individually furnished bedrooms (making it one of the larger hotels in this guide), all with en suite facilities and colour TV. There is also a very pretty honeymoon suite.

Sharon and Attilio Savasi met when she was a chef and he a waiter at the same hotel. They provide a friendly relaxed service. Sharon is a cordon bleu trained cook and provides an excellent five-course table d'hôte menu whilst Attilio, who is something of an amateur but enthusiastic wine expert, will advise you on a suitable choice of wine. Vegetarian and special diets are catered for.

Easily Accessible: The surrounding area is one of the most beautiful in the whole country and of course attracts tourists in their multitudes. Just step outside the hotel and look at the sheep–dotted hills, whilst above birds of prey hover and swoop. The fields and woods contain squirrels, badgers and red deer. The little village of Grasemere has inspired many of our great artists and poets including Wordsworth, Coleridge and Ruskin. If you feel like a gentle lakeside stroll Grasmere Lake is to hand, or for the more energetic, Helvellyn, the most climbed peak in England, rises up only a short distance from the village. The local council organises walks with leaders who are very knowledgable about the area. Within an hour's drive you can visit the seaside. Northwards in a couple of hours you can visit Edinburgh, Gretna Green and Hadrian's Wall – but most people linger in Lakeland.

Local Activities: fell walking, rowing, power boating, canooing, wind-surfing, water-skiing, pony-trekking, horse-riding, fishing, swimming.

Greenways   Chauffeuring available
Wharfeside Avenue
Threshfield
Grassington Skipton
North Yorkshire
BD23 5BS

☎ Grassington (0756) 752598

Mike and Jill Popplewell

Surrounded by the glorious scenery of the Yorkshire Dales National Park, on the banks of the river Wharfe and with views to the ancient forest of Grass Wood, Greenways has a near perfect setting. A secluded garden completes the tranquil atmosphere. There are five bedrooms, a lounge with a television, and a dining room with spectacular views.

Food at Greenways is wholesome, fresh and plentiful (Jill and Mike count on their guests working up a good appetite from walking) with herbs and vegetables from the kitchen garden. If you wish to eat out there are several pubs and restaurants nearby: the Angel Inn at Hetton is well recommended. Packed lunches are available on request.

If an aspiring artist, you will enjoy the special painting and sketching week held three times a year at Greenways by local artist Ted Gower. Ted, who has lived for over thirty years in Yorkshire, will guide you to a different beauty spot every day.

Easily Accessible: For walkers the Dales Way passes by and the Pennine
Way (stretching for 185 miles from Derbyshire to the Scottish borders)
can be reached near Malham. In Grassington there are several popular
special events during the year, including the Dickensian weekends held
on three Saturdays prior to Christmas Day, the music festival in late
June, and in August, the annual exhibition of Dales paintings and
crafts. Skipton, just twenty minutes away, has a castle and canal. A
forty-minute drive will take you to Haworth Lane, home of the Brontë
sisters now open to the public.

Local Activities: walks, fishing (trout and grayling), bird-watching,
horse-riding, caving, ballooning and crafts.

Grove House   A 'no smoking' house
Hamsterley Forest
Redford
Nr Bishop Auckland
Co Durham
DL13 3NL

☎ Witton-le-Wear (038888)203

Helene and Russell Close

From A68 to Hamsterley, right in village then 2 miles into forest

Grove House shelters in the middle of a forest, surrounded by 5000
acres of woodland, moors and becks where deer, squirrels and many
birds can be seen. From Hamsterley village, it is approached through
the forest and finally a spectacular tree-lined avenue. It is not surprising
to learn that the naturalist David Bellamy lives nearby.

The house itself is an elegant early 19th-century stone building which
was originally an aristocratic shooting lodge. It has been carefully restored and retains many original features, with a beamed ceiling in the
lounge and an open fire and superbly ornate ceiling in the dining room.
There is a separate reading room. The large garden is bordered by two
rivers. With its formal rose garden, large lawns and a wooded area with
a pigeon house and herbaceous borders, it is altogether an ideal place for
just sitting and listening to the birdsong.

Helene and Russell Close are friendly and outgoing. Helen does all
the cooking, discussing the menus beforehand with her guests. Game
– pheasant and venison from the forest – is a regular feature. Helen
considers her home-made soups the speciality of the house. Lunch or
packed lunches are provided on request.

Easily Accessible: There are numerous waymarked walks through the forest which has designated picnic areas. A tree library next to the house will interest any amateur naturalists. There are many beautiful walks over the surrounding dales. Britain's highest waterfall, High Force, is quite spectacular. The Bowes Museum at Barnard Castle houses an exquisite collection of objets d'art. Nearby are the ruins of Egglestone Abbey. Durham has an outstanding 11th-century cathedral with a Norman castle, now part of the university, next door. It is an attractive town and one in which it is still pleasant just to wander around its streets and along the banks of the River Wear.

Local Activities: walks, golf, horse-riding, bicycle hire, bird-watching.

Holme Castle Country Hotel

Holme Village
Nr Holmfirth
West Yorkshire
HD7 1QG

A 'no smoking' house
Sorry, no pets

☎ Holmfirth (0484) 686764

Jill Hayfield and John Sandford

On A6024, 2½ miles south of Holmfirth.

Located in a conservation area within the Peak National Park, the charming village of Holme is home to a traditional Pennine community of hill farms and stone-built weavers' cottages. In this tranquil setting stands the distinctive form of Holme Castle, an impressive Victorian stone house built in 1820. The castle tower (added in 1870) gives the building its name.

The décor inside is classical and, at the same time, very comfortable. Jill Hayfield was a design student and has used her considerable flair and artistic skill in decorating the house. The drawing room is particularly notable for its splendid oak panelling and parquet floor which was a wedding gift to the wealthy mill owner occupier in 1924. All rooms have extensive views of the surrounding moorlands and hills. The eight bedrooms are elegantly furnished and equipped with colour TV.

Outside there is an attractive walled garden with mature sycamore trees, herbaceous borders and a lawn which is home to a wide variety of birds, who are encouraged to visit the dining room window, where guests may observe them with the aid of the proprietor's binoculars and telescope!

Jill Hayfield and John Sandford are very gregarious hosts. If you are a sociable person, then you will delight in the all pervasive convivial atmosphere. The three-course dinner is served at one table where Jill and John often join their guests. The food is very good, with organic, wholefood and local produce (including locally made yogurt and goats cheese) regularly featured on the menu.

Easily Accessible: Walks spiral out in every direction, including the Pennine Way, which runs across Black Hill and can be joined one mile from the house. In nearby Holmfirth you can visit the popular post-card museum, antiques and craft shops. Seven miles to the north-east lies Huddersfield, with its famous choral society, art gallery, and a contemporary music festival in November. Twenty-five miles away, in the small moorland village of Haworth, you can visit the Brontës' house, still full of their personal possessions. Take a day trip to York, 45 miles away.

Local Activities: walks, golf, horse-riding, cycling, bird-watching, pony-trekking, fishing.

Wellfield House Hotel   Sorry, no pets
33 New Hey Road
Marsh
Huddersfield
HD3 4AL

☎ Huddersfield (0484) 25776

John and Paulaine Whitehead

Within easy reach of Huddersfield town centre and M62

Situated in the foothills of the Pennines and near to the centre of Huddersfield, Wellfield House is ideally located for enjoying both the history and beauty of Yorkshire. Although it has been modernised, it remains an exceptional example of Victorian architecture with many of its original fixtures and fittings intact, including stained glass windows, ornate plaster ceilings, oak panelling and marble fireplaces. The large, mature garden is always very much enjoyed by guests in summmer. There are two comfortable lounges with open fires, one with a large collection of books for guests to read. The five bedrooms are attractive, spacious, each with a marble fireplace and colour TV.

John and Polly take great pleasure in making Wellfield House seem like home to their guests and are more than willing to give advice on sight-seeing, walks etc. The food is delicious: home-baked bread, cakes and pastries, the excellence of which can be explained by the fact that

John and Polly were both bakers in John's father's business. Fruity jams and marmalades are also home-made and the vegetables and herbs are fresh from the kitchen garden.

Easily Accessible: Wellfield House is situated in the foothills of the Pennines, and local walks take in Calderdale and the Holme and Colne Valleys. The Pennine Way is accessible 10 miles from the house. Eight miles away you can visit the Oakwell Country Park with 87 acres of parkland, nature trails and bridleways. The Colne Valley Museum exhibits restored weavers' cottages, and has a weaving workshop and clogger's shop. The whole landscape is dotted with picturesque weaving villages such as Holey, Holme and Netherthong, and attractive mill towns such as Marsden and Slaithwaite.

Local Activities: walks, golf, swimming, squash, badminton, bowling, sauna and solarium at Huddersfield Sports Centre.

Manor House Farm   Children over 7 by arrangement
Ingleby Greenhow   Award winner
Great Ayton   Transport provided to meet
North Yorkshire   public transport
TS9 6RB

☎ Gt Ayton (0642) 722384

Margaret and Martin Bloom

Phone for directions

This secluded sandstone farmhouse of a 164-acre sheep and corn farm is reached by way of a large, wooded drive. Situated in the North York Moors National Park it is surrounded by hills, primitive woodland and elegant parkland from the adjacent manor house. Peacocks, ducks, geese, deer and rare sheep can be seen in the immediate environs.

Inside the farmhouse the décor is simple and attractive with white walls and dark beams. There are three individually decorated guest bedrooms, a lounge with an extensive library and colour TV, and a dining room with a wood-burning fire and pleasant views of the garden. Recipes for the delicious four-course home-cooked evening meal are often created by the Blooms themselves, and are influenced by Continental cuisine.

Easily Accessible: There are many beautiful signposted walks which start almost directly from the house and which take you through forests, and others which take you over the moors and dales. A visit to Helmsley town and castle (where walkers can take up the Cleveland

Way long–distance footpath), with a stop–off at Rievaulx Abbey, makes
for an enjoyable outing. There are numerous pretty towns and villages
which hold open–air markets. Blakey Ridge and Hutton–le–Hole with
the outdoor Ryedale Folk Museum are at the heart of the moor, and only
thirty–five minutes' drive from the farm. The beautiful city of York,
forty–five minutes away, has a famous Minster and popular Yorvik
(Viking) Centre. Castle Howard, a splendid 17th–century mansion with
an exquisite art collection and 1000–acre park, and Flamingo Zoo, the
largest private zoo in the country, are both easily reached for day trips.

Local Activities: walks, horse–riding, golf. Stabling and grazing are
offered for a fee at Manor Farm House for people wishing to bring
their own horses.

The Courtyard
Fairbank
Kirkby Lonsdale
Cumbria
LA6 2AZ

☎ Kirkby Lonsdale (05242) 71613

Gill and Timothy Grey

10 mins from M6 (exit 36)

Sorry, no pets
Bed and Breakfast only
Children over 10 welcome

This elegant listed Georgian house stands near to the centre of a picturesque market town in a quiet yet central position. It has very fine views
over the rooftops of the town, and the large garden has beautiful views
of the fells. It is a large house, newly decorated, curtained and carpeted,
and furnished elegantly with antiques, porcelain, and paintings. There
are three bedrooms, one with a four–poster bed, and a TV room.
   There is no evening meal, but there are restaurants and pubs within
a few minutes walk including the Royal Hotel, an old coaching house,
with an elegant dining room equipped with pianist, and also the Snooty
Fox, a charming pub with attractive beamed ceilings.

Easily Accessible: Kirkby Lonsdale is situated between the Lake District
and the Yorkshire Dales, and is ideally placed for visiting both. Local
walks take in moorland, the banks of the river Lune and its valley.
There are many stately homes to visit including Levens Hall, a beautiful
Elizabethan mansion with topiary gardens; and Sizergh Castle, built in
1340, with the later addition of a Tudor Great Hall and a fine portrait
collection. A trip on the Settle to Carlisle Railway takes you through
some stunning countryside. The coast and the resort of Morecambe with

its seaside attractions and four-mile promenade is easily reached for a day trip. Arnside Knott, a piece of wooded land owned by the National Trust, has superb views of Morecambe Bay and the Lake District mountains and a wide variety of wildlife including red squirrels and deer.

Local Activities: walks, golf, fishing, tennis.

New Capernwray Farm
Capernwray
Carnforth
Lancashire
LA6 1AD

Award winner
Unlicensed, guests welcome
to bring own wine
Children over 10 welcome

☎ Carnforth (0524) 734284

Sally and Pete Townend

Just off M6, exit 35

Situated deep in the Keer Valley, this charming white house, dating back to 1697, has thick stone walls and oak beams. Originally a simple rectangular building, a wing was later added to the rear, and within the angle of the two wings a dairy was constructed – this is now the dining room. The pretty garden has fine views (particularly towards the Pennine Way), a table and chairs for guests, and enough room for dogs to run around in. The three bedrooms are attractive and decorated to a high standard, equipped with private bathrooms and colour TV. The beamed lounge with its log fire is elegantly furnished in a country-house style.

Dinner is served at a candlelit table decked out in fine linen and porcelain. The cuisine is a mixture of English and Continental and fresh ingredients are used.

Easily Accessible: There is lots of walking to be done as New Capernwray is only half an hour from both the Lake District and the Yorkshire Dales and the immediate area has much unspoilt countryside to explore. Try the Lancaster canal towpath from Capernwray to Borwick with views of the Lakeland Fells and the nearby beauty spots of Arnside-Silverdale and the Trough of Silverdale. The coastal resort of Morecombe is twenty minutes away and has all the amenities of a seaside resort including an open-air leisure park and Oceanarium. Popular places to visit are the historic town of Lancaster with its medieval castle and maritime museum, and, for railway enthusiasts, Steamtown at Carnforth, where visitors can take a ride on a steam locomotive. Blackpool is 34 miles away.

Local Activities: trout and salmon fishing, golf, horse-riding, clay pigeon shooting, walks, canal cruises, beaches, bird-watching.

Mains Hall
Mains Lane
Little Singleton
Nr Blackpool
Lancashire
FY6 7LE

Dinner by arrangement but
not on Sundays
No smoking rooms available

☎ Poulton le Fylde (0253) 885130

Robert and Beryl Owen

Entrance to drive off A 585

Set back from the road by a long drive and framed by a crescent of trees, Mains Hall is both an imposing and yet secluded 16th-century manor house with a romantic past – it was here that George IV courted his wife to be, Marie Fitzherbert. Despite extensive modernisation, its inherent air of historical grandeur shines through with the fine wood panelling, oak beams, a splendid staircase, ruined moat and pretty walled garden. The beamed lounge has a roaring log fire in winter. All the bedrooms are en suite or with private facilities; one has a four-poster and another a half-tester bed.

Bob and Beryl Owen bought the Hall in 1978 and they both greatly enjoy the guest house business. Bob is a lecturer at a local college, and so it is his wife Beryl who runs the hotel. Her favourite hobby is of particular interest as she studies wine and treats her guests to informal wine tastings. The three-course dinner is delicious. As far as possible fresh and home-grown produce is used and old fashioned puddings (the ones that do not count the calories) are a speciality. Dinner is served at 7pm but if you miss it, there is a range of tasty snacks available at the bar.

Easily Accessible: The Hall is situated on the banks of the River Wyre and so river walks (wellies almost always essential) are popular with guests. Half an hour way, the stunning countryside of Beacon Fell offers some lovely walks over hills and through woods. The Lake District is only an hour away. A very pleasant day can be spent touring the Fylde villages with their market days and craft exhibitions. Salisbury Hall is a magnificent black and white house, set in beautiful grounds and selling antiques. Blackpool with its seven miles of sandy beaches, spectacular autumn illuminations and 518ft high tower is only 7 miles away. Both Manchester and Liverpool are within easy reach.

Local Activities: swimming, horse-riding, golf, sports centre, sailing.

Greystones

Market Place   No smoking in bedrooms
Middleham   Reduced rates 30 days or more
North Yorkshire
DL8 4NR

☎ Wensleydale (0969) 22016

Keith and Frances Greenwood

This attractive Georgian house stands in an elevated position above a cobbled market place. In its lifetime it has been a grocer's shop and a bank. Its present owners, Keith and Frances Greenwood, are Yorkshire 'born and bred' but spent most of their adult lives in Bedfordshire. When they returned, one summer, to visit relatives, they saw and fell immediately in love with Greystones. It is a happy, friendly house, with a relaxed atmosphere where one is pleasantly greeted with a refreshing cup of tea and home-made biscuits. There are four bedrooms, each with en suite facilities, and a large comfortable lounge with a log fire and colour TV.

The evening meal consists of a set starter, a set main course, a choice of sweets and some delicious Wensleydale cheese and biscuits followed by after-dinner coffee in the lounge. The food is fresh and herbs, vegetables and fruit come from their allotment. Special diets can be catered for.

Easily Accessible: Middleham nestles in the heart of the Yorkshire Dales. Much of the town is built from stones pillaged from its splendid castle, once the seat of Richard III. It is also a racehorse training centre, and every morning around 7.30, stable lads can be seen leading the horses through the town and up onto the moors for training. Last but not least, much of the BBC series 'All Creatures Great and Small' is filmed here. There are many interesting walks around the town and on the Dales and it is also possible to take a mini-bus tour from Middleham of the popular areas of Wensleydale and Swaledale, with a local resident acting as guide. The eerie remains of Jervaulx Abbey (where, incidentally, Wensleydale cheese was first made) is just 4 miles away. Seven miles away, the Aysgarth Falls make a spectacular sight. Fifteen miles away, you can visit the Lightwater Valley with its amusement park for children.

Local Activities: walks, pony-trekking, fishing, swimming.

The Mill Hotel
Mungrisdale
Penrith
Cumbria
CA11 0XR

No pets in public rooms
Closed Dec–Feb
Award winner

☎ Threlkeld (059683) 659

Richard and Eleanor Quinlan

Situated at the foot of a mountain and bordered by a trout stream, this is an easy place to feel completely relaxed in. Inside it is comfortable and attractive and decorated in traditional English fabrics, with an open fire and oak beams contributing to the fresh country mood. There are eleven cosy bedrooms, most with private bathrooms and colour TV.

The proprietors Richard and Eleanor Quinlan found this, their ideal property, in 1985. Richard has a wealth of experience in catering as for twenty years he was manager of a large company hotel. Running a small, intimate hotel was his dream. He is the 'front of house' person at The Mill, and enjoys chatting to guests over drinks in the lounge before dinner.

Dinner is excellent; there are five courses described by the proprietors as a mixture of English and French cuisine. The sweets in particular are quite spectacular, and are sometimes decorated with fresh flowers. A popular speciality of the house are the freshly baked wholewheat and herb soda breads.

Easily Accessible: The small unspoilt village of Mungrisdale lies towards the north of the Lake District but is still well-placed for touring. Of course walking is the chief activity. Everywhere one goes, there are mountains, lakes and sheep-dotted valleys. The nearest lakes are Derwentwater and the larger Ullswater where you can take a cruise. Nearby places to visit include the Lingholm Gardens, Carlisle Castle built in 1092 to watch over England's border with Scotland, and Wordsworth's house in Cockermouth which was his birthplace and houses some of his personal effects. At Ambleside you can take a steam train through the lake and river scenery of the Leven valley. The gardens at Dalemain, developed over the centuries from a medieval herb garden, contain many unusual plants and shrubs and a wide variety of roses.

Local Activities: walks, fell-walking, rock-climbing, pony-trekking, bird-watching, sailing, fishing, hang-gliding, golf.

Old Farmhouse
Raskelf
Nr York
North Yorkshire
YO6 3LF

Closed Christmas
Advance booking must include
dinner

☎ Easingwold (0347) 21971

Bill and Jenny Frost

Off A19, 2 miles north of Easingwold

This old farmhouse resting in the village of Raskelf (the name means 'the shelf of the roe deer'), probably dates back to the 18th century. When Bill and Jenny bought it in 1977, it was in need of a lot of tender loving care – today, much restored and refurbished it has a wealth of beams, stripped pine and attractive brick fireplaces. There is a small but colourful garden with a large patio. The ten bedrooms are very prettily decorated with fine furniture and some antiques, one has a four-poster bed, all have en suite facilities. There are two lounges, one with a TV. All the main rooms have open fires. It is run as a collaborative effort by the Frost family, and this includes the friendly intervention of the family pets, two dogs, three cats, and two rabbits, all kept well under control. The service is excellent and very personal too – morning and afternoon tea are brought to one on a tray.

The food is imaginative and delicious – so good in fact that unless you have pre-booked it is virtually impossible to get in for dinner at week-ends. There is a choice of six starters, and six main courses with specialities such as Honey Roast Quail and Beef Sassay, which consists of braising steak stuffed with cheese and herb paté, wrapped in bacon and cooked in red wine. The puddings, such as the notorious 'Boozey Prunes', are just as appetising.

Easily Accessible: The village of Raskelf is a rural community lying at the northern end of the Vale of York, a few miles from the Hambleton Hills which form the southern edge of the North York Moors. There are many fine walks such as the Cleveland Way, which passes within 7 miles and the Lyke Wake walk, starting at Osmotherly, some 15 miles away. A pleasant footpath to Sessey, 3 miles away, starts directly from the house. York is just 15 miles away. Castle Howard, a palatial 18th-century country house with 1000 acres of grounds, and Beningbrough Hall, with over one hundred portraits from the National Portrait Gallery, are just two of the historic houses in the area. For horse-racing fans, Catterick, Ripon, York, Thirsk, and Wetherby racecourses are all within a short drive's distance.

Local Activities: walks, golf, horse-riding, fishing, swimming.

The Fat Lamb

Crossbank
Ravenstonedale
Kirkby Stephen
Cumbria
CA17 4LL

Three ground-floor rooms
　suitable for the disabled
Will collect guests from
　station

☎ Newbiggin-on-Lune (05873) 242

Paul and Helen Bonsall

Off A683 between Sedbergh and Kirkby Stephen

At an outstanding elevation of 1000 feet, the Fat Lamb has had its fair share of battles with the elements, and its proprietors, Paul and Helen Bonsall, admit that the garden's survival has been something of a minor miracle. Near hurricane force winds and free-roaming sheep put paid to early attempts at planting flowers and shrubs. Instead, rockeries and crazy paving abound and, after much tender loving care, a lawn has emerged triumphant. A strange assortment of livestock roam outside the garden's fenced perimeter and amongst the Nubian goats, geese, and miniature Shetland ponies, a strange creature, a Langrake (otherwise known as a Cumbrian Long-Necked Sheep), can be spotted. The Langrake, named Carlos, is over six feet high and is believed (by Paul and Helen) to be the last survivor of its breed. Looking more like a lumpy llama than a sheep, poor Carlos is all alone in the world – and quite understandably, a mate is being sought. Any suggestions gratefully received!

Inside the Fat Lamb, the visitor will find comfort and warmth. Although Helen and Paul have completed extensive renovations, they have intentionally retained the original character of what was a 17th-century inn. All nine bedrooms have private bathrooms. There are two lounges, one with a TV, the other with books and games. The cosy bar has an open fire.

The restaurant is open to guests and non-guests for lunch and dinner and offers both a table d'hôte and à la carte menu. Good home-cooking is prepared, using fresh and local produce.

Easily Accessible: The Fat Lamb is situated on the edge of the Howgill Fells at the foot of Wild Boar (2,324 feet). Thus the hill walker has a challenge right on his or her doorstep. Further afield, the Lake District and North Yorkshire Dales provide some breathtakingly beautiful and exciting walks. There are many pretty villages and market towns to explore including Appleby, where in June each year the famous horse fair sees the largest gathering of gypsies in Britain. At the Acorn Bank Garden, owned by the National Trust, you can see a fascinating collection of medicinal and cooking herbs.

Local Activities: walks, fishing, golf.

Burgoyne Hotel
Reeth
Richmond
North Yorkshire
DL11 6SN

☎ Richmond (0748) 84292

Steve and Pat Foster

10 miles west of Richmond on B6270

This attractive stone house dates from the 1750s, and has been a hotel since the 1930s. It rests in the heart of the dramatic scenery of Swaledale, one of Yorkshire's most beautiful areas, in the village of Reeth. The spacious, airy rooms have exhilarating views of the surrounding hills and dales. There is a TV lounge, a lounge bar, a dining room and a small garden. Many of the bedrooms are large and have en suite facilities with colour TV available on request.

Pat and Steve came rather unexpectedly to the hotel trade after sixteen years in the Royal Air Force – Steve as a pilot, and Pat as an education and administrative officer. At Burgoyne, Steve is chef, describing himself as an enthusiatic amateur. This is overly modest as the food is very good, with the choice of starter always including a home-made soup, lots of fresh vegetables, and a choice of delicious sweets.

Easily Accessible: Reeth is a large village with good amenities, including shops and cafés and a local folk museum detailing the history of the region over the last two centuries. Walks abound: the Pennine Way passes within ten miles of the village, and the coast to coast path passes right through. The surrounding countryside is quite dramatic with the legacy of the vast lead mining industry still evident. There are numerous picturesque villages, each with its own traditional arts and crafts, which include glass-making, spinning, embroidery, pottery and rope-making. A short drive to Arkengarthdale and you can down a pint in the highest pub in England. There are numerous historic houses of great interest including Bolton Castle, built in the 14th century. Children will enjoy

Lightwater Valley which has, amongst other attractions, a miniature railway, grand-prix track and fun rides.

Local Activities: walks, pony-trekking, fishing.

Whashton Springs Farm
Whashton
Richmond
North Yorkshire
DL11 7JS

Sorry, no pets
No dinner Thursday

☎ Richmond (0748) 2884

Gordon and Fairlie Turnbull

Whashton Springs Farm is set high in the hills, with superb views of the Yorkshire Dales. Guests are welcome to explore the 300-acre mixed farm (worked by Gordon Turnbull and his two sons) at their leisure.

The south-facing Georgian house is a most attractive listed building with unusual bow windows which overlook the gently sloping lawn. The pretty stone bridge which crosses the stream at the end of the walled garden is also listed. Three bedrooms overlook this charming scene. Six further bedrooms (all with en suite facilities) are situated in a converted stone courtyard. The conversion upset one member of the family. Snoopy the donkey was left without quarters and paid several unsuspecting guests a visit in a attempt to re-occupy her old home. All the bedrooms have a colour TV and one has a four-poster bed.

The Turnbulls are very friendly and welcoming. Gordon enjoys running the small bar and serving in the dining room which his wife says he took to like a 'duck to water'. Dinner is excellent: locally produced meat, vegetables and cheeses, and after dinner coffee and mints are served very elegantly in the drawing room.

Easily Accessible: There are numerous pretty villages to visit in the area and all are surrounded by the lovely unspoilt countryside. Walkers can enjoy both the dales and the moors and the Pennine Way, which can be reached 15 miles away. Among the many historic places to visit are Richmond's Norman castle and Easby Abbey (reputedly linked by an underground passage which is haunted by a drummer boy) and Aldborough Roman town with houses, courts, a forum and a temple. Richmond, 3 miles away, is a delightful town, full of history and housing the only Georgian theatre in the country. York, Durham and the Lake District are an hour's drive away.

Local Activities: walks, golf, fishing, pony-trekking, canoeing.

Stanhope Old Hall
Bishop Auckland
Co Durham
DL13 2PF

☎ Weardale (0388) 528451

Phyllis and Keith Robson

On A689 at the west end of Stanhope

Stanhope Hall must be one of the most extraordinary houses in this book. It was built way back in 1135 as a fortified manor house. In 1976 it was purchased by Phyllis and Keith who restored it, quite miraculously, from an almost derelict state to its present form in which it resembles its original appearance to an extraordinary degree. The thick stone walls, solid oak beams, cantilever oak staircase and mullioned windows are all exceptional, and the décor and style of furnishing is so absolutely 'right' that it is not difficult to imagine that one has just 'stepped back in time'. Features are continually being rediscovered; just one week before my arrival yet another brick fireplace complete with original bread corner oven was discovered. In 1989 Phyllis and Keith joined forces with Neville Spiers and purchased the adjoining Elizabethan extension and formed the banquet hall which can seat sixty. There are ten attractive bedrooms, thoughtfully decorated in keeping with the rest of the house. Eight are en suite.

All meals are available in the Feathertonehaugh dining room. The food is wholesome, plentiful and traditionally English. Bread and cakes are home-baked daily. Vegetarians and special diets are catered for.

Easily Accessible: Weardale was recently classified an 'area of outstanding natural beauty' and there is considerable scope in the immediate vicinity for fell walking, as well as more gentle ambles along the river Wear. Stanhope itself is an old market town; its centre has many 18th and 19th-century buildings, and was designated a conservation area in 1972. It also has a mock-medieval castle erected in 1798, and even more extraordinarily a 250-year-old fossilised tree. All around its industrial heritage can be seen, in the lead mining centre at the Dale Killhope Wheel, Britian's finest lead mining site, which is dominated by a 30ft water wheel. The Weardale Museum at nearby Ireshopeburn is a small museum in the Minister's House adjacent to a Methodist chapel where John Wesley once preached. It displays exhibitions of Weardale history and local life.

Local Activities: walks, mountain cycling, pony-trekking, fishing.

Shire Cottage

Benches Lane, Ernocroft Farm
Marple Bridge
Stockport
Cheshire
SK6 5NT

Bed and Breakfast only
Early breakfast for airport
     travellers

☎ daytime, Manchester (061427) 2377;
evening, Marple (04574) 66536

The Sidebottom Family

Off A626, Stockport and Glossop 6 miles.

This is a comfortable modern bungalow set in a large garden in peaceful countryside, with magnificent views overlooking Etherow Country Park. It is very conveniently situated for Manchester.

Monica Sidebottom says she took in guests as she was tired of talking to her animals! She is a friendly and helpful hostess who will book horse-riding, golf and fishing for her guests. She does not provide dinner, but there are thirteen eating places within two miles, ranging from pubs to classy restaurants. The three bedrooms have private facilities and TV.

Easily Accessible: The pleasures of Etherow Country Park – excellent views, wild flowers and wildfowl – are almost on your doorstep. Four miles away at Kinder Scout you can join the Pennine Way. Lyme Park, 4 miles away, has several hundred acres of parkland dotted with deer, and fine views of expansive moorland. It also has a very fine collection of clocks dating back to 1658. At Paradise Mill, 10 miles away, silk was handwoven from the 1750s until 1981 – today an exhibition gives you an idea of the skills and working conditions involved. There are many stately homes, including Adlington Hall, a stunning Elizabethan manor with an elegant Georgian portico; Arley Hall and Gardens, a Victorian residence set in twelve acres of gardens; and Bramwell Hall, a 15th-century black and white manor house. Eighteen miles away in Manchester you can visit Castlefield, Britain's first urban heritage park, which includes the Air and Space Museum and the Greater Manchester Museum of Science and Industry.

Local Activities: walks, fishing, golf, horse-riding, cycle hire.

Braemount House   Closed Jan and Feb
Sunny Bank Road
Windermere
Cumbria
LA23 2EN

☎ Windermere (09662) 5967

Tony and Mary Eley

A short car journey from railway station

Situated in the heart of the Lake District, away from main roads and close to some of the most beautiful countryside in the British Isles, Braemount House has much to offer anyone who appreciates comfort, hospitality and the great outdoors. When Tony Eley and his Irish wife Mary purchased Braemount House in 1986 they were newcomers to the hospitality business; Mary had retired from the nursing profession and Tony from the Royal Air Force. Together they have created a warm and welcoming atmosphere, with Tony (when he is not trying to improve his golf handicap) working front of house, and Mary preparing the meals.
    The house is Victorian, fairly small but with a marvellous homely feel to it. The four bedrooms are prettily furnished, all are en suite and well-equipped and each has a colour television. Dinner is a set menu meal served each evening at 7pm. The cooking is described by the Eleys as a mixture of English and Continental cuisine with a touch of Irish here and there.

Easily Accessible: Braemount House is situated in the Lake District National Park within easy walking distance of Windermere and Bowness villages. It is ideally located for exploring the beautiful scenery of Lakeland by car or, as most people prefer, by foot. If you have a literary bent, there is a lot that will appeal to you here; Wordsworth, Ruskin and Beatrix Potter all made their homes in the vicinity and today these 'shrines' are open to the public. In a very different vein, Sellafield nuclear plant has a visitors' centre, which is surprisingly popular with tourists.

Local Activities: walks, boat trips on the lakes, horse-riding, fishing, golf, fell-walking, bird-watching.

White Doves   Bed and Breakfast only
20 Claremont Terrace
off Gillygate
York
YO3 7EJ

☎ York (0904) 625957

Espie Bleasdale

5 minutes from city centre

White Doves is a Victorian terraced house situated only a few minutes from the famous Minster, in a quiet cul-de-sac. Its proprietor, Espie, is a former schoolteacher who taught in Australia for four years before retiring to York to establish this most pleasant and comfortable guest house. Charming and friendly, she will help you make the most of your visit. There are four tastefully furnished bedrooms, each with its own facilities, and colour TV. Dinner is not provided but there are many eating establishments within easy walking distance.

Easily Accessible: White Doves is ideally situated for exploring the very best of the 1,900-year-old city of York, with its Minster (the largest Gothic church in England), the Yorvik Viking Centre, and the famous 'shambles', an area of winding medieval streets. Among the many tours available, the Ghost Walk of York will take you on a quite literally 'haunting' tour, while a river tour along the Ouse takes you right through the city centre. There are also excellent tours from York into the surrounding area, where you can walk a number of the dales and moors, and see ancient abbeys, castles and fine stately homes.

Local Activities: sports amenities in city.

Jefferson Arms

Thorganby
York
YO4 6DB

☎ Wheldrake (090 489) 316

Robert Mason

6 miles east of York on Selby road (A19)

The Nutcracker suite in this charming 17th-century inn is so called because the low-ceilinged doorway has an exposed beam which has caught out the unwary and cracked a few heads in its time. The whole house is low-ceilinged, and furnished with antiques and pretty fabrics, with lots of fresh cut flowers and old world charm and character. It has very much the feel of a traditional (but rather special) coaching inn. Robert Mason, who has many years experience in catering, has an excellent idea of how to welcome his guests: a small decanter of sherry, fresh fruit and chocolate, await you in your room.

There are six cosy bedrooms (two have four-poster beds); each has a colour TV and en suite shower. The garden is colourful with an interesting original feature – a huge stone arch from an old church that resembles an ancient ruin and which spurts water into the garden pond.

The Poacher's Restaurant serves traditional English food, with a taste of France here and there. Desserts and bread are home-made; herbs come from the garden. A good English breakfast is served in the pleasant conservatory.

Easily Accessible: The tranquil village of Thorganby stands just fifteen minutes from York and near to the Wolds. There are numerous picturesque villages, ruined abbeys, and historic houses within easy driving distance, including Sledmere House which was built in the 1750s and rebuilt after a devastating fire, using the original plans, in 1911. Here, among the many magnificent rooms, you can see the splendid library, exotic Turkish room, modelled on an Istanbul mosque, a beautiful chapel and acres of Capability Brown's landscaped grounds dotted with follies. Twelve miles south of here you can see Britain's oldest horse races, the Kiplingcotes Derby at South Dalton. The first race was held here in 1519, and today it takes place once a year, on the third Tuesday of each March.

Local Activities: walks, golf.

SCOTLAND

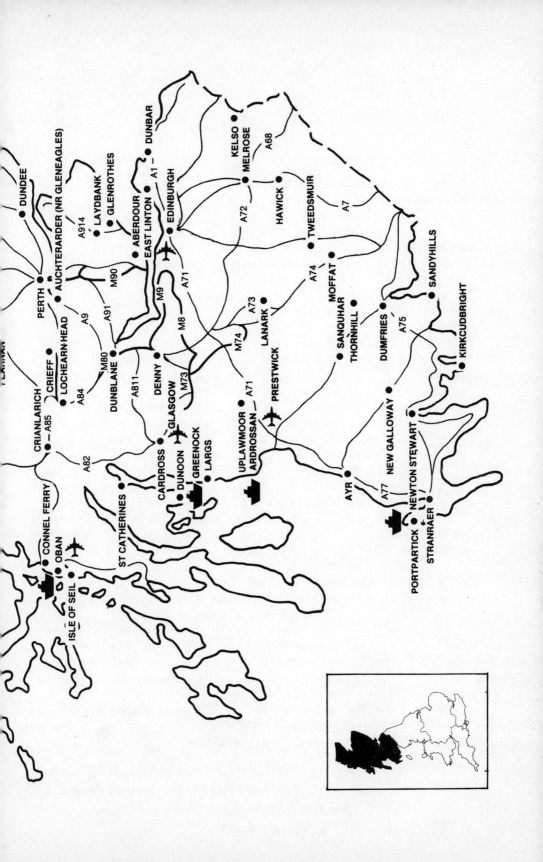

Scotland

There is a certain romanticism in most people's minds about Scotland. Although much of this has been inspired by one of its greatest writers, Sir Walter Scott, it is also a quite natural response to the dramatic, vivid, and for the most part unchanged landscape. For who can fail to be moved by the snow-capped mountains, tranquil lochs, sweet-scented pine forests, and purple, heather-clad hills? And in the depths of the lonely Highlands, rare wildlife flourishes: the golden eagle and opsrey, reindeer, red deer, stags and wild cats which sweep and roam over and across its terrain. Off the coasts of the Isles of Orkney and Shetland, seals frolic, and in the St Kilda Isles, the even rarer Soay sheep wanders freely, the only wild sheep in the British Isles.

In the more densely populated south, Scotland's two greatest cities are located: its capital Edinburgh has a wealth of architecture, particularly fine in the elegant Georgian New Town and in the 1,000-year-old castle which sits impressively high on a rock overlooking the city. In summer a different Edinburgh emerges when its streets, theatres and art galleries play host to an internationally acclaimed arts festival. Fifty miles west sprawls Glasgow, Scotland's largest city. No less cultural than Edinburgh, with excellent art collections and fine Victorian architecture, its people are famed for their gritty yet generous character. The most beautiful city of the Highlands must be Perth, once Scotland's capital. Much praised by Sir Walter Scott, Perth is steeped in history: James I of Scotland was murdered here, Bonnie Prince Charlie once stayed in its hostelry; and the famous minister John Knox preached on the 'idolatory of the church' in its kirk.

The bloody and often tragic history of Scotland has left its mark on the land, particularly in the many grim-looking castles and ruined abbeys that dot the countryside. In this eerie atmosphere the ghosts of murdered lairds are said to roam their ancient lands, and it is no wonder that fact and fiction tend to merge. Is there, or is there not, a strange prehistoric monster lurking in the depths of Loch Ness? Today, hundreds of years after Nessie was first spotted, no one, not even the scientists, can prove or disprove her existence. Other legends revolve around Scotland's great warriors; it is said that brave King Arthur lies asleep in a cave tomb in the Eildon Hills; and legend has it that the sturdy heart of Robert the Bruce lies buried in the ruins of Melrose Abbey.

It is not, however, only the romantic who will enjoy Scotland: sportspeople come here in their droves for the excellent hiking, mountaineering, golf, trout and salmon fishing, and, of course, for the increasingly popular sport of skiing – the premier skiing resort is in the Cairngorms, and the season there lasts from early December to the end of May.

Last but by no means least, many people are drawn to Scotland to sample its most popular export, malt whisky. Scotland's 'water of life' has a special place in the hearts of most of her people, and visitors invited to join the Whisky Trail soon find their very own place for it.

Scottish Tourist Board:
25 Ravelston Terrace, Edinburgh EH4 3EU
Tel: (031) 332 2433

ABERDEEN   CRAIGLYNN HOTEL
36 Fonthill Road, Aberdeen AB1 2UJ. *Tel*: Aberdeen (0224) 584050. *Hosts*: Hazel & Chris Mann.
Rates: B   Vouchers accepted.
(See page 220 for description)

ABERDOUR   THE WOODSIDE HOTEL
High Street, Aberdour, Burntisland, Fife, KY3 0SW. *Tel*: Aberdour (0383) 860328. *Telex*: 72165 G ref WOODSIDE. *Fax*: 0383 860920. *Host*: Andy Morris.
Rates: C/D
   Comfortable and spacious recently renovated Victorian house opposite 18-hole golf course, in historic picturesque village. Only 20-min drive from Edinburgh. Easy access M90 and many golf courses. Fishing, yachting and beaches near. 4-poster.

AUCHTERARDER (Nr Gleneagles)   SEATHAUGH
Orchil Road, Blackford, Auchterarder, Perthshire PH4 1RG. *Tel*: Blackford (076482) 493. *Hosts*: David & Connie Montgomery.
Rates: B
   Very comfortable, recently restored, stone-built farmhouse in 5 acres gardens and paddock. Panoramic views over Orchil hills. Golf arranged. Riding available. Off Auchterarder (Gleneagles 2 miles) to Braco road. Not suitable for children. Dinner by arrangement only. Sorry, no pets.

AULTBEA   DRUMCHORK LODGE HOTEL
Aultbea, Ross-shire IV22 2HU. *Tel*: Aultbea (044582) 242. *Hosts*: The Cooper Family.
Rates: C/D
   Comfortable Highland hotel with unequalled panoramic views overlooking Aultbea and Loch Ewe. Sauna, solarium. Few miles famous Inverewe

Gardens. Sea, loch and salmon fishing by arrangement. Golf, hill-walking, climbing. Fine sandy beaches nearby.

AYR (Coylton)   LOW COYLTON HOUSE
Manse Road, Coylton, Ayrshire KA6 6LE. *Tel*: Ayr (0292) 570615. *Hosts*: The Hay Family.
Rates: B   Vouchers accepted.
Very comfortable and spacious country house (1880) in lovely garden. Croquet lawn and paddock. Lovely safe sandy beaches. Golfers' paradise, incl Troon and Turnbury. Culzean Castle NT. Dinner by arrangement only. Prestwick 8 miles, Ayr 6.

BALLATER   INVERCAULD ARMS HOTEL
5 Bridge Square, Ballater, Aberdeenshire AB3 5QJ. *Tel*: Ballater (03397) 55417. *Telex*: 94015973. *Hosts*: James & Laddawan Anderson.
Rates: D
Victorian mansion nicely situated near town centre with views over River Dee and Riverside Gardens; Balmoral Castle 7 miles, may be visited May-Aug. Aberdeen 40 miles. Glenfiddich, Glenlivet and other famous distilleries within reach. Limited opening Jan-Mar. 4-poster room.

BALLATER   MOORSIDE HOUSE
Braemar Road, Ballater, Aberdeenshire AB3 5RL. *Tel*: Ballater (03397) 55492.
Hosts: Ian & Ann Hewitt.
Rates: A
(See page 221 for description)

BANFF   THE COUNTY HOTEL
32 High Street, Banff, Grampian AB4 1AE. *Tel*: Banff (02612) 5353. *Hosts*: Richard & Barbara Forster.
Rates: C/D   Vouchers accepted.
Elegant Georgian mansion overlooking Banff Bay. Richard and Barbara specialise in fresh local produce. Central for golf and fishing. Whisky and Castle Trails arranged. Beautiful coast and countryside. Reduced rates for 3 nights or more. Four-posters. All rooms with colour TV, telephone, en suite or with private bathroom.

BONAR BRIDGE   BRIDGE HOTEL
Bonar Bridge, Sutherland IV24 3EB. *Tel*: Ardgay (08632) 204. *Fax*: 086 32 686 *Host*: Mrs Ann Stevens.
Rates: D
Situated at head of Dornoch Firth; ideally located for touring; 1hr drive from Inverness (1hr airport; 2hrs Orkney ferry). Trout fishing and golf available locally. Bird-watching, forest and hill-walking. Freephone Bridge Hotel.

BRAEMAR   CALLATER LODGE
9 Glenshee Road, Braemar, Aberdeenshire AB3 5YQ. *Tel*: Braemar (03397) 41275. *Hosts*: William & Jean Rose.

Rates: A   Vouchers accepted.
   Spacious lodge standing 1,100 feet above sea level in over an acre of grounds on south side of this Royal Deeside village. Pleasant views of surrounding hills. Skiing (9 miles Glenshee) packages available. Balmoral 8 miles. Golf, fishing.

CARDROSS   KIRKTON HOUSE

Darleith Road, Cardross, Dumbartonshire G82 5EZ. *Tel*: Cardross (0389) 841951. *Hosts*: The Macdonald Family.
Rates: A/B   Vouchers accepted.
   Comfortable, informal, 160-year-old converted farmhouse with stable and paddock. Lovely panoramic views. Tranquil setting. Near Loch Lomond, Trossachs and Highland routes. Reduced rates 7 nights or more. 18 miles to Glasgow centre and airport.

CARRBRIDGE   KEEPER'S HOUSE PRIVATE HOTEL

Carrbridge, Inverness-shire PH23 3AT. *Tel*: Carrbridge (047984) 621. *Hosts*: Penny & Peter Rawson.
Rates: A/B   Vouchers accepted.
(See page 221 for description)

CONNEL FERRY   FALLS OF LORA HOTEL

Connel Ferry, by Oban, Argyll PA37 1PB. *Tel*: Connel (063171) 483. *Hosts*: Mrs C. M. Webster & Miss A. M. M. Innes.
Rates: C/D   Vouchers accepted.
   Traditional comfortable hotel in elevated position overlooking Loch Etive and Connel Bridge. Set back off A85, 5 miles from Oban. 'Gateway to the Highlands and Islands'. Sea and coarse fishing. Gliding, stalking, pony-trekking courses. 4-poster and half-tester available.

CRIANLARICH   ALLT-CHAORAIN HOUSE

Crianlarich, Perthshire FK20 8RU. *Tel*: Crianlarich (08383) 283. *Host*: Roger McDonald.
Rates: D (incl dinner)   Vouchers accepted.
(See page 222 for description)

CRIEFF   GALVELMORE HOUSE

Galvelmore Street, Crieff, Perthshire PH7 4BY. *Tel*: Crieff (0764) 2277. *Hosts*: John & Rosemary Kirby-Jones.
Rates: A
   Comfortable Georgian house in quiet street in centre of Crieff. Walled garden. Many golf courses, shooting, fishing, pony-trekking, water-skiing nearby. Transport available. Gleneagles 12 miles, Edinburgh 45 miles. Sorry, no pets.

CRIEFF   MURRAYPARK HOTEL

Connaught Terrace, Crieff, Perthshire PH7 3DJ. *Tel*: Crieff (0764) 3731. *Fax*: 0764 5311. *Hosts*: Noel & Ann Scott.

Rates: D   Vouchers accepted.
Friendly hotel in quiet residential area of bustling town, heart of beautiful Perthshire. Views over Strathearn to Ochil hills. Twenty golf courses, fishing nearby. Proprietors are proud of their reputation for good food and attentive service. BTA commended restaurant.

CROMARTY   THE ROYAL HOTEL

Marine Terrace, Cromarty, Ross-shire IV11 8YN. *Tel*: Cromarty (03817) 217. *Hosts*: The Morrison Family.
Rates: B/C   Vouchers accepted.
Small, friendly, waterside hotel overlooking Cromarty Firth in unique and unspoilt former royal and ancient burgh on Black Isle peninsular. Informal and relaxed atmosphere. Safe beach. Salmon and sea fishing. Exceptional for bird-watching. Log fires. All outdoor activities can be arranged. Good value.

DENNY   THE TOPPS FARM

Fintry Road, Denny, Stirlingshire FK6 5JF. *Tel*: Denny (0324) 822471. *Hosts*: Jennifer & Alistair Steel.
Rates: A/B   Vouchers accepted.
New farmhouse in superb position, specialising in sheep and Cashmere goats. Tastefully furnished en suite room for the disabled. Easy access off M80. Stirling 7 miles. Edinburgh or Perth 40 mins. Trossachs, Loch Lomond, Burrell Collection (Glasgow) 30 mins. Taste of Scotland 1989. Tennis court, fishing. Riding and golf nearby. Phone for directions.

DUMFRIES (Newtonairds)   BROUGHSHANE

Newtonairds, Dumfries DG2 OJL. *Tel*: Newbridge (0387) 720467. *Host*: Angela Duffin.
Rates: B   Vouchers accepted.
Comfortable, attractive modern farmhouse surrounded by hillside fields. Trout farm. Castles, lead mines, Caerlaverock Wildfowl Trust, NT gardens and houses nearby. No smoking in bedrooms. From Dumfries – A76, B729, left fork towards Newtonairds, 2 miles on right. Sorry, no pets.

DUMFRIES   CAIRNDALE HOTEL

English Street, Dumfries DG1 2DF. *Tel*: Dumfries (0387) 54111. *Hosts*: The Wallace Family.
Rates: D
Originally two Victorian town houses, the hotel is situated close to the centre of bustling market town of Dumfries. Ideally situated for touring Burns' country and the Borders. Gateway to Galloway and its many historic houses and gardens. Golf, fishing, shooting available by arrangement. 4 syndicate rooms. Queen-size beds available. Jacuzzi, spa baths, mini-bars.

DUNBAR BAYSWELL HOTEL AND RESTAURANT
Bayswell Park, Dunbar, East Lothian EH42 1AE. *Tel*: Dunbar (0368) 62225.
Host: Anne Creedigan.
Rates: C/D Vouchers accepted.
Clifftop country house hotel with breathtaking views across the Firth to
Dunbar Castle, May Island and Bass Rock. Just off the A1 and near mainline
BR station. Within 30 mins Edinburgh. Taste of Scotland cuisine. Quiet and
relaxing. Numerous golf courses within easy reach.

DUNBLANE STIRLING ARMS HOTEL
Stirling Road, Dunblane, Perthshire FK15 9EP. *Tel*: Dunblane (0786) 822156.
Fax: 0786 822648. *Hosts*: Jane & Richard Castelow.
Rates: B/C Vouchers accepted.
17th-century coaching inn in centre of historic Dunblane. Central to
Scotland. Excellent rail, road and air connections. International restaurant
including 'Taste of Scotland' cuisine. Reduction for 3 nights or more incl
dinner.

DUNDEE (Broughty Ferry) BEACH HOUSE HOTEL
22 Esplanade, Broughty Ferry, Dundee, Tayside DD5 2EN. *Tel*: Dundee
(0382) 76614. *Fax*: 0382 480241. *Host*: Lynne Glennie.
Rates: B/C
(See page 223 for description)

DUNOON ABBOT'S BRAE HOTEL
Bullwood, West Bay, Dunoon, Argyll PA23 7QJ. *Tel*: Dunoon (0369) 5021.
Hosts: Keith & Laura Cronshaw.
Rates: C
Imposing country house in wooded grounds on edge of town. Spectacular
sea views. 2 different short ferry crossings from Gourock off A8 and M8.
Honeymoon packages available. Rates include en suite facilities. Reductions
for 3 nights or more. Meals use local produce. Golf/fishing nearby.

EAST LINTON THE HARVESTERS HOTEL AND
RESTAURANT
East Linton, East Lothian EH40 3DP. *Tel*: East Linton (0620) 860395. *Hosts*:
Harry, Elaine & Carol Hyde.
Rates: D Vouchers accepted.
Lovely, extremely comfortable Georgian house in 3½ acres attractive
gardens with river frontage. Small village just off A1, 22 miles Edinburgh,
34 Berwick. Proprietors are proud of their reputation for good country food.
Also a coach house annexe.

EDINBURGH THE DRUM
Gilmerton, Edinburgh EH17 8RX. *Tel*: Edinburgh (031) 664 7215. *Hosts*: Alan
& Patrea More Nisbett.
Rates: D Vouchers accepted.

Fascinating William Adams house set in 500 acres of farmland, yet still within the city. All rooms en suite. Four-posters. Breakfast in 15th-century armoury. Shooting, tennis, croquet, riding, superb walks. Helicopter pad. Off Edinburgh ring route between A7 and A68.

EDINBURGH   THE MEADOWS
17 Glengyle Terrace, Bruntsfield, Edinburgh EH3 9LN. *Tel*: Edinburgh (031) 229 9559. *Hosts*: Gloria & Jon Stuart.
Rates: A/C
   Comfortable, early Victorian terraced house in quiet situation overlooking park near A702 and A68 junction at Tollcross. Princes Street 10 mins. Castle 25 mins walk. Theatres and university near. Plenty of pubs and restaurants nearby. Min 3 nights (except businessmen).

EDINBURGH   NOVA HOTEL
5 Bruntsfield Crescent, Edinburgh EH10 4EZ. *Tel*: Edinburgh (031) 447 6437/7349. *Telex*: 727364 NOVA G. *Fax*: 031 452 8126. *Host*: Jamie McBride.
Rates: D
   In quiet residential cul-de-sac, overlooking Bruntsfield Links with putting green with views of Pentland hills from the rear. Attractive walled garden. Bar/lounge. Easy walking distance Princes Street and castle. Easy parking. Sorry, no pets. 4-poster and half-tester available.

EDINBURGH   (A 'no smoking' house)   TEVIOTDALE HOUSE
53 Grange Loan, Edinburgh EH9 2ER. *Tel*: Edinburgh (031) 667 4376. *Hosts*: Mr & Mrs J. Coville.
Rates: B/C   Vouchers accepted.
   25 years of loving care have made this beautifully restored town house luxuriously comfortable; quiet residential location. 'Breakfast is a banquet!' Access from the 'by-pass' on to A702 City South. Princes Street 10 mins.

FEARNAN (by Aberfeldy)   TIGH-AN-LOAN HOTEL
Fearnan, by Aberfeldy, Perthshire PH15 2PF. *Tel*: Kenmore (08873) 249.
Hosts: David & Shenac Kelloe.
Rates: B/C   Vouchers accepted.
   Peaceful, lochside hotel with panoramic views. Own fishing rights. 18-hole golf at Kenmore 3 miles, 9-hole at Aberfeldy and Killin. On A827 9 miles west of Aberfeldy.

FETTERCAIRN   RAMSAY ARMS HOTEL
Fettercairn, Kincardineshire AB3 1XX. *Tel*: Fettercairn (05614) 334. *Host*: Jeff Evans.
Rates: C
   Comfortable and relaxing old coaching inn, on edge of Deeside and Grampian Highlands. Perth 40 miles, Aberdeen 34. Golf, trout and salmon

fishing, shooting, pony-trekking, hill-walking. Free use of spa, bath, sauna, solarium and exercise facilities.

FORRES   BROUGH HOUSE
Milton Brodie, Forres, Moray IV36 0UA. *Tel*: Alves (034 385) 617. *Hosts*: Mark & Rosemary Lawson.
Rates: B   Vouchers accepted.
(See page 224 for description)

FORT AUGUSTUS   THE BRAE HOTEL
Fort Augustus, Inverness-shire PH32 4DG. *Tel*: Fort Augustus (0320) 6289.
Hosts: Andrew & Mary Reive.
Rates: A/B
(See page 225 for description)

FORT WILLIAM (Banavie)   MOORINGS HOTEL
Banavie, Fort William, Inverness-shire PH33 7LY. *Tel*: Corpach (03977) 550.
Fax: 03977/441. *Host*: Norman Sinclair.
Rates: D
(See page 226 for description)

GLENROTHES (Freuchie)   LOMOND HILLS HOTEL
Parliament Square, Freuchie, by Glenrothes, Fife KY7 7EY. *Tel*: Falkland (0337) 57329. *Fax*: 0337/57498. *Hosts*: The van Beusekom Family.
Rates: C   Vouchers accepted.
(See page 227 for description)

GRANTOWN-ON-SPEY   (A 'no smoking' house)   DUNSTAFFNAGE
  HOUSE
Dunstaffnage Brae, Grantown-on-Spey, Morayshire PH26 3JR. *Tel*: Grantown (0479) 2000. *Hosts*: David & Martha Hunt.
Rates: B   Vouchers accepted.
(See page 228 for description)

GRANTOWN-ON-SPEY   COPPICE HOTEL
Grant Road, Grantown-on-Spey, Morayshire PH26 3LD. *Tel*: Grantown-on-Spey (0479) 2688. *Hosts*: Mike & Pat Warnes.
Rates: C
  In own wooded grounds, 200 yards from main street. Spey Valley is an area of great scenic beauty. Easy reach of six golf courses. Salmon and trout fishing, sailing, canoeing, pony-trekking. Hill-walking and skiing in Cairngorms. Kincraig Wildlife Park.

HAWICK   (A 'no smoking' house)   BURNSIDE COTTAGE
Wilton Dean, Hawick, Roxburghshire TD9 7HY. *Tel*: Hawick (0450) 73378.
Host: Elspeth Scott.
Rates: A   Vouchers accepted.
(See page 229 for description)

HAWICK KIRKLANDS HOTEL
West Stewart Place, Hawick, Roxburghshire TD9 8BH. *Tel*: Hawick (0450)
72263. *Host*: Barrie Newland.
Rates: D Vouchers accepted.
  Charming, comfortable hotel in quiet residential area, with views. Beautiful
  Scottish Borders touring area of historic interest. Good leisure centre 3 mins
  walk. Golf, salmon and trout fishing and pony-trekking arranged. BTA
  commended.

INVERNESS CRAIGSIDE HOUSE
4 Gordon Terrace, Inverness IV2 3HD. *Tel*: Inverness (0463) 231576. *Hosts*:
Mr & Mrs Skinner.
Rates: A/B Vouchers accepted.
  Comfortable, spacious Victorian house with wonderful views from lounge
  of castle, river and countryside. In quiet residential area. Sun terrace, small
  garden, parking. Excellent touring centre by coach or car. Home-cooking.
  Sorry, no pets.

ISLE OF SEIL WILLOWBURN HOTEL
Clachan Seil, by Oban, Argyll PA34 4TJ. *Tel*: Balvicar (08523) 276. *Hosts*:
Archie & Maureen Todd.
Rates: B Vouchers accepted.
  Friendly, small hotel with spectacular views. Setting for 'Ring of Bright
  Water'. Approached via Atlantic Bridge. Wildlife including sea otters and
  sea trout. Via A816 and B844 signposted Easdale. Oban 20 mins drive.

ISLE OF SKYE (Portree) KING'S HAVEN HOTEL
Portree, Isle of Skye, Inverness-shire IV51 9DJ. *Tel*: Portree (0478) 2290. *Host*:
Judith Vaughan-Sharp.
Rates: B/C Vouchers accepted.
  Comfortable and friendly old Georgian house in centre of village near
  harbour and bus terminal. Ideal centre for exploring Skye. Fishing, golf and
  other activities available. All rooms have bathrooms en suite and colour TV.
  Good pubs and restaurants nearby.

KELSO CROSS KEYS HOTEL
The Square, Kelso, Roxburghshire TD5 7HL. *Tel*: Kelso (0573) 23303. *Fax*:
0573 25792 *Host*: Marcello Becattelli.
Rates: C
  The majestic façade of this rebuilt coaching inn dominates one side of
  the ancient cobbled square, in this attractive market town on the Scottish
  border. Fishing in Tweed and Teviot. Golf, curling and riding.

KIRKCUDBRIGHT ANCHORLEE GUEST HOUSE
95 St Mary Street, Kirkcudbright DG6 4EL. *Tel*: Kirkcudbright (0557) 30793.
Hosts: Marina & George Anderson.
Rates: A/B Vouchers accepted.
This elegant detached Victorian house in conservation area retains much of its

original character and provides spacious accommodation. Large walled garden. Private parking. 5 mins walk from town centre. Golf course a pitch away. STB highly commended.

KIRKMICHAEL (by Pitlochry)   THE LOG CABIN HOTEL

Kirkmichael, Perthshire PH10 7NB. *Tel*: Strathardie (0250 81) 288. *Host*: Alan Finch.

Rates: D

In the heart of the Scottish Highlands, relaxed, all-year-round centre for skiing, climbing, golfing, sailing, water-skiing with own stalking and shooting. Near Pitlochry. Easy access of M90 and A9.

LADYBANK (Nr Cupar)   REDLANDS

By Ladybank, Fife KY7 7SH. *Tel*: Ladybank (0337) 31091. *Hosts*: Jane & Ronald Keanie.

Rates: B   Vouchers accepted.

(See page 230 for description)

LANARK (Sandilands)   EASTERTOWN FARM

Sandilands, Lanark, Lanarkshire MLll 9TX. *Tel*: Douglas Water (055 588) 236. *Hosts*: The Tennant Family.

Rates: A/B

18th-century farmhouse on working sheep farm with panoramic views. Private trout fishing. Falls of Clyde and and New Lanark restored industrial village nearby. Centrally situated for Southern Scotland. M74 3miles, Lanark 7. Sorry, no pets.

LARGS   GLEN ELDON HOTEL

2 Barr Crescent, Largs, Ayrshire KA30 8PX. *Tel*: Largs (0475) 673381. *Hosts*: Dewar & Mary Paton.

Rates: C   Vouchers accepted.

Family-run hotel with a warm welcome. Near promenade at north end of this attractive resort. Easy reach of sports centre and golf. All bedrooms with bathroom en suite and telephone. Some 'no smoking' areas. Sorry, no pets.

LOCHEARNHEAD   MANSEWOOD COUNTRY HOUSE

Lochearnhead, Perthshire FK19 8NS. *Tel*: Lochearnhead (05673) 213. *Hosts*: Jeff & Sue Jeffery.

Rates: B   Vouchers accepted.

200-year-old stone manse, with friendly, cosy atmosphere in stunningly beautiful countryside and watersports area. South of Lochearnhead on A84. Walking, sailing. Proprietors are proud of their good standard of food. All bedrooms double-glazed. 4-poster. Off-peak breaks available. No TV.

MELROSE   (A 'no smoking' house)   DUNFERMLINE HOUSE

Buccleuch Street, Melrose TD6 9LB. *Tel*: Melrose (089682) 2148. *Hosts*: Susan & Ian Graham.

Rates: A   Vouchers accepted.

(See page 231 for description)

MOFFAT   MOFFAT HOUSE HOTEL
High Street, Moffat, Dumfriesshire DG10 9HL. *Tel*: Moffat (0683) 20039.
Hosts: The Reid Family.
Rates: C/D   Vouchers accepted.
(See page 232 for description)

NAIRN   MILLFORD HOTEL
Mill Road, Nairn, Inverness-shire IV12 5EW. *Tel*: Nairn (0667) 53941. *Hosts*:
Audrey & Kent Grant.
Rates: B
   Spacious Victorian house, 3 acres garden with putting green, on edge
   of town. Extensive views. 10 mins walk good sandy beaches. Two golf
   courses. Salmon and trout fishing arranged. Cawdor Castle and Culloden
   nearby. Inverness 14 miles.

NEW GALLOWAY   CAIRN EDWARD
New Galloway, by Castle Douglas, Kirkcudbrightshire DG7 3RZ. *Tel*: New
Galloway (06442) 244. *Hosts*: Donald & Penny Murray.
Rates: A/B   Vouchers accepted.
(See page 233 for description)

NEWTON STEWART   ROWALLAN HOUSE HOTEL
Corsbie Road, Newton Stewart, Wigtownshire DG8 6JB. *Tel*: Newton Stewart
(0671) 2520. *Hosts*: Adam & Ethel Imrie.
Rates: C   Vouchers accepted.
   Comfortable, spacious Victorian house in 1½ acres lovely gardens. Quiet
   residential area, 5 mins walk town centre. Walking, golf, bird-watching,
   fishing. Historic area. Bar lounge. All rooms colour TV.

OBAN   THE BALMORAL HOTEL
Craigard Road, Oban, Argyll PA34 5NP. *Tel*: Oban (0631) 62731. *Hosts*:
Robert & Elizabeth Pollock.
Rates: B/C
   Centrally situated hotel, very convenient for shops, with piers, harbour
   and esplanade a few mins walk. Ferries for island cruises. Most watersports,
   sailing centre, fishing. Owners take pride in varied selection in restaurant.
   Colour TV all rooms.

ONICH (Fort William)   CUILCHEANNA HOUSE
Onich, Nr Fort William, Inverness-shire PH33 6SD. *Tel*: Onich (08553) 226.
Hosts: Andrew & Margaret Dewar.
Rates: B   Vouchers accepted.
   Large 16th-century farmhouse, in 120 acres beef farmland, overlooking Loch
   Linnhe. 10 miles south of Fort William, off A82. Tranquil surroundings.
   Fishing, boat hire, sailing, climbing. Glencoe 12 miles. Home-cooking, local
   produce. No TV. With cottage annexes.

PERTH (A 'no smoking' house)   ALPINE GUEST HOUSE
7 Strathview Terrace, Perth, Tayside PH2 7HY. *Tel*: Perth (0738) 37687. *Hosts*:
David & Ina Gray.
Rates: A/B   Vouchers accepted.
 Welcoming, friendly house with superb views over Little Glenshee. Ideal
 situation for many golf courses. 15 mins walk from leisure centre. Colour
 TV all rooms. Edinburgh and Glasgow within 1 hr drive. Children over 5
 welcome. Sorry, no pets.

PERTH (Glencarse)   NEWTON HOUSE HOTEL
Glencarse by Perth, Perthshire PH2 7LX. *Tel*: Glencarse (073 886) 250. *Fax*:
073 886 717. *Hosts*: Mr and Mrs Geoffrey Tallis.
Rates: C/D   Vouchers accepted.
 Comfortable former dower house in 1½ acres gardens. Slip road off A85.
 Easy access M90. Perth 6 miles, Dundee 13. Glasgow, Edinburgh, Aberdeen
 and Inverness within 2 hrs drive. Heart of beautiful Carse of Gowrie. Golf,
 fishing and historic area.

PITLOCHRY   AIRDANIAR HOTEL
160 Atholl Road, Pitlochry, Perthshire PH16 5AR. *Tel*: Pitlochry (0796) 2266.
Hosts: Andrew & Sue Mathieson.
Rates: C   Vouchers accepted.
 Comfortable hotel with friendly atmosphere, set in 3 acres gardens, with
 lovely views. Within few minutes walk Pitlochry with its many facilities.
 Home-cooking, own and local produce. 3-day autumn and spring breaks
 available.

PORTPATRICK   RICKWOOD HOTEL
Heugh Road, Portpatrick, Stranraer, Wigtownshire DG9 8TD. *Tel*: Portpatrick
(077681) 270. *Hosts*: Allan & Kay Dickson.
Rates: B   Vouchers accepted.
 Detached corner house in nice position, overlooking pretty countryside,
 picturesque village and bustling little harbour. Golf, tennis, fishing, riding,
 watersports. Botanical gardens. Gulf Stream temperature climate. Ground-
 floor rooms available. Reduced rates after 3 nights.

ROSEHALL BY ARDGAY   INVEROYKEL LODGE HOTEL
Rosehall, Strathoykel, by Ardgay, Ross-shire IV24 3DP. *Tel*: Rosehall (054984)
200. *Hosts*: Derek & Rita Hatherton.
Rates: B
 Northern Highlands sporting lodge in 16 acres grounds, overlooking River
 Oykel. Magnificent views. 1 mile off A837. 12 miles Ardgay. Free salmon
 fishing in grounds, two trout hill-lochs nearby. Children over 12 welcome.
 Stalking and fishing packages available.

ST CATHERINES   THISTLE HOUSE
St Catherines, by Cairndow, Argyll PA25 8AZ. *Tel*: Inverary (0499) 2209.
Hosts: Sandra & Donald Cameron.

Rates: A/B Vouchers accepted.

Spacious country house in peaceful location with magnificent loch views across to Inverary and castle. Display gardens nearby. On the A815 between Cairndow and Strachur. Home-cooking. Bring own wine. Reduced rates 2 nights or more. BTA commended.

SANDYHILLS CAIRNGILL HOUSE HOTEL
Sandyhills, Dalbeattie, Kirkcudbrightshire DG5 4NZ. *Tel*: Southwick (038778) 681. *Hosts*: Brian & Anne Downs.
Rates: C
(See page 234 for description)

SANQUHAR DRUMBRINGAN GUEST HOUSE
53 Castle Street, Sanquhar, Dumfriesshire DG4 6AB. *Tel*: Sanquhar (0659) 50409. *Hosts*: Margot Innes, Doreen Connolly.
Rates: A Vouchers accepted.

Homely Georgian house with garden, edge of ancient village with oldest post office in Britain. Fishing, golf, bowling. Lovely Nithsdale valley, walking Southern Upland Way. Home-cooking. Drumlanrigg Castle and Wanlockhead Mining Museum nearby. Sorry, no pets.

SCOURIE SCOURIE HOTEL
Scourie, Sutherland IV27 4SX. *Tel*: Scourie (0971) 2396. *Hosts*: Ian & Mary Hay.
Rates: C

Occupying the site of fortified house of the Mackays of Scourie, overlooking tiny crofting village. Rugged and beautiful countryside. Touring, bird-watching Apr-June, walking, fishing, climbing. No TV.

STRANRAER NORTH WEST CASTLE HOTEL
Royal Crescent, Stranraer, Wigtownshire DG9 8EH. *Tel*: Stranraer (0776) 4413. *Telex*: 777088. *Fax*: 0776 2646. *Hosts*: The McMillan Family.
Rates: D

Very comfortable friendly hotel in gardens, with magnificent views over Loch Ryan. Many features include indoor heated swimming pool, sauna, solarium, curling rink Oct-Apr, carpet bowling and 4-poster bed. Ferry points to Larne, Northern Ireland. Exhibitions accommodated.

THORNHILL GEORGE HOTEL
Thornhill, Dumfriesshire DG3 5LU. *Tel*: Thornhill (0848) 30326. *Hosts*: Robert & Rachael Saville.
Rates: C

Old coaching inn in beautiful Nithsdale. Burns and Borders touring. Private fishing on George Loch and salmon fishing on River Nith. Shooting, three golf courses. Many historic houses and gardens. On A76 easy reach A74.

TUMMEL BRIDGE KYNACHAN LODGE
Tummel Bridge, by Pitlochry, Perthshire PH15 5SB. *Tel*: Tummel Bridge (08824) 214. *Hosts*: Valerie & Peter Hampson.

Rates: B/C   Vouchers accepted.
Warm, comfortable and spacious house, once a whisky baron's shooting lodge, in 12 acres lochside grounds. Luxury bedrooms all en suite with colour TV. Hosts are proud of their cuisine and wine list. Sorry, no pets.

TWEEDSMUIR MENZION FARMHOUSE
Tweedsmuir, Tweeddale ML12 6QR. *Tel*: Tweedsmuir (08997) 247. *Hosts*: Mary & David Brett.
Rates: B   Vouchers accepted.
(See page 235 for description)

UPLAWMOOR CARSWELL HOUSE FARM
By Neilston, Renfrewshire G78 3DH. *Tel*: Uplawmoor (050 585) 676. *Hosts*: Iain & Mary Edgar.
Rates: C   Vouchers accepted.
Remote stone-built 18th-century house on working farm. Quiet and secluded yet only 12 miles from Glasgow city centre. Home and local produce in traditional cooking. Special diets catered for. Burns country, fishing and golfing nearby. Glasgow airport 10 miles, Paisley 7. Sorry, no pets.

Craiglynn Hotel   Sorry, no pets
36 Fonthill Road
Aberdeen
AB1 2UJ

☎ Aberdeen (0224) 584050

Hazel and Chris Mann

Easy reach city centre and port, off Bon-accord Street

This spacious house was built at the turn of the century of Aberdeen granite and has a most unusual roof structure which incorporates a domed tower – the tower bedroom below is very popular with guests. There is a large colourful garden. Inside, several original features remain, including the stained glass windows, oak and rosewood panelling, and parquet flooring. All nine bedrooms are comfortable, well-equipped and have remote-controlled TV.

Dinner is served between 7 and 7.30pm. All meals are prepared to order, and local meat, fish and fresh vegetables are used. Specialities of the house are home-made soups and delicious main-course sauces.

Easily Accessible: Craiglynn is situated in a quiet residential area but within a short bus ride of the centre of Aberdeen. The city has a wealth of things to do and see; historic monuments, a harbour, and all the amenities expected of a modern city including extensive sports facilities, art galleries, theatres and museums. It also has some lovely sandy beaches and is surrounded by the beautiful wild scenery of the Grampian Highlands. You can take the Malt Whisky Trail and visit seven excellent distilleries and enjoy the stunning countryside at the same time. Local events include sheepdog trials, cattle markets and Highland games, and in certain pubs you will be treated to Scottish evenings and folk music.

Local Activities: extensive sports facilities in Aberdeen, hill-walking, horse-riding, pony-trekking.

Moorside House   Closed Dec/Jan/Feb
Braemar Road   Dogs (prior arrangement only)
Ballater
Aberdeenshire
AB3 5RL

☎ Ballater (03397) 55492

Ian and Ann Hewitt

Situated 200 yds from centre of Ballater on A93 to Braemar

Moorside House lies on the banks of the River Dee in the burgh of Ballater. Built in 1883 of locally hewn pink and grey granite, it has an attractive landscaped garden with fine views stretching to the distant mountains. The wooded hills of Craigendarroch and Craig Coillach rise up around it.

It is run by Ian and Ann Hewitt who met in Trinidad, where Ann's relatives were established in the hotel business. This gave Ian the idea of setting up a similar, small-scale, homely establishment in the Highlands. They both love the business; Ian enjoys meeting new people and for Ann, cooking is a pleasure. All nine bedrooms have private or en suite facilities and colour TV and are decorated in pleasant pastel colours. There is a guest dining room and lounge.

The four-course dinner menu is a mixture of traditional and modern Scottish cooking. Fresh and local produce is used. For breakfast the full Scottish menu includes a particularly good bowl of porridge. Ann is, she says, greatly rewarded, 'by the return of empty plates'.

Easily Accessible: The lovely countryside is obviously the main attraction for visitors and walking is a real pleasure here, partly because the area is not over-crowded. Try walking up Craigendarrock Hill (meaning Hill of Oaks); the views from the top are excellent. Balmoral Castle grounds 8 miles away are open to the public; adjacent to Balmoral is the Royal Lochnager Distillery. The 16th-century ruins of Knock Castle, 2 miles away, have a murky past – all the sons of the Laird were murdered by a neighbouring Forbes of Strath girnock; when the Laird was informed he was so overcome by grief that he fell down a staircase to his death. Glen Muick is very lovely with roaming red deer, beautiful waterfalls, and a peaceful loch. The Malt Whisky Trail, a one day car tour, will take you to world-famous distilleries.

Local Activities: walks, golf, fishing, hill-walking, tennis/bowls, horse-riding, pony-trekking.

Keeper's House Private Hotel
Carrbridge
Inverness-shire
PH23 3AT

☎ Carrbridge (047984) 621

Peter and Penny Rawson

Closed 1 Nov–20 Dec
Unlicensed, guests welcome to
  bring own wine

This was once a gamekeeper's cottage belonging to a large estate . It is situated in the small highland village of Carrbridge and surrounded by beautiful countryside of sweet-smelling pine trees, dark mooorland and mountain peaks. There is wildlife here in abundance; deer, wild cats, red squirrels, golden eagles, ospreys and reindeer.

The hotel is full of charm and character and Penny Rawson's beloved and rare plants. The Rawsons (a brother and sister team) have worked hard on the property creating a games-room from a garage, an Alpine section in the garden and adding private facilities to three of the five rooms. The spacious dining room is often sunny and is filled with antiques and heirlooms. The cosy lounge is lit by log fires in the cold winter months and has a colour TV.

The food is traditional Scottish fare and ingredients are fresh. Vegetables and fruit (raspberries, blackcurrants and gooseberries) come from the garden and eggs from the Rawsons' hens. The delicious kippers and haddock come from Portsoy. Vegetarians will be offered alternatives by arrangement.

Easily Accessible: Local walks are varied and numerous and will take you through lochside and forest, field and riverbank, moor and mountains. Golfers will enjoy the nine-hole golf course opposite the hotel. In September for one week Carrbridge hosts its own festival of Scottish music. The Carrbridge Landmark Centre provides nature trails, an excellent shop and a good selection of books. Six miles away at the RSPB reserve at Loch Garten, you can see the nesting ospreys and in the adjoining Abernethy Forest you can walk in 21,000 acres of mountain, moorland and native pine forest. Seven miles away at Aviemore there is a visitor centre and entertainment complex with a full range of sports facilities. The nearest large town is Inverness, 23 miles away. Resting on the banks of the River Ness with a castle (now the county court) it has a variety of shops, a cinema and a theatre. Twenty-five miles away, Cawdor Castle, home of the Thanes of Cawdor, has some beautiful gardens. The Whisky Trail, visiting several famous distilleries, can be picked up nearby.

Local Activities: skiing, water sports on Loch Morlich and Loch Insh, pony-trekking, walking, bird-watching, golfing, fishing, mountaineering.

Allt-Chaorain House
Crianlarich
Perthshire
FK20 8RU

Price of dinner included.
Will collect guests from station
Closed 5 Nov to 10 March
Children over 5 welcome

☎ Crianlarich (08383) 283

Roger McDonald

Off A82 towards Tyndrum

No smoking in dining room and bedrooms

Allt-Chaorain is a warm and attractive house lying spectacularly in an elevated position among forest-clad hills and rugged mountains. Just five hundred yards from the A82, it makes an ideal base from which to tour the Central Highlands. The house was built at the turn of the century as a country home and used for many years as a shooting lodge. It has ten acres of land and a pretty garden of roses and rhododendrons. There is a comfortable lounge with a log fire and bar and a south-facing sunroom with superb views of the wild rugged landscape dominated by the mountain, Ben More. All nine bedrooms have private facilities.

All the food is prepared from fresh produce. The menus are discussed with guests at breakfast time. Heavily influenced by traditional Scottish recipes, they are cooked to perfection. Packed lunches are available on request.

Easily Accessible: The surrounding countryside is a walker's paradise with hills mountains,lochs, and the West Highland Way to enjoy. There is an enormous variety of birdlife and the natural flora of the area (which includes Alpine plants) is fascinating. There are several castles to explore including Inverary, a sumptuous baronial-type castle, and Doune with an interesting motor museum. The small, peaceful island of Iona has been a centre of Christianity since St Columba founded his monastery there. Today the abbey church is a thriving Christian community. Both Glasgow and Perth are under 60 miles away.

Local Activities: walks, salmon and trout fishing, bowls, golf, sailing, tennis, wind-surfing, water-skiing.

Beach House Hotel

22 Esplanade
Broughty Ferry
Dundee
Tayside
DD5 2EN

☎ Dundee (0382) 76614

Lynne Glennie

4 miles east of Dundee city centre

Beach House hotel is a small, warm and wonderfully comfortable Victorian terraced house in the old fishing village of Broughty Ferry just outside Dundee. It has a small patio garden overlooking a sandy beach and a very attentive and friendly proprietor, Lynne Glennie. There are five bedrooms all en suite with colour TVs, and an attractive lounge. Snacks are available all day and a full home-cooked dinner is served in a small dining room from 6pm to 9pm – Lynne's soups are a speciality.

Easily Accessible: Dundee is the heart and capital of the Tayside region which encompasses the counties of Angus, Fife and Perthshire. It is a coastal city with a fine historical heritage and offers all the amenities one would expect, including a castle museum, a botanical garden and the frigate *Unicorn* (the oldest British-built warship afloat). The picturesque village and castle of Glamis (a royal residence since 1374 and the family home of the Earl of Strathmore) are half an hour from Dundee. 700-year-old Blair Castle, and Earlshall Castle and gardens are 8 miles away. Just outside Dundee there are several country parks ideal for gentle walks. Dundee is well placed for visiting Aberdeen, Edinburgh, St Andrews and Perth (a town described by Sir Walter Scott as the 'most varied and beautiful in Scotland').

Local Activities: swimming, golf, tennis, coarse and sea-fishing, flying, skiing and sailing.

Brough House

Milton Brodie
Forres
Moray
IV36 0UA

Sorry, no pets
Unlicensed
Will collect guests from station

☎ Alves (034385) 617

Mark and Rosemary Lawson

4 miles east of Forres, off A96, follow sign for East Grange

This lovely country house lies well secluded off the road between Forres and Elgin in the magnificent countryside of Morayshire (which has one of the highest sunshine levels in the UK). The house is beautifully furnished with antiques and warm colours. There are two twin-bedded rooms, one with a bathroom en suite and the other with a private bathroom. A third twin room is available with a shared bathroom. The cosy drawing room has a TV and open fire. There is a pretty garden with a large kitchen garden providing fresh vegetables.

Dinner is taken by candlelight at a well-dressed table in the elegant dining room. Rosemary and Mark often eat with their guests. Game, local fish and fresh vegetables are frequently on the menu. If guests wish to eat out Rosemary will recommend local restaurants.

Easily Accessible: The whole area is full of natural beauty ranging from wild untutored countryside to spotless sandy beaches, from ancient forests to rugged cliffs. But man also has made his mark in the many ancient monuments, castles and churches that dot the countryside and small villages. Walks vary from gentle lakeside ambles to the arduous long-distance footpath, known as the Speyside Way. Morayshire is the heart of the whisky industry and you can take the famous Whisky Trail to seven distinctive malt whisky distilleries. The capital of the region is Elgin with its ruined medieval cathedral. Nearby is the 13th-century Pluscarden Abbey which is being restored by Benedictine monks. On the coast the maritime museums of Buckie and Lossiemouth record the history of the Moray fishing industry. The 17th-century Brodie Castle in Forres has a fine collection of furniture and paintings.

Local Activities: walks, sandy beaches, golf, fishing, horse-riding.

The Brae Hotel   Closed Dec/Jan

Fort Augustus
Inverness-shire
Scotland
PH32 4DG

☎ Fort Augustus (0320) 6289

Andrew and Mari Reive

The Brae Hotel is situated in the midst of the Great Glen just outside the village of Fort Augustus. It stands in its own grounds of approximately one and a half acres and from its elevated position has spectacular views. The house is warm and comfortable. There are eight bedrooms, five of which have private facilities. A couple of bedrooms overlook Loch Ness, and others the village and the Caledonian Canal.

The Reives are kind and solicitous hosts who obviously enjoy the challenge of making their guests' holidays as relaxing and pleasant as possible. They came to Fort Augustus having (like many others) fallen in love with the stunning natural beauty of the highland scenery and atmosphere when Andrew was based here with the Royal Navy.

There is good, wholesome home-cooking on offer. Dinner is taken in the elegant dining room accompanied by candlelight, fine linen, flowers and classical music. After dinner coffee and mints are served on the verandah. Specialities of the house include Stilton and grape pastry and marinaded roast venison.

Easily Accessible: You can step outside the door and embark on a walk which will take in the expansive, mountainous, forest-clad scenery. Fort Augustus has a Benedictine Abbey and a nine-hole golf course. Nineteen miles away at the Loch Ness Centre, you can see evidence and theories about the elusive monster, and take a 'Jacobite Cruise' from the Clansman Marina to Urquhart Castle. Inverness, 34 miles away, is the administrative capital of the Highland region. The Landmark Highland Heritage and Adventure Park has some excellent nature trails, exhibitions and an adventure playground for children.

Local Activities: walks, bird-watching (buzzards, kestrels) golf, pony-trekking, mountaineering, fishing.

Moorlands Hotel
Banavie
Fort William
Inverness-shire
PH33 7LY

Sorry, no pets
Chalet annexe

☎ Corpach (03977) 550
Norman Sinclair

Off A830 to Mallaig on B8004, 3 miles outside Fort William

Situated beside the Caledonian Canal, Moorlands Hotel has magnificent views of the Scottish Highlands and Ben Nevis, and is ideally positioned as a touring centre. It is an attractive modern hotel, run pleasantly and professionally by the Sinclair family who originally came from Orkney. Its Jacobean-style restaurant, cellar bistro, and lounge area are all new and a main lounge bar has been recently refitted to a split-level design with a nautical theme, with wood panelling and brass fittings, a ship's figurehead and pictures of canal scenes. There is entertainment every night.

The rooms are modern and comfortable with functional and tasteful décor. All the bedrooms have private facilities and colour television, one has a four-poster.

The menu is based around traditional Scottish fare and ingredients are fresh. The chef makes tasty bread rolls and grows his own herbs. There is both an à la carte and table d'hôte menu.

Easily Accessible: Walking in the wild unspoilt scenery is a favourite occupation of most guests. Moorlands is conveniently situated at the end of the West Highland Way and near to Ben Nevis (Britain's highest peak) and so provides plenty of walks of varying levels which take in woods, hills, mountains, lochs and ruined castles. The Caledonian Canal is right on the hotel's doorstep and nearby Loch Eil and Loch Linnhe provide opportunities for boat trips. Moorlands is also well placed for visiting many of the Highland attractions including Loch Ness, famous for its elusive monster; the Sea Life Centre; and the Highland Wildlife Park. Once a year, in September, the very fit (and maybe a little mad) take part in the Ben Nevis Hill Race.

Local Activities: walks, fishing, bird-watching, boat cruises.

Lomond Hills Hotel

Parliament Square
Freuchie
Fife
Scotland
KY7 7EY

☎ Falkland (0337) 57329

The van Beusekom Family

Off A914 Dundee/Kircaldy Road, 3 miles north of Glenrothes

This hotel, originally an 18th-century wayfarers inn, stands on the site of medieval parliament buildings. Part of the buildings used to be an old cobbler's shop, hence the 'Cobblers' wine bar and restaurant. The décor is functional and comfortable. There are twenty-five bedrooms, all en suite and with colour TV, an attractive lounge, a sauna, and a function room which can accommodate up to two hundred people. The honeymoon suite has a four-poster bed trimmed with lace.

Dinner is available all nights (this is one of the few places in this guide where no prior notice is necessary). There is an à la carte and table d'hôte menu, flambé dishes, and home-baked bread and shortbread are house specialities.

Easily Accessible: Freuchie is a picturesque village with pretty 16th-century buildings against a backdrop of the Lomond Hills. It is well situated for touring the centre of Scotland. The countryside is beautiful, with rivers, streams, and rolling farmlands. Close to Freuchie there are some waymarked Forestry Commission walks.

Two miles away, you can visit Falkland Palace, the country residence of the Stuart kings and queens, with gardens containing the oldest tennis court in Great Britain. Seven miles away at Cupar, you can visit the Scottish Deer Centre, and view the magnificent red deer at close quarters. A circular tour of Fife will take in the univeristy town of St Andrews, 18 miles from Freuchie, the picturesque fishing villages of Anstruther and Crail, the Fishery Museum, the folk museum in Ceres and the Scottish Trust properties of the Hill of Tarvit and Kelly Castle. Edinburgh, a centre of culture and history, is 32 miles away.

Local Activities: golf, walk, pony-trekking, fishing, gliding, cycling.

Dunstaffnage House

Dunstaffnage Brae
Grantown-on-Spey
Morayshire
PH26 3JR

A 'no smoking' house
Vegetarians by arrangement

☎ Grantown (0479) 2000

David and Martha Hunt

Dunstaffnage House is set in an acre of pretty garden with wonderful views across the open land to the Cairngorms, yet only a few minutes drive from the centre of Grantown. The house is very charming in a typically Victorian style with many original features – high ceilings, cornices and two attractive stained glass windows intact. The fireplace in the lounge came from Sir Thomas Lipton's yacht, *The Endeavour*. Throughout the house the large windows give fine views of the surrounding countryside. The lovely south-facing Victorian conservatory with its wisteria and fig tree is ideal for quiet relaxation. All six bedrooms are en suite or have private bathrooms.

David and Martha came to Dunstaffnage House after eight years of teaching sports in the Alps. They chose this area because it reminded them of the Alps and afforded them the chance to continue with their much loved skiing. Being sports enthusiasts they will arrange activities for their guests including skiing holidays, guided walking tours, cycle trips, golf and fishing.

The evening meal is served at a set time and is cooked to cordon bleu standard by Martha and is served by candlelight. Packed lunches are available on request.

Easily Accessible: The surrounding scenery is quite beautiful with a thick pine forest right on your doorstep. There are numerous walks in the Cairngorms and Speyside, and local walks around Grantown and the Cromdale Hills. Apart from taking in the scenery and the many outdoor pursuits available, there are several places of historical interest well worth a visit including Cawdor Castle, 25 miles away, with its 14th-century keep and associations with Macbeth; and Elgin, 40 miles away, a fascinating medieval town with a ruined cathedral, and a museum notable for its fine fossil collection. The Aviemore sports centre is 12 miles away.

Local Activities: walks, golf, trout and salmon fishing, tennis, bowling, wind-surfing, bird-watching (RSPB reserve, 5 miles), canoeing, pony-trekking, skiing.

Burnside Cottage

Wilton Dean
Hawick
Roxburghshire
TD9 7HY

Sorry, no pets
A 'no smoking' home
Unlicensed

☎ Hawick (0450) 73378

Elspeth Scott

Phone for directions

Elspeth Scott, the charming proprietor of this small, cosy and bright establishment, welcomes visitors as if they were, in her own words, her 'personal guests'. Her aim is to make you feel as welcome, comfortable and relaxed as possible, with the expectation, constantly fufilled, that you will return again and again.

Built in 1813, Burnside Cottage lies on a hill, in the beautiful wilderness of the Scottish Borders. It is close to the town of Hawick, the centre of the Borders knitwear industry. It has a small front and back garden where the occasional strutting pheasant can be seen, and a sunny patio much appreciated by guests. There are two guest bedrooms each decorated in a country house style with dark wood furniture. As access to the guest bathroom (once a stocking factory) is through the kitchen, Elspeth, concerned for one's modesty, provides bathrobes.

A wholesome breakfast is served and dinner and packed lunches are provided on request. If guests wish to eat out there are several reasonably priced local restaurants. At night, your favourite hot drinks – hot chocolate, Ovaltine and Bovril, plus Elspeth's home-made shortbread – are offered. There are very few house rules but the ban on smoking is very definite.

Easily Accessible: The surrounding countryside is stunning with plenty of scope for gentle ambles and, for the more energetic, hill walking. Elspeth is prepared (her schedule permitting) to drop guests at the start and collect them at the end of walks. Among the many places to visit are: the 12th-century abbeys of Jedburgh and Melrose; Abbotsford House, the stately home of Sir Walter Scott which was financed by the Waverley novels; and the 16th-century Thirlestone Castle, home to a fine collection of china, furniture and paintings and the Borders Country Life Museum. Edinburgh, Carlisle and Berwick-on-Tweed are well within reach for day trips.

Local Activities: walks, fishing, horse-riding, golf, swimming, mountain cycling.

Redlands

By Ladybank
Nr Cupar
Fife
KY7 7SH

Closed March
Sorry, no pets

☎ Ladybank (0337) 31091

Jane and Ronald Keanie

20 minutes from St Andrews

Here you can relax in a pine lodge overlooking a lovely garden, or sun yourself on the semi-circular sun terrace. The landscape of woodland and fields is very beautiful and if you like golf, you may well feel you have died and gone to heaven – there are an astounding twenty-five golf courses within a 20-mile radius and the local Ladybank course is an Open qualifier.

The lodge, which was rebuilt by Ronald Keanie, has four bedrooms each with its own facilities and colour TV. There is a comfortable and spacious sitting room.

The three-course dinner menu makes good use of Scottish produce, namely game and seafood, and whilst some recipes are traditional, others are home-brewed. Vegetables are from the garden or locally grown and bread and rolls are home-baked. Packed lunches are available but please give prior notice.

Easily Accessible: Redlands is half a mile outside Ladybank village which is served by British Rail and buses. There are walks to suit everyone. The nearby Falkland hills are delightful and not too strenuous. There is a stunning 10-mile coastal walk from St Andrews to Crail. If you feel like something a little on the wild side, the glens of North Angus and Perthshire will interest you. Falkland, 4 miles away, is an ancient town with a 16th-century palace which was the country residence of Stuart kings and queens. Twelve miles away at St Andrews is a fine cathedral and a ruined priory, and pristine beaches. Ceres, only 6 miles from Redlands, is a very pretty village with a medieval hump-back bridge. There are numerous National Trust properties, such as Kellie Castle and Balmerino, both 15 miles away. Children will enjoy the adventure farm, museum and nature trail at Cambo, 15 miles away. Take a day trip to Edinburgh, 45 miles away.

Local Activities: golf, loch and river fishing, pony-trekking, riding, tennis, swimming, flying, parachuting, flying, bowling.

Dunfermline House

Buccleuch Street
Melrose
TD6 9LB

Unlicensed
Sorry, no pets
A 'no smoking' house

☎ Melrose (089682) 2148

Susan and Ian Graham

Off A68/A7 junction

With an aviary, a fish pond, a rabbit, a guinea pig, a watchful cat and a 'prize leek' patch, Dunfermline House is obviously very much a family home. It is situated in the small town of Melrose, which nestles comfortably between the Eildon Hills and the silvery River Tweed in the beautiful rolling countryside of the Scottish Borders.

The house is tastefully decorated and each room has an individual character, each with its own colour TV. There is a cosy guest lounge and a dining room where breakfast and dinner are served.

The three-course table d'hôte menu makes good use of local produce; Border lamb and fresh trout from the River Tweed are firm favourites.

Easily Accessible: Walks abound; the Southern Upland Way passes through Melrose. 210 miles long, it runs from the west to the east coast of southern Scotland. A climb up the Eildon Hills will present the energetic with stunning panoramic views of the surrounding gentle rolling countryside. Just fifty yards from the hotel, you can visit the ruins of Melrose's 12th-century Abbey where lies the heart of Robert the Bruce, King of Scots. Adjacent to the ruins are the Priorwood gardens which specialise in growing plants for drying and flower arranging. Nearby is Galashiels, a centre for the 19th-century textile industry, where you can still visit the 'mill shops'. Within 15 miles you can visit numerous abbeys, castles, historic houses and craft centres. The marvellous historic and cultural cities of Edinburgh, Berwick-on-Tweed, and Glasgow are under two hours' drive away.

Local Activities: walks, riding, golf, salmon and trout fishing, swimming.

Moffat House Hotel
Closed mid-Nov to mid-March

High Street
Moffat
Dumfriesshire
DG10 9HL

☎ Moffat (0683) 20039

The Reid Family

Easy access off A74 to Glasgow or A701 to Edinburgh

Surrounded by the soft, rolling hills of Armadale, Moffat House is set in two acres of mature garden and has magnificent views of the Annan valley. It is a mid-18th-century mansion built by the famous architect, John Adam, and typically consists of a main building with two connecting wings. It is situated in the charming old spa town of Moffat, a recent winner of both the 'Best Kept Village' and the 'Scotland in Bloom' awards.

Whilst the exterior of the house is largely unaltered since its earliest days, the interior has been completely refurbished, although the main architectural feature, a stunning central spiral staircase, remains. There has been much modernisation and recently a new bar/lounge and conservatory have been added. All fifteen bedrooms have private facilities and colour TV. It is worth saying that, with fifteen bedrooms, Moffat House is one of the largest hotels in this book, but in common with the others, the service is warm and personal.

An à la carte menu and bar meals are served in the evening. The food is of a high standard with fresh local produce such as Solway salmon, Galloway beef, venison and wild duck regularly featured.

Easily Accessible: There are many stunning local walks on the Annandale Hills along the river Annan, and through Greenhillstairs and Rivox Forests. Fourteen miles away you can visit Grey Mare's Tail, a great waterfall, and here you may catch sight of a herd of wild goats which live in the area. You can take a day trip to visit Wanlockhead, the highest village in Scotland, with its Museum of Lead Mining, where you can visit an underground mine gallery, and not far away, Drumlanrig Castle, the magnificent 17th-century home of the Duke of Buccleuch and Queensbury. Twenty-five miles away, at the Caerlaverock Nature Reserve, along the shore of the Nith Estuary and Solway Firth, you can see natterjack toads and great flocks of wildfowl.

Local Activities: walks, golf, tennis, bowls, fishing, pony-trekking.

Cairn Edward
New Galloway
by Castle Douglas
Kircudbrightshire
DG7 3RZ

Closed Nov–Easter
Unlicensed, guests welcome
 to bring own wine
No dinner June–Aug

☎ New Galloway (06442) 244

Donald and Penny Murray

One mile south of New Galloway on the A762 road

Lying on the edge of the Galloway Forest Park, this building of solid granite remains pretty much unaltered since its origin in 1872 as the country home of the descendants of Viscount Kenmure (the ruins of Kenmure Castle stand half a mile away). Around the house is an acre of garden and beyond this eight acres of rough ground with rocky outcrops and mature trees and squirrels and deer from the forest paying occasional shy visits. The lovely Loch Ken is just across the way.

The house is spacious and comfortable with a large drawing room and a dining room with separate tables. All bedrooms have en suite or private facilities and colour TV; their attractive wooden shutters are always appreciated as they block out the dawn chorus – traffic noise is *not* a problem!

Dinner is offered from Easter (when Cairn Edward opens) to the end of May and again from September to October (when it closes). The food is home-cooked; local produce such as the delicious Solway salmon, free-range eggs and chickens and locally cured bacon are regular features. If guests wish to eat out, there are several eating places in New Galloway, just one mile away.

Easily Accessible: The location is excellent both for touring south west Scotland by car and as a centre for walking. Thirty miles away, you can visit Drumlanrig Castle, built in the 17th century and home to an exquisite art collection. Dumfries, 26 miles away, has several interesting museums and the house of Robert Burns. Walkers will find a great deal of variety, from short forest walks to the long Southern Upland Way. Much of the walking is fairly rugged and a climb to the top of Merrick (2,766 feet), 35 miles away, is a challenge for the adventurous. Almost straight from the doorstep of Cairn Edward you can embark on a day's walking in the Galloway Forest.

Local Activities: walks, watersports on Loch Ken, coarse and game fishing, bird-watching (RSPB reserve), golf.

Cairngill House Hotel   Closed Jan/Feb
Sandyhills
Dalbeattie
Kirkcudbrightshire
DG5 4NZ

☎ Southwick (038778) 681

Brian and Anne Downs

Take A710 coast road, Dumfries 18 miles

This hotel is quite gloriously situated in an elevated position just fifty yards from a sandy beach. It has one of the finest outlooks on the Solway coast; the views of the bay and beaches are panoramic and in the far distance Lake District peaks can be seen.

A grand Victorian building, it has three acres of garden with a pond and hard tennis court. It was once owned by a cotton baron from Lancashire; today it belongs to Brian and Ann who left Australia (where they worked as wool buyers) to fufil their long-time ambition of opening their own hotel. There are six comfortable and spacious bedrooms, tastefully furnished.

An evening meal of good home-cooking is served.

Easily Accessible: The countryside is waiting to be explored; the lochs, rolling heather-covered moors, peaceful woods and long, unspoilt coastline provide tremendous scenic variety. There are many castles, churches, abbeys and ancient monuments and public gardens to visit. Kirkcudbright, once an active port, is an attractive town, particularly along the waterfront. It has a ruined castle, an interesting local history museum, and its own school of painters. Nearby are the National Trust's Threave Gardens, and at the Threave Wildfowl Refuge on the River Dee you can see many bird varieties.

Local Activities: walks, fishing, golf, pony-trekking, bird-watching.

Menzion Farmhouse
Tweedsmuir
Tweeddale
Peebleshire
ML12 6QR

☎ Tweedsmuir (08997) 247

Mary and David Brett

Off A 701 Moffat 15 miles

Children over 12 welcome
No TV
Chauffeuring available

Menzion farmhouse, in the Tweedsmuir Hills, lies in an area officially designated of 'outstanding natural beauty' and 'special scientific interest.' It is remote (but accessible) and sparsely populated, providing a perfect retreat for the beleaguered city dweller, or indeed anyone who feels like getting away from it all.

A farmhouse probably stood on this site at the time of the Great Plague. The present house is old, with a west gable wall, 8 feet thick and built of solid stone. There are five acres of grounds with a walled garden and croquet green. Adjacent to these grounds lies 7,000 acres of forest accessible to walkers. Inside Menzion is old-fashioned and comfortable with blazing log fires in cold weather. A five-course dinner is served at a large refectory table seating twelve, so guests have a chance to get to know one another. Fresh produce is used from the kitchen garden (except for the more exotic items from abroad), and cakes and bread rolls are home-baked. Packed lunches can be provided. If guests arrive too late for dinner, there is a local inn which provides very good fare.

Mary and David have travelled extensively and enjoy meeting their guests, who hail from all quarters of the world. They will do whatever they can to make your stay as comfortable as possible – provide chauffeuring as required, offer advice on the area and book fishing and golf. Tuition in trout fishing is provided at no charge, along with waders and tackle.

Easily Accessible: Walking is a delight here as the area is never crowded and the walker can truly be alone with nature. To the rear of Menzion, Broad Law rises some 2,750 feet and is the highest point in the Scottish Borders. It is ideal for sighting rare arctic-alpine species of plant life. Fifteen miles away from Menzion you can join the Southern Upland Way, which runs for 212 miles from the south-west coast of Scotland to the eastern seaboard. Apart from the abundance of nature to keep you busy, there are several historic and archaeological sites, museums and botanic gardens to visit. The beautiful historic city of Edinburgh is only forty minutes away by car, and Glasgow just a little further.

Local Activities: walks, bird-watching, fishing, golf, skiing in winter.

WALES

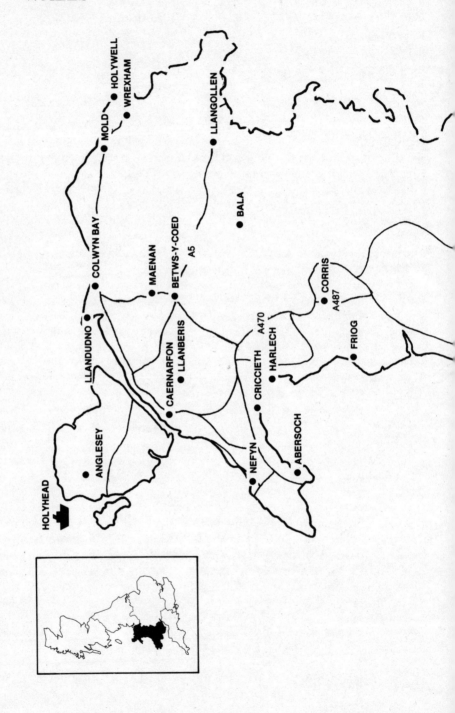

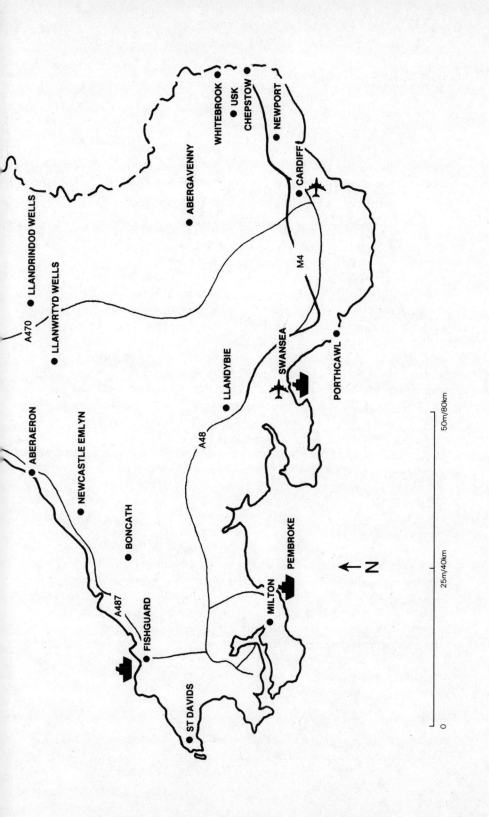

Wales

There can be no better indication of the wealth of natural beauty in Wales than the fact that this small country boasts three of Great Britain's National Parks: Snowdonia in the north, the Brecon Beacons in the south-east, and the Pembrokeshire National Park in the south-west. The latter is designated an area of outstanding natural beauty and is renowned for its magnificent cliff scenery, its long sandy beaches, and its 167 miles of long-distance footpath. But it is really the mountains that reign supreme over the landscape – the Black Mountains, the Brecon Beacons, Snowdonia, and the vast Cambrian range. And an integral part of the mountain scenery are the great cascading waterfalls, and the abundance of rare and varied wildlife including polecats, red squirrels, deer and buzzards.

The people, too, demand our attention and admiration. Some of Britain's brightest lights have hailed from this sparsely populated land: Dylan Thomas, poet and writer, who lived, worked and was buried in Laugharne in Dyfed; the great statesman, David Lloyd George who grew up in and never forgot Llanystumdwy; and T.E. Lawrence, better known as Lawrence of Arabia, who was born in Tremadog. The Welsh people as a whole are renowned for the excellence of their singing voices, and indeed the Treochy Male Voice Choir is world-famous.

For the historian and archaeologist, amateur and professional, Wales is a treasure trove. There are Roman remains, like the fortress at Caerleon; mysterious standing stones like those in the Preseli hills; ancient Celtic crosses like those in the church of Llanbadarn Fawr; and the great Welsh fortresses such as the border castles of Powis, Chirk, and Raglan (the latter a very fine example of a medieval fortification) which are spread throughout the landscape.

Situated often rather incongruously alongside these ancient relics are those of the more recent past – the great slate quarries, the ruined iron-works and the derelict mills of Wales' industrial heritage. A fascinating insight into the reality of coal mining can be seen at the Big Pit Museum in Gwent where visitors are allowed to descend its shaft and experience – as hundreds of miners have – the atmosphere, sights and sounds of a coal mine.

Wales is also a land shrouded in myth and legend. King Arthur often plays a large part in the many fantastic stories. Tales of his bravery in defending the Celts against the Saxons and ferocious monsters are legion. One of the most poignant must be that concerning Merlin, his magician, who – it is said – sleeps on Bardsey Island awaiting the king's return.

Wales is also home to one of the greatest follies in the British Isles: Clough Williams-Ellis built Portmeirion, a mock Italian town complete with campanile and statues representing figures from Roman mythology, on the Lleyn Peninsula. Portmeirion has a decidedly fantastical atmosphere – one could almost be in Disneyland.

Wales Tourist Board
Brunel House, 2 Fitzalan Road, Cardiff CF2 1UY
Tel: (0222) 499909

ABERAERON (Pennant)   BIKEREHYD FARM
Rose Villa, Pennant, Llanon, Dyfed SY23 5PB. *Tel*: Nebo (09746) 365. *Hosts*: Sheila & John Goddard.
Rates: B

Charming, comfortable award-winning farmhouse and adjacent en suite bedrooms converted from 14th-century cottages. Gourmet country-house food, local and national recipes. Children over 8 welcome. From A487 north of Aberaeron take B4577 to Pennant village, turn left at crossroads.

ABERGAVENNY   BELCHAMPS
1 Holywell Road, Abergavenny, Gwent NP7 5LP. *Tel*: Abergavenny (0873) 3204. *Hosts*: Stella & Eddy Perrin.
Rates: A   Vouchers accepted.

Comfortable house overlooking park, views of Blorenge mountain and castle. Ideal centre Black Mountains, Usk and Wye Valleys, Brecon Beacons, Offa's Dyke, historic castles. Pony-trekking. Local pubs and restaurants. Family rooms available. Sorry, no pets.

ABERGAVENNY   LLANWENARTH HOUSE
Govilon, Abergavenny, Gwent NP7 9SF. *Tel*: Gilwern (0873) 830289. *Hosts*: Bruce & Amanda Weatherill.
Rates: D   Vouchers accepted.
(See page 247 for description)

ABERSOCH   RIVERSIDE HOTEL
Abersoch, Pwllheli, Gwynedd LL53 7HW. *Tel*: Abersoch (075881) 2419/2818. *Hosts*: John & Wendy Bakewell.
Rates: D

Attractive hotel, nicely located overlooking pretty river and harbour. Proprietor-chefs proud of reputation for fine cuisine. Lovely sandy beaches. All water-sports. Five golf courses nearby. Heated covered swimming pool. Closed Nov–Feb. Sorry, no pets. BTA commended.

ANGLESEY (Nr Holyhead)   THE OLD RECTORY COUNTRY HOUSE

Rhoscolyn, Nr Holyhead, Anglesey LL65 2DQ. *Tel*: Trearddur Bay (0407) 860214. *Host*: Edna Aldred.

Rates: B

Lovely and very comfortable Georgian house in 1½ acres gardens. Beautiful views. Coastal walks, sandy bay. Bird-watching. Home-cooking, own and local produce. Near ferry to Ireland. Reduced rates 2 nights or more.

ANGLESEY (Llanerchymedd)   LLWYDIARTH FAWR

Llanerchymedd, Isle of Anglesey, Gwynedd LL71 8DF. *Tel*: Llanerchymedd (0248) 470321. *Hosts*: The Hughes Family.

Rates: A   Vouchers accepted.

Warm, comfortable, secluded Georgian mansion in 900 acres farmland. Perfect for exploring Anglesey. Views to Snowdonia. Trout fishing nearby. All rooms en suite or with private bathrooms, colour TV, radio. Log fires. Fresh local produce. Children welcome. Phone for directions. Sorry, no pets.

BALA (Llandderfel)   DEWIS CYFARFOD

Llandderfel, Bala, Gwynedd LL23 7DR. *Tel*: Llandderfel (06783) 243. *Hosts*: Barbara & Peter Wilde Reynolds.

Rates: B

17th-century house set in 7 acres of woods overlooking the magnificent Dee valley. South-facing terrace. Wildlife abounds – binoculars provided. Some rooms en suite. Licensed. Children over 10 welcome, under 12 free accommodation. All rooms colour TV and radio. Most European languages spoken or comprehended. Phone for directions.

BALA   LLIDIARDAU MAWR

Llidiardau, Bala, Gwynedd LL23 7SG. *Tel*: Bala (0678) 520555. *Host*: Mrs Shirley May.

Rates: A

(See page 248 for description)

BALA   WHITE LION ROYAL HOTEL

61 High Street, Bala, Gwynedd LL23 7AE. *Tel*: Bala (0678) 520314. *Hosts*: Dougal & Patricia Bannerman.

Rates: C/D

Comfortable half-timbered coaching inn (1754) prominent in the High Street. Coaching house fare. Welcoming atmosphere. Centre of North Wales. Castles, lakes, slate mines, narrow-gauge railways all within 1½ hrs.

BETWS-Y-COED (Dolwyddelan)   ELEN'S CASTLE HOTEL

Dolwyddelan, Gwynedd LL25 OEJ. *Tel*: Dolwyddelan (06906) 207. *Hosts*: John & Elaine Barker.

Rates: C/D   Vouchers accepted.

Tastefully restored former coaching inn centrally situated in the Snowdonia National Park. Spectacular scenery, fishing and walking. No television. Near Betws-y-Coed to the south in between Blaenau Ffestiniog and Betws-y-Coed on the A470. Reduced rates 3 nights or more (except July and August).

BONCATH PANTYDERI FARM AND GUEST HOUSE
Boncath, Dyfed SA37 0JB. *Tel*: Boncath (023974) 227. *Hosts*: Max, Janet & Noela Jones.
Rates: A/B Vouchers accepted.
Sixteenth-century country mansion, now an 800-acre working farm. Lovely views overlooking trout lake. Own pony-trekking and river fishing. Rough shooting. Home-cooking, own and local produce. Off B4332. Cardigan 6 miles. Sorry, no pets.

CAERNARFON (Seion) TY'N RHOS FARM
Llanddeiniolen, Caernarfon, Gwynedd LL55 3AE. *Tel*: Portdinorwic (0248) 670489. *Hosts*: Lynda & Nigel Kettle.
Rates: B
(See page 249 for description)

CARDIFF (Penarth) THE WALTON HOUSE HOTEL
37 Victoria Road, Penarth, South Glamorgan CF62 2HY. *Tel*: Penarth (0222) 707782. *Host*: E. Ferrandez.
Rates: B
Spacious and comfortable Edwardian hotel in quiet residential area, 10 mins walk from Penarth seafront. 4 miles Cardiff city centre and lovely old castle. Airport 5 miles. Gold and Welsh Folk Museum nearby. Fishing. Home-cooking, fresh local produce.

CHEPSTOW CASTLE VIEW HOTEL
Bridge Street, Chepstow, Gwent NP6 5EZ. *Tel*: Chepstow (02912) 70349. *Telex*: 498280 Ref CV/H *Fax*: 0291 62 5614. *Hosts*: Martin & Vicky Cardale.
Rates: D Vouchers accepted.
(See page 250 for description)

COLWYN BAY LYNDALE HOTEL & RESTAURANT
410 Abergele Road, Colwyn Bay, Clwyd LL29 9AB. *Tel*: Colwyn Bay (0492) 515429. *Hosts*: Marirose & Roger Livesey.
Rates: C
Superior, comfortable coastal hotel. Near sandy beaches. Ideal for Snowdonia. Roger and Marirose are proud of their reputation and menus in restaurant. All rooms en suite with full facilities. 4-poster. 2–3 day breaks available all year.

CORRIS BRAICH GOCH HOTEL
Corris, Nr Machynlleth, Powys SY20 9RD. *Tel*: Corris (065473) 229. *Hosts*: Dave & Wendy Kay.

Rates: B

Old 17th-century coaching inn, now a friendly, fully licensed hotel, in tiny village overlooking beautiful Dulas River valley. Near Snowdonia National Park on A487 south of Dolgellau. Two-day winter breaks available.

CRICCIETH NEPTUNE HOTEL

Min y Mor, Criccieth, Gwynedd LL52 0EF. *Tel*: Criccieth (0766) 522794. *Hosts*: Mr & Mrs E. Williams.
Rates: A/B   Vouchers accepted.

Friendly, well-located hotel, situated right on the seafront in popular seaside resort. Views over Cardigan Bay, Snowdonia and Lleyn Peninsula. Golf, tennis, bowling, fishing. Portmeirion and Ffestiniog (slate caverns) nearby. Home-cooking; fresh and local produce.

FISHGUARD (Llanychaer)   PENLAN OLEU AND RESTAURANT

Llanychaer, Fishguard, Dyfed SA65 9TL. *Tel*: Puncheston (0348) 881314. *Hosts*: Ruth & Andrew Stuart-Lyon.
Rates: B

Comfortable converted Welsh farmhouse which was the subject of an article in *The New York Times*. Off B4313 (Fishguard 3½ miles) towards Puncheston. Proprietors are proud of their awards for good food. Rates include bathroom en suite. No TV. BTA Commended. Sorry, no pets.

FRIOG (Nr Fairbourne)   (A 'no smoking' house)   SEA VIEW GUEST HOUSE

Friog, Nr Fairbourne, Gwynedd LL38 2NX. *Tel*: Fairbourne (0341) 250388. *Hosts*: Roger & Mary White.
Rates: A   Vouchers accepted.

Detached, old stone-built house on edge of Snowdonia National Park with views to sea. On A493, 8 miles Dolgellau. Vegetarian and diabetic food available. Dinner by arrangement. Children over 6 welcome. Sorry, no pets.

HARLECH (Llanbedr)   PENSARN HALL

Llanbedr, Gwynedd LL45 2HS. *Tel*: Llanbedr (034123) 236. *Hosts*: John & Maureen Weiss.
Rates: B

Splendid, tastefully restored house in extensive grounds overlooking the Artro estuary in Snowdonia National Park. Near beaches. Distinctive home-cooking and wines. Two miles south of Harlech on A496.

HOLYWELL   THE HALL

Lygan-y-Wern, Pentre Halkyn, Holywell, Clwyd CH8 8BD. *Tel*: Halkyn (0352) 780215. *Host*: Davinia Vernon.
Rates: A   Vouchers accepted.
(See page 251 for description)

LLANBERIS PADARN LAKE HOTEL
High Street, Llanberis, Gwynedd LL55 4SU. *Tel*: Llanberis (0286) 870260.
Host: Mr Ashes.
Rates: C
  Nice friendly hotel, usefully situated just off A4086 on edge of town adjacent
  to Lake Padarn. Lovely views of lake and mountains. Shooting, salmon and
  trout fishing arranged. Own private rough shoot. Mountain railway nearby.

LLANDRINDOD WELLS GRIFFIN LODGE HOTEL
Temple Street, Llandrindod Wells, Powys LD1 5HF. *Tel*: Llandrindod Wells
(0597) 2432. *Hosts*: Alan & Jean Benbow.
Rates: A/B Vouchers accepted.
  Comfortably modernised Victorian house in this mid-Wales spa, well
  situated for touring from the Welsh borders to the sea. Near Elan Valley
  reservoirs. Home-cooking, local produce.

LLANDUDNO HEADLANDS HOTEL
Hill Terrace, Llandudno, Gwynedd LL30 2LS. *Tel*: Llandudno (0492) 77485.
Hosts: George & Brenda Woods.
Rates: C Vouchers accepted.
  Comfortable, relaxed and friendly hotel with outstanding views over
  Conwy Bay. All bedrooms have sea or country views. In quiet cul-de-sac,
  residential area, 5 mins walk from sea-front and shops. Three 4-posters.
  Closed Jan and Feb.

LLANDUDNO THE SHERWOOD HOTEL
Promenade, Llandudno, Gwynedd LL30 lBG. *Tel*: Llandudno (0492) 75313.
Hosts: Mike & Linda Bentley.
Rates: B Vouchers accepted.
  Comfortable double-fronted Victorian property at the quiet end of prom-
  enade with seaward views over the Ormes. Easy walking distance local
  amenities, and near Conference and Leisure Centre. All rooms en suite and
  colour TV. Own car park.

LLANDYBIE THE MILL AT GLYNHIR
Llandybie, Ammanford, Dyfed SA18 2TE. *Tel*: Llandybie (0269) 850672.
Hosts: Donald & Thelma Gittins.
Rates: D
  Beautifully converted 250-year-old mill, on the side of Loughor Valley
  with extensive views. Heated indoor pool, jet stream. Free 18-hole golfing.
  Own fishing. Pony-trekking nearby. M4 20 min. At Llandybie, take Golf
  Club turning, then right after 1½ miles at first tiny crossroads. Children
  over 11 welcome.

LLANGOLLEN TY'N-Y-WERN HOTEL AND RESTAURANT
Llangollen, Clwyd LL20 7PH. *Tel*: Llangollen (0978) 860252. *Host*: Barbara
Evans.
Rates: C

Warm and friendly country house hotel (1750) in its own gardens, with spectacular views of Vale of Llangollen, River Dee and castle. 1 mile town centre off A5. Free fishing (1 trout, 1 salmon). Golf. Rambling, pony-trekking arranged. Mark Sebastian resident chef-partner.

LLANWRTYD WELLS LASSWADE HOUSE

Llanwrtyd Wells, Powys LD5 4RW. *Tel*: Llanwrtyd Wells (05913) 515. *Hosts*: Sandy & Barry Sharples.

Rates: C   Vouchers accepted.

Hospitality in handsome Edwardian country house. Unrivalled position, views rugged Welsh hills. All rooms either en suite or with private bathroom and TV. Licensed. Honesty bar. CC Access, Visa. No smoking in dining room. Outdoor swimming pool. Winter breaks. Home-cooking. Off A483, near station (5 trains daily!) BTA commended.

MAENAN MAENAN ABBEY HOTEL

Maenan, Llanrwst, Gwynedd LL26 0UL. *Tel*: Dolgarrog (049269) 247. *Telex*: 61362. *Host*: Richard Scott.

Rates: D

Lovely historic country house set in own grounds in heart of Conwy valley. Ideally situated for coastal resorts and touring Snowdonia National Park and North Wales. Log fires. Proprietors proud of reputation for excellent cuisine. Adjacent to A470.

MILTON (Nr Tenby) MILTON MANOR HOTEL

Milton, Nr Tenby, Pembrokeshire SA70 8PG. *Tel*: Carew (0646) 651398. *Fax*: 0646 651897. *Hosts*: Barrie & Elizabeth Richardson.

Rates: C   Vouchers accepted.

Georgian manor in 6 acres of private grounds. Secluded traditional garden. Peaceful countryside bordering Pembrokeshire National Park. Close to Milford Haven, Pembroke and Haverfordwest business centres. On A477 between Pembroke and Carmarthen.

MOLD (Nr Chester) THE CHEQUERS HOTEL

Chester Road, Northophall Village, Nr Mold, Delyn, Clwyd CH7 6HJ. *Tel*: Deeside (0244) 816181. *Telex*: 617112. *Fax*: 0244 814661. *Host*: Brian Green.

Rates: D

Welsh manor house of charm and distinction in 40 acres woodland and parkland setting in beautiful North Wales area. On A55, Chester 9 miles, Hawarden airport 5. Golf special rates, trout fishing, spa bath. Rooms for disabled.

NEFYN DOLWEN HOUSE

Nefyn, Gwynedd LL53 6LS. *Tel*: Nefyn (0758) 720667. *Hosts*: Roy & Menna Barnes.

Rates: A   Vouchers accepted.

Situated in a small village on the north side of Lleyn Peninsula overlooking

Caernarfon Bay near mountains, sandy beaches and cliff walks. Off A499 or A497 on B4417.

NEWCASTLE EMLYN (Rhydlewis)   BRONIWAN

Rhydlewis, Llandysul, Dyfed SA44 5PF. *Tel*: Rhydlewis (023975) 261. *Hosts*: Carole & Allan Jacobs.

Rates: A

(See page 252 for description)

NEWPORT (Gwent)   ANDERLEY LODGE

216 Stow Hill, Newport, Gwent NP9 4HA. *Tel*: Newport (0633) 266781. *Hosts*: David & Hilda Smith.

Rates: A/B   Vouchers accepted.

Secluded Victorian house with garden in residential area. Large comfortable rooms with showers, colour TVs and writing desks. Own car parking. Good access to M4 exit 27 (1½ miles). Reduced rates 3 nights or more. Ideal for business travellers and tourists alike. Sorry, no pets.

PORTHCAWL   MINERVA HOTEL

52 Esplanade Avenue, Porthcawl, Mid-Glamorgan CF36 3YU. *Tel*: Porthcawl (065671) 2428. *Hosts*: Rosemarie & Tony Giblett.

Rates: A/B   Vouchers accepted.

Edwardian end-of-terrace hotel, just off seafront and harbour in attractive small seaside town. Close Royal Porthcawl Golf Club. Splendid coastal walks on Heritage Coast. Colour TV in all rooms. Good value. Easy drive Swansea or Cardiff.

ST DAVIDS   REDCLIFFE HOUSE

17 New Street, St. Davids, Dyfed SA62 6SW. *Tel*: St Davids (0437) 720389. *Hosts*: Terry & Lala Clarke.

Rates: A

Comfortable and excellent value, in this smallest cathedral city of Britain. Peace and quiet, superb coastline, lovely cliff walks, many local sandy bathing beaches. Bird-watching, boat trips, sea fishing, golf. Sorry, no pets.

USK   TY-GWYN FARM

Gwehelog, Usk, Gwent NP5 1RG. *Tel*: Usk (02913) 2878. *Host*: Jean Arnett.

Rates: A/B   Vouchers accepted.

Charming farmhouse with lovely views, sunny conservatory and secluded garden with fish-pond. Touring Wye Valley and Brecon Beacons. Sailing, fishing, gliding nearby. Easy access M4, M5 (M50). Take A449 and A472 to Usk, follow Gwehelog sign. Farm award winner. Children over 12 welcome. Sorry, no pets.

WHITEBROOK (Nr Monmouth)   THE CROWN AT WHITEBROOK

Whitebrook, Nr Monmouth, Gwent NP5 4TX. *Tel*: Monmouth (0600) 860254. *Telex* 498280 Attn CROWN. *Hosts*: Roger & Sandra Bates.

Rates: C/D   Vouchers accepted.
(See page 253 for description)

WREXHAM THE BEECHES

Chester Road, Gresford, Wrexham LL12 8PW. *Tel*: Wrexham (097 883) 3838.
Hosts: The Toner Family
Rates: A/B   Vouchers accepted.

Comfortable attractive house in rural area with spacious gardens/parking. Set back off A483. Wrexham 2 miles, Chester 9. All rooms en suite and with colour TV. Snooker and pool rooms. Family rooms. Children under 12 half price. Dinner by arrangement only.

Llanwenarth House

Govilon
Abergavenny
Gwent
NP7 9SF

Closed February
Children over 5 welcome
Award winner

☎ Gilwern (0873) 830289

Bruce and Amanda Weatherill

three miles from Abergavenny, phone for directions

Surrounded by the Black Mountains in the Brecon Beacons National Park, this is a house full of historical interest with connections ranging from Charles I to Captain Henry Morgan, the infamous Governor of Jamaica, and with rumours of buried treasure in the grounds. Inside, antiques, family paintings and period furniture enhance the elegance and character inherent in this finely proportioned manor house. There are five bedrooms, all individually furnished with en suite facilities and colour TV. Both the drawing room and dining room are very attractive with large Georgian windows creating a spacious and light atmosphere. The garden is mature and colourful with a walled orchard given over to sheep and vegetables.

Amanda Weatherill, a trained cordon bleu cook, and wine-shipping husband Bruce take considerable care in the planning of menus. The food is freshly prepared and very high quality produce is used – free- range ducks, pork, chicken, vegetables and fruit from the kitchen garden, locally caught salmon and trout. If guests wish to eat out, there are several local restaurants which are recommended.

Easily Accessible: The scenery varies from rugged mountains to gentle valleys and mixed farmland. Within 15 miles of Llanwenarth there are some thirty waymarked walks and within 3 miles the mountains of Blorenge, Tyla and Sugarloaf can be approached. In the Brecon Beacons, the Pen y Fan walk can be attempted, to the highest peak in the region. Abergavenny is a bustling market town with a museum in the grounds of a ruined castle. There are famous racecourses at Chepstow and Cheltenham. Although a car is a necessity, the Brecon Mountain Railway will take you through some of the more inaccessible countryside. Castles are numerous. Wales' oldest and deepest mine is at Blaenavon, known as Big Pit, closed as a colliery in 1980 after a hundred years of production.

Local Activities: walks, mountaineering, trout and salmon fishing, horse-riding, golf, hang-gliding, bird-watching, boating on Monmouthshire canal.

Llidiardau Mawr

Llidiardau
Bala
Gwynedd
LL23 7SG

Closed Nov. to Easter
Unlicensed (bring own wine)
Sorry, no pets

☎ Bala (0678) 520555

Mrs Shirley May

Take A4212 from Bala for ½ mile, then left for 3 miles through Rhyduchaf

You have to watch your step at Llidiardau Mawr – uneven floors, low doorways and steep stairways can catch out the unwary! This 17th-century farmhouse and watermill is situated 1,100 feet up in the beautiful and rugged mountain countryside of the Snowdownia National Park. Its newly tamed garden has fine views and a fast-running mountain stream.

The building has been lovingly restored (rats evicted, rubble removed and original features unearthed) from a very sorry state. Today it is modern and comfortable whilst it still retains an 'old world' character. The rooms are painted white to complement the black beams. The dining room has a beautiful Welsh stone fireplace with original pit, and in the lounge (which incorporates the old pantry) old meat hooks remain alongside the colour TV. In the new pine kitchen, old beams are still very much at home.

Unusually, there is a choice of supper and dinner, served at 6pm and 6.30pm respectively.(The supper menu is simpler and cheaper.) The food, cooked by Shirley May herself, is fresh and wholesome and local produce such as Welsh lamb and free-range eggs are used whenever possible.

Easily Accessible: Bala lies beside a four-mile long lake (which you can take a steam-train ride around) and is surrounded by three mountain ranges. There is a local bus running once a day from Bala to the cottage. Walkers are spoilt for choice, with numerous delightful walks in the surrounding countryside. In season there are guided walks around Bala.(Your host will supply Ordinance Survey maps.) Ten miles away is Lake Vyrnwy, a reservoir and the largest RSPB nature reserve covering 17,000 acres. Pistyll Rhaedr, the highest waterfall in Wales, is again only 10 miles away. Fifteen miles away you can visit the Llechwedd Slate Caverns. There are numerous castles to visit for a day trip including the magnificent Harlech Castle built between 1283 and 1289 and perched proudly on a cliff.

Local Activities: walks, fishing, sailing, wind-surfing, canoeing, skin-diving, swimming, golf, horse-riding.

Ty'n Rhos Farm

Award winner

Llanddeiniolen
Caernarfon
Gwynedd
LL55 3AE

☎ Portdinorwic (0248) 670489

Lynda and Nigel Kettle

½ mile off B4366

This pretty slate house is situated in a tranquil hamlet on the edge of the Snowdonia National Park. It was once a dairy farm but with the introduction of milk quotas only a few cows are kept now to provide milk, cheese, cream and yogurt. Visitors are welcome to milk the cows and pat the other friendly animals – children love it.

The three-quarter acre garden has a pond with ducks and views across the 72 acres of farmland and lakes. Inside the house all the bedrooms have magnificent views across the lovely countryside, over to the Snowdonia mountains and in the other direction to Anglesey. The interior is furnished simply but very pleasantly in keeping with the old-world cottage ambience of the house. The nine bedrooms are all individually decorated and locally crafted wood is a feature; all are equipped with a colour TV and are en suite.

The food is fresh, wholesome and imaginative and the menu provides an excellent choice of dishes. Individual diets are catered for.

Easily Accessible: There are several gentle walks in the immediate vicinity, starting from Llanddeiniolen church (with reputedly the oldest yew trees in Europe), and at Pen Dinas, an Iron Age hill fort. Llanddeiniolen is situated on the very edge of Snowdownia National Park and here the more energetic will find numerous walks taking in the mountainous scenery. The summit of Snowdon can be climbed on foot or by train. The views when not shrouded in cloud are magnificent. Of the many interesting places to visit, try Caernarfon Castle, 6 miles away; Llandudno, a Victorian seaside resort; Harlech Castle; and Portmeirion, the dream village of Clough Williams-Ellis and the setting for the TV series 'The Prisoner'. To the east lies Betws-y-coed with its craft and woollen shops.

Local Activities: walks, cliff walks, golf, sea and river fishing, skin-diving, sailing, pony-trekking.

Castle View Hotel
Bridge Street
Chepstow
Gwent
NP6 5EZ

☎ Chepstow(02912) 70349

Martin and Vicky Cardale

Easy Access M4 and 10 mins M5 intersection

This charming ivy-clad building was built over three hundred years ago with stones from Chepstow castle. It has massive walls six feet thick, a beautiful hand-turned oak staircase, 18th-century wall paintings, and a delightful secluded garden. All eleven bedrooms are en suite and are equipped with a mini-bar and TV. There is a lounge bar, residents lounge, and dining room.

Martin and Vicky Cardale came to Castle View with a wealth of valuable experience, having built up a chain of hotels in Australia. They run Castle View with their family of four, including their eight-year-old daughter, Zara, whose speciality is making the hotel's home-made ice-cream, and Holly, the friendly much-loved golden retriever.

Food is freshly cooked, with all meals available and a choice of bar snacks or restaurant meals. The cuisine is home-cooked British with local produce – salmon, Welsh lamb and fresh vegetables regularly featured. A full vegetarian menu is available.

Easily Accessible: Chepstow is an interesting and historical town set in the outstanding natural beauty of the Wye Valley. It was a port from Norman times to the 19th century, and has an 11th-century castle perched high on the cliffs above the River Wye and a pretty church with a Norman nave. There are numerous places of historical interest to visit nearby including Tintern Abbey, a 12th-century Cistercian abbey, and Caldicot, Raglan, and Penow Castles. Four miles away at Caerleon, the ruins of one of the three main military bases in Roman Britain, the Legionary Fortress of Isca can be explored. The Forest of Dean and Clearwell Caves (a natural cave system mined for 2,500 years for iron ore) are a twenty-minute drive away. Walkers can enjoy the Wye Valley walk covering 34 miles, and Offa's Dyke path which runs from the Severn Estuary to Prostatyn – 168 miles north.

Local Activities: walks, golf, horse-riding.

The Hall   Bed and Breakfast only
Lygan-y-Wern
Pentre Halkyn
Holywell
Clwyd
CH8 8BD

☎ Halkyn (0352) 780215

Davinia Vernon

Easy access off A55, junction B5123 to Bagillt

This charming house is prettily and conveniently set in a rural position, just a few miles outside Chester. The main house is believed to date from 1690 and there are traces of an earlier farmhouse in the grounds. One of the outbuildings, a listed dovecote, has been renovated and is now home to two splendid white doves. There are thirteen acres of grounds, with extensive views over the estuary of the River Dee, a large vegetable plot, and formal gardens. Bantams, geese, ducks and hens roam the grounds.

Accommodation is provided in a neatly converted cottage with five bedrooms and two bathrooms, a sitting room with a wood-burning stove and colour TV, a dining room and kitchen. It is very simply but tastefully furnished with white walls, pine furnishings and flowery fabrics. The walls are adorned with locally painted watercolours.

Whilst no evening meal is provided there are plenty of local pubs and restaurants within a two-mile radius.

Easily Accessible: You can walk for miles and miles on the nearby Halkyn mountains and a little further afield, the Denbigh moors and Snowdonia provide many challenging walks. Chester, 15 miles away, is an attractive historical city with some beautiful black and white buildings, an 11th-century cathedral, a famous zoo, and some Roman remains. You can take a day trip to Bodelwyddan Castle with its walled garden, aviary, maze and adventure woodland. The popular Victorian resort of Llandudno, 29 miles away, is fairly unspoilt, and has a sandy beach, an attractive park, and an open-air theatre.

Local Activities: walks, fishing, pony-trekking, golf, Holywell leisure centre with sauna, spa pool, sunbed, trimnasium, swimming pool, squash, tennis, bowls.

Broniwan

A 'no smoking' home

Rhydlewis
Llandysul
Dyfed
SA44 5PF

☎ Rhydlewis (023975) 261

Carole and Allan Jacobs

From A487 onto B4334 to Rhydelwis, left in village, passing village shop on right then first on right.

A stay at Broniwan in the heart of Wales can be an educational experience; guests staying at this small Victorian stone farmhouse are given the opportunity to feed the calves, milk the cows, make friends with the donkey and tend the hens.

The farmhouse rests on a rocky slope and is surrounded by beech trees. The surrounding area is very beautiful with gentle hills, waterfalls and purple heather. The house faces south towards the Frenni Fawr hills, famous in Welsh legend. The pretty garden with rhododendrons, irises, ferns and Victorian 'immortelles' surrounds the house. The interior is furnished in period style with a pleasing 19th-century watercolour collection completing the picture. There are three double bedrooms, one with en suite facilities. The drawing room and dining room are furnished prettily in Laura Ashley décor and have very fine views. There is a playroom in the barn with paints, records and books.

The food is plentiful and very wholesome (I enjoyed an impromptu and delicious kedgeree); much of the produce served at dinner comes from the farm including the delicious beef. Carole and her American, jazz-loving husband Allan enjoy meeting their guests and are keen to give advice on anything from milking a cow to pointing out the best walks available. They will also meet you at the train stations.

Easily Accessible: You can step outside the door and walk around the farm and the village. Five miles away the Ceredigion heritage coast stretches for miles and miles. The Preselli hills present more of a challenge, especially if you attempt the Carn Ingli summit. There are numerous pretty villages with markets. The woollen mills at Dre-fach Felindre, 10 miles away, were once a centre of the Welsh woollen industry. There are numerous historic and archaeological sites to visit including the fascinating ancient burial chambers at Pentre Ifan, 20 miles away.

Local Activities: walks, fishing (sea trout), sailing and golf, sandy beaches.

The Crown at Whitebrook

Meetings room available

Whitebrook
Nr Monmouth
Gwent
NP5 4TX

☎ Monmouth (0600) 860254

Roger and Sandra Bates

Off A466 at Bigsweir Bridge, 17 miles Severn Bridge

The Crown has been an Inn since the 18th century and its widely acclaimed restaurant now occupies the original part of the building. It is set in the Whitebrook Valley, just a mile from the Tintern Forest where the peace and quiet is disturbed only by a gently babbling brook and birdsong.

There are twelve cosy bedrooms, all with en suite bathrooms and colour TVs. There is also a small room available for executive meetings of two to twelve delegates.

Sandra Bates is a trained caterer who has run three restaurants. Her experience is brought to bear in the Crown's superior restaurant where she is particularly proud of the French cuisine. Ingredients are fresh and many, such as the fresh salmon from the Wye, are locally produced. Specialities of the house are home-made rolls, chocolate truffles and home-made ice-creams and sorbets.

Easily Accessible: There is plenty to do and see in this beautiful area; within a 15-mile radius there are ten castles to explore and the Forest of Dean is only 5 miles away. Take a day trip to the Brecon Beacons, Hereford, Gloucester, Bristol, Cardiff, Newport or the Black Mountains. Walking is a main attraction; the countryside is varied and walkers can enjoy gentle lakeside ambles, rugged hill climbing, or strolls along easy paths. The Tintern Forest, the Wye Valley Walk, and Offa's Dyke are all within 2 miles and there are over thirty waymarked walks within 5 miles of the Crown.

Local Activities: walks, trout and salmon fishing, caving, canoeing, boating, pony-trekking, horse-riding.

The Authors

Mike Stone was born in Hove in 1935. After a varied career, he found himself as a freelance hotel inspector travelling extensively around Britain. In the course of his travels he realised how useful a reliable guide to good rooms and personal care at reasonable rates would be, and embarked on The *Guestaccom* booklets, followed by *Country Homes* and *ExecHotels*. Until recently he ran his own hotel in Hove, but has now given it up in order to concentrate full time on his expanding guidebook interests. He still lives in Hove.

Roger Russell was born in Ipswich in 1944. He joined forces with Mike Stone, after several years travelling through Britain in the computer industry, as the job of inspecting new locations for the guidebooks grew. He is married and lives in Brighton.

David & Charles

£5 VOUCHER

With the compliments of your hosts.
Please present this voucher <u>on arrival</u>

For conditions please see over

David & Charles

£5 VOUCHER

With the compliments of your hosts.
Please present this voucher <u>on arrival</u>

For conditions please see over

David & Charles

£5 VOUCHER

With the compliments of your hosts.
Please present this voucher <u>on arrival</u>

For conditions please see over

David & Charles

£5 VOUCHER

With the compliments of your hosts.
Please present this voucher <u>on arrival</u>

For conditions please see over

CONDITIONS OF USE

1. Voucher valid at any of the 321 places as indicated in the area index, until 30 June 1991.
2. To be used against bed and breakfast for a stay of at least 3 days for 2 people.
3. Only one voucher to be used at any single establishment.
4. Not valid on Bank Holidays.
5. Allowable against rack rates only
   (Not against discounted rates).

CONDITIONS OF USE

1. Voucher valid at any of the 321 places as indicated in the area index, until 30 June 1991.
2. To be used against bed and breakfast for a stay of at least 3 days for 2 people.
3. Only one voucher to be used at any single establishment.
4. Not valid on Bank Holidays.
5. Allowable against rack rates only
   (Not against discounted rates).

CONDITIONS OF USE

1. Voucher valid at any of the 321 places as indicated in the area index, until 30 June 1991.
2. To be used against bed and breakfast for a stay of at least 3 days for 2 people.
3. Only one voucher to be used at any single establishment.
4. Not valid on Bank Holidays.
5. Allowable against rack rates only
   (Not against discounted rates).

CONDITIONS OF USE

1. Voucher valid at any of the 321 places as indicated in the area index, until 30 June 1991.
2. To be used against bed and breakfast for a stay of at least 3 days for 2 people.
3. Only one voucher to be used at any single establishment.
4. Not valid on Bank Holidays.
5. Allowable against rack rates only
   (Not against discounted rates).